"This book brings heart, clarity, insight, and practical tools to the complex work of equity-focused improvement. It's a must-read for school and district leaders who are ready to move from intention to sustainable, systemic action."
    David R. Schuler, *Executive Director, AASA, The School Superintendents Association, USA*

"This volume will empower educational leaders to use a leading approach to local innovation – improvement science – to address a fundamental societal commitment: equity in-and-through public education. The volume benefits from Prof. Marci Shepard's unique experience straddling K-12 and higher education to produce practical knowledge for educational improvement."
    Donald J. Peurach, *Professor of Educational Policy, Leadership, and Innovation, University of Michigan; Senior Fellow of the Carnegie Foundation for the Advancement of Teaching, USA; and Co-Director of the Improvement Scholars Network*

Where the Science of Improvement Meets the Heart of Leadership

Where the Science of Improvement Meets the Heart of Leadership is a hands-on roadmap for leading meaningful school and district change. Grounded in the proven framework of improvement science, it offers a step-by-step process to transform systems and build a positive, collaborative culture. More than an informational book, this is a facilitation guide—complete with learning targets, icebreakers, leadership strategies, reflection prompts, and practical tools throughout. Real leaders coach you through every step, sharing insights, challenges, and successes to show what's truly possible. At the heart of it, this book helps close the vision–implementation gap—the disconnect between leaders' aspirations to create equitable, improvement-focused environments and the day-to-day staff experience, which too often lacks ownership and psychological safety to engage in authentic, vulnerable inquiry. Whether you're a current or aspiring superintendent, principal, or district leader that's leading teams, transforming departments, or improving systems at scale, this exciting book gives you the strategies and support to turn vision into action—and lead lasting, equity-centered change with those closest to the work.

Marci Shepard is Assistant Professor of Instruction for Educational Leadership and Director of the Ohio University Leadership Project, at Ohio University, USA.

Also Available from Routledge Eye on Education
(www.routledge.com/eyeoneducation)

A Blueprint for Teacher Retention: Leading Schools that Teachers Don't Want to Leave
James A. Bailey

Your School Leadership Edit: A Minimalist Approach to Rethinking Your School Ecosystem
Tamera Musiowsky-Borneman, C.Y. Arnold

Game-Changing Leadership in Action: An Educator's Companion
Kim Wallace

How to Have Difficult Conversations as an Educational Leader: Self-Reflections and Strategies for Success
Patty Corum

The Respected School Leader: Developing your Character Traits and Transformational Leadership Skills
Howard J. Bultinck, Lynn H. Bush, Noreen A. Powers

The International Education Leadership Companion: Lessons and Best Practices from Expert Leaders
Lindsay Prendergast, Catarina Song Chen, Colin Brown

Leadership Teams in America's Best Schools: Improving the Lives of All Students
Joseph F. Johnson, Jr., Cynthia L. Uline, Stanley J. Munro, Jr., Francisco Escobedo

Making Community Schools a Reality: Harnessing Your Power as a School Leader through Collaboration
Emily L. Woods

Wholehearted School Leadership: Rewiring our Schools for Courage, Justice, Learning, and Connection
Kathryn Fishman-Weaver

Data Analysis for Continuous School Improvement, 5th Edition
Victoria L. Bernhardt

Culturally Conscious Decision-Making for School Leaders: A Toolkit for Creating a More Equitable School Culture
Shauna McGee

Teacher Leadership Practice in High-Performing Schools: A Blueprint for Excellence
Jeremy D. Visone

Where the Science of Improvement Meets the Heart of Leadership

Leading Equity-Focused School and District Improvement

Marci Shepard

Routledge
Taylor & Francis Group
NEW YORK AND LONDON

Designed cover image: Design Buckets

First published 2026
by Routledge
605 Third Avenue, New York, NY 10158

and by Routledge
4 Park Square, Milton Park, Abingdon, Oxon, OX14 4RN

Routledge is an imprint of the Taylor & Francis Group, an informa business

© 2026 Marci Shepard

The right of Marci Shepard to be identified as author of this work has been asserted in accordance with sections 77 and 78 of the Copyright, Designs and Patents Act 1988.

All rights reserved. The purchase of this copyright material confers the right on the purchasing institution to photocopy or download pages which bear a copyright line at the bottom of the page. No other parts of this book may be reprinted or reproduced or utilised in any form or by any electronic, mechanical, or other means, now known or hereafter invented, including photocopying and recording, or in any information storage or retrieval system, without permission in writing from the publishers.

For Product Safety Concerns and Information please contact our EU representative GPSR@taylorandfrancis.com. Taylor & Francis Verlag GmbH, Kaufingerstraße 24, 80331 München, Germany.

Trademark notice: Product or corporate names may be trademarks or registered trademarks, and are used only for identification and explanation without intent to infringe.

ISBN: 978-1-041-14297-3 (hbk)
ISBN: 978-1-041-14296-6 (pbk)
ISBN: 978-1-003-67380-4 (ebk)

DOI: 10.4324/9781003673804

Access the Support Material: www.routledge.com/9781041142966

Typeset in Warnock Pro
by SPi Technologies India Pvt Ltd (Straive)

Improvement happens in community, and I've been blessed to learn and lead with some of the best. Thank you:

To my Superintendent Improvement Network, for creating a thoughtful space to learn and explore improvement science alongside incredible leaders.

To my Superintendent's Cabinet teammates, for putting that learning into practice by co-leading with curiosity and innovation.

To the leaders who shared their stories, for inspiring and teaching through lived experience.

To my research partners, for keeping the learning going.

To my family, for giving me the support and space to write.

And to Zeke the Doodle, for doing the opposite by staying permanently glued to my side.

Contents

Support Materials   xi
AI Statement   xiii
Meet the Author   xiv
Preface   xv

PART I THE WHY: EQUITY, WORKPLACE CULTURE, AND LEADERSHIP VALUES   1

▶ 1   **Introduction: Workplace Culture and Improvement Science**   3

▶ 2   **Meet Three Educational Leaders Who Use Improvement Science**   17

PART II THE WHAT: THEORIES, PRINCIPLES, AND LEADERSHIP PARADIGM SHIFTS   35

▶ 3   **Theory behind Improvement Science**   37

▶ 4   **Principles of Improvement**   68

▶ 5   **Six Paradigm Shifts for Leading Continuous School System Improvement**   85

PART III THE HOW: STRUCTURED PROCESSES, TOOLS, AND LEADERSHIP STRATEGIES 123

▶ 6 Processes and Tools for Leading through Disciplined Inquiry 125

▶ 7 Addressing the Vision–Implementation Gap of a Positive Workplace Culture 157

▶ 8 Addressing the Vision–Implementation Gap of Staff Ownership (User-Centered) 183

▶ 9 Addressing the Vision–Implementation Gap of Staff Vulnerability (Problem-Specific) 218

▶ 10 Zooming Out: Leading with a Systems Lens 257

Appendix 1: Icebreaker Group Activity Facilitation Guide 276
Appendix 2: Chapter 6 Try This—Tools for Leading Disciplined Inquiry 278
Appendix 3: Connecting NELP Standards to Improvement Science in Schools and Districts 302

Support Materials

The "Try This" activities in this book are also available on the book product page online, so you can easily print them for use. To access these downloads, go to www.routledge.com/9781041142966 and click on the "Support Material" link.

  Try This: Self-Assessment—Where Are You on Your Improvement Journey? (Preface)
  Try This: Build a Workplace Culture for Continuous Improvement (Chapter 1)
  Try This: Identify Your Leadership Values (Chapter 2)
  Try This: Apply Deming's PDSA Cycle to Your Own Leadership Practice (Chapter 3)
  Try This: Apply the Six Principles of Improvement (Chapter 4)
  Try This: Apply the Six Leadership Paradigm Shifts (Chapter 5)
  Try This: Tools that Support Disciplined Inquiry (Chapter 6)
    Assemble a Team Check-In (Chapter 6)
    Identify an Issue (Chapter 6, Phase 1)
    Data Analysis Protocol (Chapter 6, Phase 1)
    5 Whys Protocol (Chapter 6, Phase 1)
    Fishbone Diagram (Chapter 6, Phase 1)
    Process Mapping (Chapter 6, Phase 1)
    Empathy Interviews (Chapter 6, Phase 1)
    Research and Evidence to Understand the Problem (Chapter 6, Phase 1)
    Affinity Protocol (Chapter 6, Phase 1)
    Setting an Aim (Chapter 6, Phase 2)
    Driver Diagram (Chapter 6, Phase 2)
    Change Ideas (Chapter 6, Phase 3)
    Theory of Action (Chapter 6, Phase 3)
    PDSA–Plan (Chapter 6, Phase 4)
    PDSA–Do (Chapter 6, Phase 4)
    PDSA–Study (Chapter 6, Phase 4)
    PDSA–Act (Chapter 6, Phase 4)

Support Materials

Spread and Scale Decision-Making Tool (Chapter 6, Phase 5)

Networked Improvement Community (NIC) Shared Learning Tool to Support Spreading and Scaling (Chapter 6, Phase 5)

Try This: Deepen a Positive Improvement Culture (Chapter 7)
Try This: Empower Staff as Improvers (Chapter 8)
Try This: Create Space for Staff Vulnerability (Chapter 9)
Try This: Be the Leader Who Changes the System (Chapter 10)

AI Statement

I conducted the literature review, original research, and drafted the full 10-chapter manuscript without the use of generative AI. During drafting, the following AI tool was used:

- Microsoft 365—Embedded spell check and grammar check

During revision, the following AI tools were used:

- Grammarly for Windows—Grammar and mechanics check
- ChatGPT Pro 4.0 (Private Mode)—Used selectively to refine tone, reduce redundancy, and provide feedback

After completion, the following AI tools were used:

- Turn-It-In—Plagiarism check (Result: 6% match, primarily due to proper nouns and common terms)
- Quilbot Premium—AI detection (Result: 100% human-written)

Meet the Author

Marci Shepard, PhD, EdD, is an award-winning educator committed to closing equity gaps by helping leaders improve systems. Her work and research live at the intersection of continuous improvement, positive culture, and educational leadership.

She has served as a teacher, school leader, central office leader, and superintendent in both Washington State and Ohio, and has held leadership roles in several state and national education organizations.

Marci's journey with improvement science began as a superintendent, first learning with a Superintendent Improvement Network, then implementing it in her district. She now researches how educational leaders use it to lead change.

Dr. Shepard is currently a faculty member and coordinator in Educational Leadership at Ohio University, and she is the Director of the Ohio University Leadership Project, which provides professional development and support to school and district leaders across Ohio.

Preface

> **CASE VIGNETTE**
>
> Mrs. Kruckeberg became a principal to make a bigger impact. She believed strong leadership could create a school where both students and staff loved and learned. But despite her team's dedication, they often felt like they were spinning their wheels. Initiatives felt irrelevant and disconnected. Professional development and collaboration focused more on keeping up with constant change than on what staff actually needed to make a meaningful impact. Teachers were overwhelmed. The desire for progress was real, but momentum rarely lasted, and it was exhausting.
>
> Kruckeberg didn't want isolated wins or short-term efforts. She wanted Wolf Creek Elementary School to be a place where educators worked together to solve the real, pressing challenges their students faced and where that learning was shared across the building to strengthen the school as a whole. She was committed to reprioritizing joy in the work, so she wanted to do all of this in a culture where people felt supported, empowered, and connected to a shared purpose.
>
> Sound familiar? Principal Kruckeberg is not alone. Many educational leaders feel the same tensions—the passion to make a difference, the pressure to improve, and the frustration of trying to move forward without the processes, tools, strategies, or culture to do so effectively. That's why I wrote this book.

▶ PURPOSE

Leaders shape culture. Culture fuels improvement. Equity ensures it matters.

Educational leaders are committed to leading school and district improvement while fostering a caring culture. Still, over the last several decades, many improvement initiatives have failed to create lasting change. This is because the urgency of the work pressures leaders to fall back on swift mandates or sweeping initiative roll-outs. However, rather than being a quicker fix, this top-down leadership approach causes improvement efforts to feel disjointed, fails to meet the just-in-time needs of students and staff, and inhibits the staff ownership and vulnerability required to address systemic challenges, especially those addressing inequities.

This book offers educational leaders a different approach, using improvement science to provide a practical, research-based way for leading change. More importantly, we are not after a one-size-fits-all solution. This book will help you customize strategies for leading a culture of continuous, equity-focused improvement in your school or district.

▶ AN UNEXPECTED SURPRISE

When I first began applying improvement science as a superintendent and later started researching it, my focus was clear. I wanted to understand the processes that drive real, system-level change. I believed that by helping adults work in a more aligned and strategic way, we could create transformative change.

But then something unexpected surfaced. As I worked alongside educational leaders, reflected on my experience, and analyzed my research data, I discovered that barriers to success were more about people than processes, and improvement was more about what happens within a culture than what is written in the strategic plan and built into the system structures. The heart of the matter became clear. Two conditions consistently determined whether improvement efforts flourished or fell flat: ownership and vulnerability. These were make-or-break attributes to improvement. As I leaned into this discovery, it illuminated how these two conditions align with core tenets of improvement science: ownership with a *user-centered* stance, and vulnerability with a *problem-specific* focus. That realization reshaped my thinking and inspired this book—a call to press toward a more user-centered and problem-specific approach to school and district improvement by increasing staff ownership and fostering vulnerability.

▶ POSITIONING EQUITY

Equity is a work of heart and the heartbeat of this book.

The phrase *equity-focused leadership* is prominently featured in the subtitle of this book because equity is positioned at the center. I made an intentional decision not to make equity a separate chapter in this book, just like it should not be a separate initiative in our school and district leadership. Every decision—whether about policy, resources, or instruction—must be viewed through an equity lens. The same is true in this book. Equity is a throughline. It is not an add-on to the work; it *is* the work. Simply defined, equity *ensures that systems regularly produce better outcomes for all students across all contexts, and that every student gets what they need to succeed.*

If equity is our purpose, improvement science is the catalyst that allows us to turn this vision into action, bringing equity to life in our schools and districts. Improvement efforts that don't center equity risk failing to reach the students who truly need us most. This makes equity more than just an abstract concept. Equity is a lived experience, and every leadership decision either reinforces or dismantles barriers to success.

As Jenny Irons (2019) points out, a general equity focus is only a starting point. Just as she presses researchers to "richly conceptualize" inequality, leaders must go beyond vague commitments and lead teams in identifying the specific disparities showing up in their schools and districts, figuring out which students are not experiencing success, how, and why (p. 2). Because of that, this book does not deeply explore specific inequities and prescribe pre-packaged strategies to address them. Doing that as an outsider would undermine the very spirit of improvement science. On the contrary, this book is a guide to help you and your team examine your own data, attending to the disparities that are showing up in your context. Then it provides processes and tools to lead your team to understand those disparities and the systems that produce or perpetuate them. With that rich conceptualization of *your* local inequities, you can select and test change ideas that directly target the root causes of the inequities in your context.

This is the heart of equity-focused leadership.

▶ WHO THIS BOOK IS FOR

This book is written for practicing educational leaders, including superintendents, central office leaders, principals, teacher-leaders, organizational leaders, and leadership coaches. It's also designed for aspiring educational leaders in graduate educational leadership programs.

The conversational, leader-to-leader tone is meant to be approachable. You'll find insights, practical strategies, and boots-on-the-ground processes and tools you can use immediately in your context. Too many books explain the *why* but don't get clear on the *how*—this one does both.

Whether you're leading professional development, facilitating a leadership team, designing system-wide improvement, leading in an organization, or preparing for a leadership role, this book is for you.

▶ WHAT PROBLEM THIS BOOK SOLVES AND WHAT MAKES IT DIFFERENT

Many leaders understand the concepts of improvement science (the *why*), but they often struggle with putting them into practice (the *how*). Leaders are left asking: How do I apply this in real time? How do I lead this work without doing it all by myself? How do I build a culture where people take ownership and feel safe to enact change? This book closes that *why–how* gap.

Where the Science of Improvement Meets the Heart of Leadership integrates improvement theory with everyday leadership. It doesn't stop there. What makes this book unique is its focus on culture. While most improvement resources focus on process, this one also centers the cultural conditions that make improvement possible, better, and sustained.

This is your system-level *roadmap* to leading equity-focused school and district improvement. It's a 3-in-1 guide that not only teaches the proven framework of improvement science but also walks you through a process to transform school systems and build a positive culture.

But it's more than an informational book. It's a hands-on *facilitation guide*. With embedded learning targets and success criteria, icebreakers, case vignettes, self-assessments, reflection tools, and implementation worksheets, you'll have practical, ready-to-use resources that turn knowledge into leadership action.

You'll also learn directly from *real leaders* coaching you every step of the way. Going beyond good ideas and wishful thinking, this book provides an inside scoop on the real-life experiences of award-winning leaders who have done this work in real systems. Through their stories, you'll see what it looks like to lead with values (Part I), dispositions (Part II), and actions (Part III) that create impactful change. This isn't pie-in-the-sky theory. It's leadership-in-action, showing us what is possible.

▶ HOW THIS BOOK IS STRUCTURED

This book is organized into three parts: The Why, The What, and The How. The parts are designed to build upon one another from foundational ideas to practical action.

Part I: The Why lays the foundation, highlighting how equity, culture, and leadership values guide our work. If *culture eats strategy for breakfast*, then this part lays the groundwork for the strategies presented later.

- The Preface introduces the core ideas and frames the rationale for centering equity in improvement.
- Chapter 1 connects the dots between workplace culture and improvement, showing how the two depend on each other.

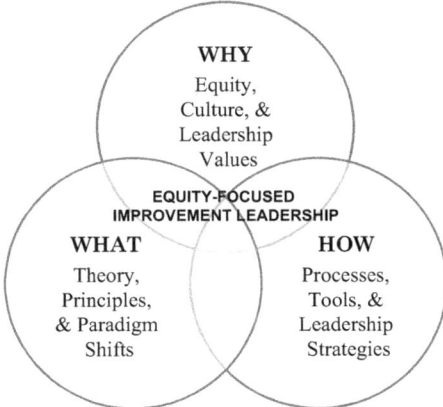

Figure P.1 Three parts: Why, How, and What.

- Chapter 2 introduces three real educational leaders who bring improvement to life through their values and systems leadership.

Part II: The What explores the theories, principles, and leadership shifts that distinguish improvement leadership from traditional change models.

- Chapter 3 examines the theoretical foundations of improvement science, especially Deming's teachings that we need to lead differently because systems, not people, are the cause of most problems.
- Chapter 4 presents the six core principles of improvement that guide systemic change.
- Chapter 5 distills improvement science literature into six paradigm shifts that help leaders move from traditional management to becoming true improvement leaders.

Part III: The How turns theory into action. It provides processes, tools, and leadership strategies to tackle common challenges and scale improvement.

- Chapter 6 introduces a five-phase improvement cycle to lead inquiry with clarity.
- Chapter 7 discusses the vision–implementation gap of workplace culture and offers strategies for aligning vision and practice.
- Chapter 8 focuses on building staff ownership, showing how to shift leadership from *doing to* to *leading with* those closest to the work.
- Chapter 9 addresses the role of vulnerability in improvement, including how leaders foster the psychological safety required for authentic equity work.
- Chapter 10 concludes with strategies for leading with systemic coherence.

This progression helps you move from understanding (Part I), to mindset (Part II), to strategies (Part III) for creating transformative change.

▶ SPECIAL FEATURES

Each chapter follows a consistent structure that guides you from insight to action through learning, dialogue, and implementation.

- Learning targets and success criteria anchor each chapter with a clear learning goal and criteria for success, modeling effective teaching and professional learning that we expect from staff.
- Relevant National Educational Leadership Preparation (NELP) standards align content to the standards to ensure relevant competencies for leadership development.
- Icebreakers kickstart engagement and connection to the content during individual reading or through a team discussion.
- Case vignettes situate each chapter in a practical leadership challenge scenario to spark reflection or discussion about the upcoming learning in context.
- Content with real leader voices draws on the experiences of leaders who are applying these ideas every day.
- Reflection questions prompt personal or group dialogue, making the learning stick.
- "Try This" tools put ideas into action with practical, ready-to-use hands-on tools that you can try yourself or use to lead teams.
- Leadership-in-action stories close each chapter with a real moment from my own leadership journey, offered as examples, not exemplars, to spark ideas and reflection.

This book is meant to be used, not just read, whether you are working through it independently or leading a team.

To start this leadership journey, use the self-assessment on the next page to reflect on where you and your team are today.

PREFACE TRY THIS: SELF-ASSESSMENT—WHERE ARE YOU ON YOUR IMPROVEMENT JOURNEY?

This self-assessment will help you determine your school or district's current strengths and areas for growth in using improvement science for equity-centered continuous improvement.

▶ INSTRUCTIONS

For each statement, rate yourself or collaboratively rate your leadership team on a scale of 1 to 5:

1. Not yet started
2. Occasionally happening
3. In progress, but inconsistent
4. Happening consistently
5. Deeply embedded in our culture

▶ PART I: THE WHY—EQUITY, WORKPLACE CULTURE, AND LEADERSHIP VALUES

- Our school/district prioritizes equity in improvement efforts, such as identifying authentic problems, listening to those experiencing or affected by the problem, applying culturally responsive solutions, and analyzing the impact on closing gaps.
- We intentionally foster a workplace culture where staff feel valued, included, and safe to engage in inquiry.
- We prioritize and support a collaborative culture, helping teams develop norms, have time to meet, and empower them to create change.
- Our leadership team embodies values of equity, collaboration, vulnerability, and a stance of continuous improvement.
- We have a clear and shared vision that centers students, and we consistently communicate and make connections between that vision and our improvement work.

▶ PART II: THE WHAT—THEORIES, PRINCIPLES, AND LEADERSHIP PARADIGM SHIFTS

- We view school/district improvement as an ongoing learning process that involves collaborative problem-solving rather than a series of professional development sessions or initiatives.
- Our leadership team understands and actively applies proven principles of improvement to shape our improvement processes.
- We recognize that achieving equity requires transforming systems that go beyond addressing individual behaviors or surface-level issues, and our improvement efforts focus on identifying and addressing root causes.
- We embrace the research-based leadership dispositions for facilitating continuous school system improvement and intentionally integrate them into our leadership practices.
- We believe that meaningful system change begins with us, and we are committed to examining and evolving our own leadership mindsets and practices as part of the improvement journey.

▶ PART III: THE HOW—STRUCTURED PROCESSES, TOOLS, AND LEADERSHIP STRATEGIES

- We use a specific and articulated cycle for inquiry, and we know and use tools that help us with each step.
- We have structures and supports in place to ensure every team is engaged in collaborative inquiry.
- Our staff takes ownership of improvement efforts and initiates inquiry rather than doing it to follow leadership expectations.
- We have a culture where it is safe to take risks, fail, and learn from mistakes without fear of shame or blame.
- We actively scale successful improvement efforts by sharing what works across teams, schools, and districts.

Copyright material from Marci Shepard (2026), *Where the Science of Improvement Meets the Heart of Leadership*, Routledge

▶ **TOTAL SCORE: ___ OUT OF 75**

- 60–75 → Your school/district has a strong foundation in continuous improvement and is well-positioned to deepen this work.
- 40–59 → Your team is progressing, but inconsistencies exist in embedding continuous improvement at all levels.
- Below 40 → There is room for growth, and this book will provide essential strategies for building a stronger improvement culture.

▶ **REFLECT**

With my teams, we talk about looking out a window (pointing to others) versus looking in a mirror (looking at ourselves). This self-assessment is a mirror. Use it to reflect or spark conversations with your team as you consider your readiness for this improvement journey:

- What are your areas of strength?
- Which areas do you anticipate needing the most attention and growth?
- Which chapter(s) of this book do you expect to be the most valuable for your current understanding of your improvement needs?

Reference

Irons, J. (2019). *Shifting the lens: Why conceptualization matters in research on reducing inequality.* New York: William T. Grant Foundation.

PART I

The Why: Equity, Workplace Culture, and Leadership Values

Preface, Chapter 1, and Chapter 2
Equity-Focused Improvement Leadership

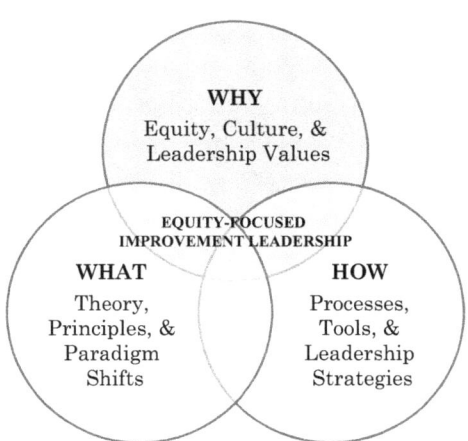

Figure PI.1 Part I—The Why.

This part lays the groundwork for transformative change by examining the essential leadership characteristics that create the right conditions for improvement. Leaders don't just implement strategies; they elevate equity, shape culture, and lead through their values.

- The Preface framed equity as the purpose of improvement.
- Chapter 1 makes a case for the importance of workplace culture and how it impacts whether improvement efforts flourish or fail.
- Chapter 2 introduces three educational leaders who have successfully embedded improvement science in their leadership, offering real-world perspectives.

By the end of this part, you will have a deeper understanding of how equity, culture, and leadership values work together to form the foundation for continuous improvement.

Introduction: Workplace Culture and Improvement Science

🎯 LEARNING TARGET

I can explain the reciprocal relationship between a positive workplace culture and improvement science, including how they influence each other to support continuous improvement.

Success Criteria

- Describe the characteristics and impact of workplace culture on staff engagement, collaboration, and system improvement.
- Analyze the improvement science framework and how it supports sustainable change in educational systems.
- Connect culture and improvement by evaluating how improvement science can be used to build and sustain a positive workplace culture.

RELEVANT NELP STANDARDS

- NELP Standard 1: Mission, Vision, and Improvement (Improvement Science Framework)
- NELP Standard 2: Ethics and Professional Norms (Workplace Culture)
- NELP Standard 7 (Building-Level): Building Professional Capacity (Collaborative Professional Culture)

ICEBREAKER: BEST JOB EVER

Think of one of your favorite places you have worked.

- What made it a great place to work?
- What were some characteristics of the leader(s)?
- How did the culture of the workplace impact your ability to grow?

(See Appendix 1 for the Icebreaker Group Activity Facilitation Guide)

CASE VIGNETTE: A PRINCIPAL'S BREAKING POINT

In the Preface, we met Principal Kruckeberg, who was committed to leading her school with a focus on both student and staff success. Despite her dedication, however, she was facing frustration with an onslaught of initiatives that never seemed to take hold. Here's the rest of her story.

Background

At Wolf Creek Elementary, Principal Kruckeberg had a staff that cared. They were working hard. But every new initiative seemed to add to the weight without moving the needle. Staff were exhausted. Staff meetings and collaboration time were bogged down with trying to navigate the changes. Even good ideas weren't getting traction.

Introduction: Workplace Culture and Improvement Science   5

Turning Point

One day, during a Building Leadership Team meeting, the kindergarten teacher let out a sigh and finally said what everyone was thinking. "It feels like we're just spinning our wheels."

Something about that struck Kruckeberg. She paused. That week, she asked her staff, "What keeps you up at night?" Responses started slowly but then trickled out. Student social-emotional needs. Low student engagement. Chronic absenteeism. Interventions that weren't working.

Rather than fix it herself, Kruckeberg helped teams explore issues they raised. Different grade levels began to identify their particular problems, test strategies to see if they made an impact on the problems, and reflect on results. Eventually, the tone of staff meetings changed. Teams came in a-buzz with what they were trying out, celebrating what they were learning together, and sharing ideas for course corrections when they ran into speed bumps or roadblocks.

Bottom Line

Transformation isn't something you do *to* staff—it's something you build *with* them. Culture shifts when people feel heard, involved, and invested in the work. Results follow.

A positive work environment isn't just a luxury. It's the foundation for meaningful school and district improvement. While improvement science gives us powerful processes and tools to lead change, they won't work without a healthy workplace culture. In this chapter, we'll connect three core ideas: (a) what workplace culture is and why it matters, (b) a brief introduction to improvement science, and (c) how the two work together.

When leaders apply top-down change, staff often feel overwhelmed, disengaged, and skeptical of new initiatives (Fullan & Quinn, 2015). The problem is that school and district leaders frequently introduce solutions before truly understanding the challenges or engaging those most affected or responsible for making the initiatives successful. If you experienced this, you may have felt:

- Confusion and frustration among staff
- Initiative fatigue, where educators feel like every year brings a new change
- Low ownership of improvement efforts

These symptoms aren't from a lack of effort or care. They are about workplace culture. Culture is shaped by leadership.

▶ UNDERSTANDING WORKPLACE CULTURE

Workplace culture is the character and personality of an organization. Whereas climate is about how people *feel*, culture is about what people *do*. Culture reflects the shared beliefs, routines, and norms that influence how people work together. Culture affects everything from job satisfaction to how management processes work to how well teams collaborate to solve problems (Seppala & Cameron, 2015). If you have been in a positive workplace culture, you likely experienced:

- A shared purpose, where employees feel their work is meaningful and connected to a larger mission.
- Trust and respect, where staff operate in an environment of mutual support and feeling valued.
- Collaboration, where people work together, knowing they are part of something bigger.
- Psychological safety, where individuals feel comfortable sharing new ideas, giving feedback, and learning from mistakes.

A positive workplace has many benefits. It increases employee commitment, engagement, satisfaction, and performance. Employees also feel better, both physically and emotionally, which improves relationships within teams. Putting in deliberate effort to improve culture is worth it for people to feel better, work better, and get more done (Seppala & Cameron, 2015).

On the other hand, a poor workplace culture also has a tremendous impact. A toxic or weak workplace culture leads to several negative consequences. For example, we want people to collaborate, but when leaders use a high-pressure approach to demand engagement, it leads to high stress and burnout. This causes staff to be more disengaged or to leave altogether. Staff turnover is actually 50% higher in more negative environments (Seppala & Cameron, 2015). On the other hand, organizations with engaged employees get 100% more job applications (Penrod, 2025).

Employees' health also suffers in high-pressure settings. According to the American Psychological Association, healthcare expenses are 50% higher in high-pressure organizations, not to mention the increased risk for heart issues (Nyberg, 2009; Seppala & Cameron, 2015).

Beyond emotional and physical impacts, a negative culture impacts productivity and effectiveness. Research by the Gallup Organization shows that disengaged staff have 37% more absenteeism in addition to more accidents and mistakes (Borysenko, 2019).

The list goes on.

As leaders, we play a crucial role in shaping the workplace environment. Research reveals that leaders need to show empathy and go out of their way to be helpful and friendly. They also need to create climates that support growth and collaboration, inviting others to talk to them and making it safe to share ideas, mistakes, and feedback (Seppala & Cameron, 2015). These are conditions where staff feel supported to improve. Ultimately, working conditions matter. That means that, as facilitators of improvement, we need to lead differently, creating a supportive, empowering, and safe work environment.

The good news is that improvement science, when done well, is a way to build a positive culture. Sure, education reform often fails when it relies on top-down approaches that do not successfully scale to wider use (Fullan & Quinn, 2015). As Li (2024) reminds us, "Reform does not necessarily involve improvement" (p. 725). So, how do we help change become improvement? Improvement science is an answer to that. It provides a structured, research-based process for addressing real problems, testing solutions, and scaling what works. At the same time, it can build a positive culture. When leaders intentionally create conditions such as shared purpose and psychological safety on the front end and use improvement science to reinforce factors like staff ownership and collective efficacy on the back end, the culture and the change process reinforce each other. Without a positive workplace culture, even the best improvement strategies will fail.

In the next section, we learn about the history and foundations of improvement science.

▶ THE EVOLUTION OF IMPROVEMENT SCIENCE—FROM INDUSTRY TO EDUCATION

Improvement science was not invented in education. In the mid-1900s, it actually emerged on the scene when industrial manufacturing, production, and assembly lines were seeking quality by putting out consistent products. In the 1980s, Deming (1982, 1994) shifted what we mean when we say *quality* by focusing on the process instead of just the products. Deming's method included less top-down management and more employee involvement in refining workflows and using data for decision-making. This approach was revolutionary. It led to significant advancements in productivity, reliability, and system efficiency.

Deming's quality improvement worked so well that, by the late 1980s, improvement science caught on in healthcare. This approach to improvement was totally new because it engaged stakeholders directly in improvement efforts. This method of improvement resulted in better patient outcomes, streamlined operations, and provided better job-embedded professional development for healthcare staff (Batalden & Davidoff, 2007).

Over time, education leaders saw its potential. They began to ask: What if we used this process to solve real problems in schools instead of chasing trends? Finally, in the early 2000s, researchers began exploring Deming's approach to quality improvement as a method for educational reform. Anthony Bryk, president of the Carnegie Foundation for the Advancement of Teaching, spearheaded its use in PK-12 school systems. He describes improvement science as a way to accelerate learning and address authentic challenges (Bryk et al., 2015). His work applied Deming's user-centered, problem-solving approach to help teams, also known as Networked Improvement Communities (NICs), drive meaningful change. When we make the change equity-focused, improvement science becomes a catalyst for social justice when superintendents, principals, and other educational leaders use it to address inequities and improve student outcomes.

Now improvement science is becoming a recognized tool for educational reform, as it applies Deming's (1982, 1994) structured, problem-centered approach to accelerate learning and support systemic change through rapid tests of improvement in school systems (Bryk et al., 2015). Specifically, educators use improvement science to ask three key questions:

1. What are we trying to accomplish?
2. How will we know that change is an improvement?
3. What change can we make that will result in improvement? (Langley et al., 2009).

The benefits of using improvement science in education include building knowledge, developing shared ownership, motivating innovators, gaining strategies by learning from variations in practice, and maintaining a focus on improvement (Lewis, 2015). Beyond these practical benefits, improvement science enhances system-wide change by influencing key areas of educational leadership, including vision, mission, equity, governance, instructional quality, and strategic planning (Li, 2021). This helps leaders move from managing outcomes to transforming the processes that produce those outcomes.

Early studies of using improvement science in education show promise. For instance, researchers collaborated with four large urban school districts to scale up math instruction improvement. Over five years, their data showed that when educators actively participated in decision-making and improvement work, teachers' instruction improved (Cobb et al., 2013).

Interestingly, while many fields have moved from theory to practice, improvement science started as a practice-based methodology that is now evolving into a formal research framework. Improvement science has become increasingly used as a research method to "define problems, understand how the system produces the problems, identify changes to rectify the problems, test the efficacy of those changes, and spread the changes (if the change is indeed an improvement)" (Hinnant-Crawford, 2020, p. 1).

Continuous improvement using improvement science is now respected and used as a way to transform schools and districts (Berwick, 2003; Bryk et al., 2015; Rother, 2009). However, despite its success across diverse sectors, education still hasn't maximized its use to scale knowledge *across* schools and districts (Lewis, 2015).

This book aims to bridge that gap by connecting Deming's industrial quality model to Bryk's application in education, offering leaders a structured way to create a culture that fosters system-wide, equity-focused improvement. For example, instead of asking, "What's wrong with this staff member?" we ask, "What about the system is making this outcome predictable?" Instead of launching one-size-fits-all solutions that we read about, we test and refine changes with real users in our real settings.

▶ CONNECTING CULTURE AND IMPROVEMENT

Here's the big idea: Culture and improvement are mutually reinforcing, not mutually exclusive. Educational leaders have tried well-intentioned improvement efforts such as new initiatives, strategic plans, and professional development designed to move schools forward. We've also seen many of these efforts fail to produce lasting change. While we have seen improvement science gaining traction in education, the process and tools alone are not enough. It's time to focus less on technical solutions and more on the human side of change.

Research has largely overlooked the role of workplace conditions, shaped by the leader, in sustaining systemic improvement (Improvement Science/Health Foundation, 2011). This leaves a critical blind spot that I call the *vision–implementation gap*. This gap is the disconnect between a leader's improvement vision and how (or if) it actually comes to life in schools and districts.

To respond to this gap, we will shift from focusing solely on *what* leaders implement to *how* they create the conditions for staff to engage in meaningful, lasting change, all driven by their compelling, equity-focused *why*. That's what makes this book about more than improvement science. It's about the leadership moves that make improvement possible! Improvement science, when led well, can be a catalyst for building an improvement culture.

A workplace culture that supports authentic improvement is not built overnight. It requires intentional leadership that fosters trust, collaboration, and a spirit of continuous learning. In the next chapter, we meet three leaders who are doing the work of successfully integrating improvement into their leadership practice and school systems. Their stories show what's possible when leaders bring together culture, values, and improvement mindsets to nurture meaningful change.

> **REFLECTION QUESTIONS**
>
> 1. Reflect on your experiences: What connections have you observed or experienced between workplace culture and successful (or unsuccessful) improvement efforts?
> 2. Leadership influence: How does leadership shape and sustain a positive workplace culture? What daily leadership actions or behaviors have you seen cultivate that positive environment?

CHAPTER 1 TRY THIS: BUILD A WORKPLACE CULTURE FOR CONTINUOUS IMPROVEMENT

A strong workplace culture is the foundation for continuous improvement. This activity will help you reflect on your current culture and consider the possibilities of using improvement science to help your school or district keep getting better.

1. Current Reality: Define Your Workplace Culture

Think about your current school or district culture.

- In a few words, how would you describe your workplace culture?
- What is one thing about your culture that positively impacts student and staff success?
- What is one aspect of your culture that limits collaboration, trust, or improvement efforts?

Copyright material from Marci Shepard (2026), *Where the Science of Improvement Meets the Heart of Leadership*, Routledge

2. Vision for the Future: Connect Culture to Improvement Science

Read the aspirational statements below and select one you most aspire to achieve.

- We have a positive workplace culture where all staff feel valued, supported, and connected to a shared purpose.
- Our teams collaborate regularly, leveraging diverse perspectives to solve the most challenging student-centered problems together.
- We ensure that improvement efforts are grounded in evidence and inquiry rather than assumptions or traditions.
- We continuously refine our approach by using small, iterative cycles of change before expanding initiatives to the whole school or district.
- We empower staff to take ownership of improvement efforts, ensuring they have a voice in identifying challenges, designing solutions, and making meaningful change.
- We embody vulnerability by acknowledging that we don't have all the answers, feeling safe to take risks, and sharing our learning and data.
- We have a culture where staff are eager to share what is working, spreading learning across teams and schools.

Then consider: Why did you select that statement? What would your team say?

Leadership Note: When you are ready to lead this journey, consider bringing this exercise to your team. Ask each person to select the aspirational statement that resonates with them, have partners share the statement they chose and why, and then come back to the whole group to hear about patterns in the team's responses. What does this tell you about your team's priorities and readiness for creating a culture of improvement?

▶ LEADERSHIP EXAMPLE: DISTRICT CLIMATE SURVEY AND STAFF FEEDBACK LOOPS

A strong workplace culture thrives on continuous feedback and reflection. Initially, our district introduced an exit interview process to gather insights from departing employees to help us understand why staff were choosing to move on. Recognizing the need to engage our current staff proactively, it dawned on us: Why are we waiting until people leave to systemically ask how they are doing?

That realization sparked a shift. We introduced an annual anonymous climate survey (a *stay*-interview, if you will) to help us better understand and have timely responses to employee experiences. Our human resources team led the work, fostering trust in the process. If *culture eats strategy for breakfast*, we knew we needed to elevate climate and culture to the same level of attention we gave our strategic improvement goals.

We asked employees to respond to statements like:

- I feel respected by my principal or manager.
- I feel valued as an employee of the organization.
- I understand the connection between my job and student success.
- I intend to stay with the district for at least the next two years.
- My school or department works together effectively toward common goals.
- I maintain a healthy balance between work and home life.
- I am given the resources needed to do my best work.

Once the quantitative ratings and qualitative comments came in, our leadership work really began. We disaggregated the results by role, school, department, and years of employment. Each leader facilitated a conversation with their team. We talked about the kind of culture we, as leaders, needed to set for this conversation – one of curiosity and not defensiveness. Our team needed to see that we weren't just taking a survey, we were using the results to get better through inquiry.

Schools and departments found that the climate survey data was a good first step in identifying areas for growth. But to truly understand the issues, teams needed to conduct further investigations through empathy interviews (one-on-one conversations that uncover people's experiences and perspectives).

From there, each team used their specific results to set culture improvement goals alongside their other strategic improvement goals. Every school and department added their goal to their improvement plan, making it public, strategic, and just as important as our other achievement and operational goals (see Table 1.1). Problems identified in the data were collaboratively solved *with* those affected, not just *for* them.

TABLE 1.1 School Improvement Plan – Climate and Culture Section

Strengths	Areas for Improvement

Strategies and Action Steps	Target Date or Timeline	Resources Needed	Vision for Success and Evidence of Effectiveness	Involvement of Stakeholders
Please provide a title, a brief overview, and a concise description of how this strategy will support your identified goal.	When will this strategy be employed at your school?	What will be needed to carry out the strategy as described?	What criteria will be used to measure success formatively and summatively? How will you progress monitor your goal?	Describe the role that the community, parents, staff, and other stakeholders are, or will be, involved in the development and/or monitoring of this goal.

Goals – Staff Engagement

When changes were made as a result of the survey input and goals, we didn't just assume staff would connect the changes they saw to the input they gave. We explicitly said, "We heard you. You told us student discipline felt inconsistent. So together, we're clarifying expectations, revising and committing to following through with the flowchart, and making sure reward systems are meaningful."

As our high school principal put it, this culture and climate work is an *all-play*. We made it a point to include everyone – bus drivers, cafeteria workers, custodial staff, teachers... Culture doesn't just live in one part of the system. It's everywhere.

In addition to our strategic improvement, we aimed to create a values-driven workplace where employees felt heard, important, and supported. We didn't get everything right, but we stayed committed to learning how our strategic focus and culture-building worked together so that improvement was something that made a difference and people liked being a part of it.

References

Batalden, P. B., & Davidoff, F. (2007). What is "quality improvement" and how can it transform healthcare? *Quality and Safety in Health Care, 16*(1), 2–3. https://doi.org/10.1136/qshc.2006.022046

Berwick, D. (2003). Improvement, trust, and the healthcare workforce. *Quality and Safety in Health Care, 12*(6), 448–452.

Borysenko, K. (2019, May 2). How much are your disengaged employees costing you? *Forbes.* https://www.forbes.com/sites/karlynborysenko/2019/05/02/how-much-are-your-disengaged-employees-costing-you/

Bryk, A. S., Gomez, L. M., Gunrow, A., & LeMahieu, P. G. (2015). *Learning to improve: How America's schools can get better and getting better.* Cambridge, MA: Harvard Education Publishing.

Cobb, P., Jackson, K., Smith, T., Sorum, M., & Henrick, E. (2013). Design research with educational systems: Investigating and supporting improvements in the quality of mathematics teaching and learning at scale. *National Society for the Study of Education, 112*(2), 320–349.

Deming, W. E. (1982). *Out of the crisis* (2nd ed.). Cambridge, MA: Massachusetts Institute of Technology, Center for Advanced Engineering Study.

Deming, W. E. (1994). *The new economics for industry, government, education* (2nd ed.). Cambridge, MA: Massachusetts Institute of Technology, Center for Advanced Engineering Study.

Fullan, M., & Quinn, J. (2015). *Coherence: The right drivers in action for schools, districts, and systems.* Ontario: Corwin Press and the Ontario Principals' Council.

Hinnant-Crawford, B. N. (2020). *Improvement Science in Education: A Primer.* Myers Education Press. Gorham, ME

Improvement science: Research scan/The Health Foundation (2011). The Health Foundation. https://www.health.org.uk/publications/improvement-science

Langley, G. J., Moen, R. D., Nolan, K. M., Nolan, T. W., Norman, C. L., & Provost, L. P. (2009). *The improvement guide* (2nd ed.). San Francisco, CA: Jossey-Bass.

Lewis, C. (2015). What is improvement science? Do we need it in education? *Educational Researcher, 44*(1), 54–61.

Li, J. (2021). Educational improvement for world-class teachers? A critical analysis of policy implementation in China. In X. Zhu & H. Song (Eds.), *Envisioning teaching and learning of teachers for excellence and equity in education* (pp. 69–85). New York: Springer.

Li (李军), J. (2024). Educational improvement science: The art of the improving organization. *ECNU Review of Education, 7*(3), 714–737.

Nyberg, A. (2009, November). Poor leadership poses a health risk at work. *Science Daily.* https://www.sciencedaily.com/releases/2009/11/091102121626.htm

Penrod, J. (2025). Understanding and nurturing organizational culture. *Kansas City Society of Association Executives.* https://www.kcsae.org/understanding-and-nurturing-organizational-culture/

Rother, M. (2009). *Toyota kata: Managing people for improvement, adaptiveness, and superior results.* New York: McGraw Hill.

Seppala, E., & Cameron, A. (December 1, 2015). Proof that positive work cultures are more productive. *Harvard Business Review.* https://hbr.org/2015/12/proofthat-positive-work-cultures-are-more-productive

Chapter 2
Meet Three Educational Leaders Who Use Improvement Science

LEARNING TARGET

I can analyze the leadership journeys and approaches of the three educational leaders and evaluate how their experiences and leadership styles inform my own growth as a leader.

Success Criteria

- Summarize the backgrounds and leadership approaches of the three featured leaders.
- Identify key leadership characteristics and common themes across the three leaders.
- Evaluate how their leadership experiences connect to my own leadership philosophy and growth.

RELEVANT NELP STANDARDS

- NELP Standard 1: Mission, Vision, and Improvement (Systems-Thinking)
- NELP Standard 2: Ethics and Professional Norms (Leadership as an Opportunity to Transform Culture, Leading with Vulnerability and Reflection, Prioritizing Collaboration)
- NELP Standard 3: Equity, Inclusiveness, and Cultural Responsiveness (Equity-Driven Leadership, Linguistic and Cultural Inclusion)
- NELP Standard 4: Learning and Instruction (Instructional Leadership)
- NELP Standard 7 (District-Level): Policy, Governance and Advocacy (System-Wide Thinking)

ICEBREAKER: LEADERSHIP IN A NUTSHELL

If someone were asked to describe your leadership style, what words would they use?

(See Appendix 1 for the Icebreaker Group Activity Facilitation Guide)

CASE VIGNETTE: THE SUPERINTENDENT WHO LED FROM A DISTANCE

Background

Dr. Callison had recently stepped into the superintendent role of Thunder Ridge Schools, a large, urban district. She moved quickly to modernize operations, implementing new data systems, streamlining central office structures, and launching initiatives aimed at improving student outcomes. On paper, the district ran more smoothly. When the Curriculum Director raised questions about instructional practice, Callison viewed that as the Director's area of responsibility. The superintendent's role, as

Callison saw it, was to ensure the district was managed well and systems operated efficiently.

Turning Point

At a regional superintendent meeting, Dr. Callison sat with three colleagues—Kyle, Melanie, and Shawn. As Callison's peers shared how they approached leadership, Callison noticed they stayed connected to the people and the work happening in schools, in addition to managing the systems.

Kyle reflected, "I spend time in classrooms to observe instruction but also to understand the experience from a teacher's lens. That's how I lead change—with the people doing the work."

Melanie shared, "If staff don't feel ownership, change won't last. I make sure they know I'm in it with them, from planning to implementation. Relationships are what make the work stick."

Shawn added, "I don't need to be the expert in every solution. My role is to model curiosity, ask good questions, and stay close enough to the work so people know they're not doing it alone."

As Callison listened, she began to recognize the gap in her own practice. She had been focused on managing the system but disconnected from the daily realities that shaped instruction and culture. That conversation shifted her thinking about leadership.

Bottom Line

Strategy matters, but so does presence. Leaders have to be in close proximity to the work, so they understand it, and to show that it's important.

Each person's leadership style is as unique as the individuals themselves. Our personal stories, previous experiences, and core values shape our leadership. In Chapter 1, we explored why workplace culture is foundational for improvement. But how do real leaders put these ideas into action? To find out, we'll meet three superintendents—Kyle, Melanie, and Shawn—who have successfully embedded improvement principles into their leadership. These leaders will be with us throughout the whole book, offering real-world insights on being improvement leaders that champion equity, inquiry, and systems change.

- Kyle leads an educational service center serving four counties.
- Melanie leads a large, urban school district.
- Shawn leads a medium-sized school district set in a rural area.

Although their paths to leadership and contexts differ, they are united by a shared commitment to equity, a belief in people, and a systems approach to improvement. Their voices help us see what it looks like to lead with clarity, humility, and courage.

The names used here are pseudonyms, but their stories, experiences, and quotes are real. Each has earned prestigious recognition at both state and national levels as Superintendent of the Year, President of an Administrator Association, and holding national leadership roles. More importantly, their leadership has earned the trust of the communities they serve.

These leaders don't just talk about improvement. They live it. They give us a behind-the-scenes glimpse of their leadership thinking and moves so we can see how they navigate the complexities of their roles, champion the cause of every student, and manage tensions. They truly embody both the heart and science of leading improvement.

After hearing the individual stories of each leader, we will look across them to identify common characteristics that bring equity-focused leadership to life. As you meet them, consider how their experiences connect to your own and how their leadership mindsets and practices spark reflections about your own leadership.

▶ KYLE'S STORY

Kyle, superintendent of an Educational Service District (ESD) supporting multiple school districts, began his career at 22 as an agriculture teacher before becoming a high school vice principal and then an assistant superintendent. He moved into the superintendent role when his superintendent retired. Kyle served there for six years before spending 12 years as superintendent in another district. Now, in his role at the ESD for six years, he leads improvement efforts at a broader, systems level. Kyle describes his region as primarily agricultural, with counties that rely on farming and host a significant migrant population.

His decision to pursue the superintendency came from a former colleague's encouragement. Although initially feeling unready when his supervisor left, he embraced the opportunity, recognizing that effective leadership is about fostering systems that enable continuous growth.

Early in his tenure, his district received a Gates Foundation grant, which exposed him to national experts in instructional leadership. This experience reinforced his belief that focused, intentional improvement efforts centered on quality instruction yield meaningful change. During a presentation for the Gates grant, he recalls a time when someone predicted, "In five years, everyone will be doing this good work." Even 20 years later, Kyle observes that many schools still struggle with focused improvement, not because they lack will, but because they lack the know-how to lead it effectively.

Kyle leads as both a communicator and a collaborator. He builds genuine relationships by getting to know people personally and fosters a low-hierarchy, flat organizational structure where staff actively participate in decision-making. He believes that the superintendent's role is to remove barriers, provide support, and ensure that those closest to students have the resources they need to succeed. Emphasizing reciprocal accountability, he believes leaders must examine their own actions when outcomes fall short.

At the heart of Kyle's work is a commitment to ensuring every child learns and graduates prepared for their chosen path. He challenges the traditional view of public education as a ranking system, urging educators to focus on moving the needle for the last 10%, those who need it most.

For Kyle, vulnerability is a leadership strength. He models how superintendents can admit when they don't have all the answers, learn alongside staff, and focus on improving practices rather than placing blame. His advice to other leaders: Tap into what excites you, focus on your passion, and lead transformative change.

▶ MELANIE'S STORY

Melanie, superintendent of a large urban school district, never set out to be a leader. She grew up in a family of public servants, which instilled in her a strong value for civic engagement and a deep commitment to teaching in her own city.

Determined to serve her community, she tailored her education to meet the unique needs of its diverse student population, where 56% of her students speak Spanish and many others are in the district's Russian bilingual program. She earned a degree in elementary education and a minor in English as a Second Language and Multicultural Education. Today, she ensures that nearly all 17 elementary schools offer dual-language programs, ensuring all students receive a culturally responsive education.

Melanie's leadership is characterized by deep listening, relationship-building, and a commitment to continuous learning for all. Instead of setting out to lead, she simply focused on becoming the best educator she could be for the children in her community. Seeking broader impact, she pursued a counseling degree and later served as a school counselor, which opened the door to leadership conversations. Encouraged by mentors who recognized strengths she hadn't seen in herself, she earned her administrator credential and eventually stepped into leadership roles, including Principal and Director of Human Resources (HR).

While serving in HR, Melanie observed a culture that was rigid, top-down, and exclusionary. She notes that this was not the *fault* of the leaders; it was the kind of command-and-control style that was expected of early women superintendents. She learned from this. Early in her career, she was told she was *too nice* and would *get eaten alive* in leadership. Although once criticized or seen as a weakness, Melanie gets compliments for her vulnerability, and she leans on it as a strength.

When the superintendent role opened, she faced a decision: step into the position to influence change or leave the district entirely. She chose to lead.

As a leader, Melanie describes herself as *heart-forward* and leads from relationships rather than titles. She tells her community, "I'm going to show up every day on your behalf," and she does so by serving those who do the heavy lifting for students.

A systems thinker at heart, Melanie ensures that improvement efforts aren't just for the sake of change; they are integrated into the district's strategic goals and supported with "accountability that is like a hug rather than a hammer."

She believes true change transforms people, not just processes. So she is deeply invested in creating systems that are not only effective but also affirming and inclusive. By centering staff and student voices, she has fostered a culture where educators feel valued, heard, and empowered to lead meaningful change.

▶ SHAWN'S STORY

Shawn, superintendent of a medium-sized school district, knew early on that he wanted to be an educator, inspired by his parents, who were both teachers. He began his career teaching sixth-grade English Language Arts and social studies during the early days of state standards and assessments. Working on curriculum and assessments alongside fellow educators sparked his passion for collaborative problem-solving.

A few years later, when a friend suggested he pursue a master's in administration and obtain a principal certificate, Shawn hesitated at first. He hadn't planned to become a principal. However, during his internship, he experienced an epiphany. He realized he could excel in a leadership role by learning from both the mistakes and successes of others. This insight propelled him to accept his first administrator position in his current district, where he has now served for 21 years.

Shawn advanced quickly, first as an assistant principal and K-12 reading specialist, then as a principal for four years, and later as the Executive Director for Teaching and Learning. In that role, he embraced a systems approach, learning to view challenges through a holistic lens rather than as isolated issues. When the longtime superintendent retired, the school board recognized Shawn's talent and named him superintendent, a position he never actively sought but has held for the past ten years.

Shawn cherishes the opportunity to develop others. He mentors new principals and supports central office leaders, believing his greatest reward is watching others grow. He values strong, two-way communication, clear vision, and consistent follow-through. His leadership style is both reflective and collaborative, openly discussing his own challenges. He strives to be a lifelong learner, encouraging his team to ask, "What is the problem we are trying to solve?" rather than chasing change for its own sake.

Understanding the pressures of his role, Shawn prioritizes self-care and transparency. He has weathered tense union negotiations, community challenges, and the politicization of current issues with resilience, acknowledging that even the toughest moments have made him a stronger leader. To foster team-care (like self-care), he gathers weekly with his administrative leaders to connect in brief stand-up meetings that blend laughter with quick strategic check-ins, reinforcing that a positive, collaborative culture is key to success.

Equity is at the heart of Shawn's work. Despite leading in a traditionally conservative community, he has championed systemic equity initiatives, even in the face of resistance. His focus remains on ensuring all students have access to high-quality opportunities, and he sees equity as a fundamental responsibility of leadership.

Shawn's leadership has three core hallmarks: relationships, communication, and follow-through. He believes superintendents must be present in every corner of the district to truly build a culture of trust and collective success. Shawn makes an effort to personally know each of his 510 staff members by name. His approach to leadership is reflective, often analyzing past decisions to refine his practice and improve outcomes and experiences for students and staff alike.

▶ FIVE COMMON THREADS AMONG THE LEADERS: LEADERSHIP APPROACHES

As I got to know Kyle, Melanie, and Shawn, five powerful themes consistently surfaced. Despite serving in different contexts, being at different stages in their careers, and having different leadership styles, these leaders share a core set of values and practices that define transformative educational leadership.

They See Leadership as an Opportunity to Transform Culture

None of these leaders set out to climb the leadership ladder. In fact, each of them was prompted by someone else to step into a leadership role. They each agreed to do so because they saw an opportunity to influence culture and create the conditions for meaningful change.

Kyle moved into leadership when a former teaching colleague, now a superintendent, encouraged him to apply for the role. Although Kyle initially felt unprepared when his superintendent retired after his first year in the central office, he embraced the challenge and now leads with a focus on support and systems improvement.

Melanie never saw herself as a leader, until others did. While working in the central office, she was asked to consider the superintendency when her retiring superintendent needed a successor. Faced with a district culture she wanted to improve or leave behind, she chose to lead it forward, determined to serve those closest to the students and change the culture for the better.

Shawn didn't plan to become a principal, let alone a superintendent. After being encouraged to pursue leadership and stepping into central office roles, he reimagined the superintendency, focusing on vision, instruction, and connection.

> *You*: How do you view your leadership as an opportunity to transform culture?

They Are Equity-Driven Leaders

Each of these leaders keeps equity front and center, ensuring that district decisions are made with the needs of students in the gaps at the forefront.

Kyle centers his efforts on ensuring every child learns and graduates ready for the future they choose. He is driven by a belief that educators must focus on the last 10% of students who we haven't yet reached.

Melanie sees inclusion and connection as defining values in her district. She actively champions programs like dual-language education, ensuring students receive culturally responsive instruction tailored to their needs.

Shawn advances equity, even in the face of resistance. In a conservative-leaning setting, he's clear. Creating opportunities for all students is non-negotiable.

> *You*: How do you lead with equity as a guiding principle?

They Lead with Vulnerability and Reflection

These leaders don't pretend to have all the answers. Instead, they model openness, reflection, and continuous growth, building the psychological safety for others to do the same.

Kyle considers vulnerability one of his core principles. He believes that openly admitting when he doesn't have all the answers and learning alongside staff invites others to take risks.

Melanie has led a cultural shift in how vulnerability is viewed in her district. Once seen as a weakness, it is now celebrated as a leadership asset. She uses reflection to make course corrections to programs and recognize where adjustments are needed to unify teams.

Shawn practices transparency, showing that leaders are human, ready to acknowledge and learn from mistakes. He openly discusses his own evaluations with principals, reflecting on where he can grow and how he has improved, making vulnerability visible and safe.

> *You*: How do you lead through vulnerability and reflection?

They Are Instructional Leaders and Systems Thinkers

These leaders understand the importance of aligning classroom instruction with broader district systems, leading with coherence from a teaching and learning stance.

Kyle sharpened his instructional leadership early by learning from experts. He focuses on the instructional core—students, teachers, and content—while fostering collaborative problem-solving.

Melanie sparked an instructional shift by reframing staff roles to show how everyone works in service of the students. She aligned hiring practices, goals, and governance with the district's core values, ensuring coherence.

Shawn mentors and coaches his staff to solve complex challenges by combining high expectations with strong support. He has moved from reactive, isolated problem-solving to a proactive, systems approach, ensuring alignment for instructional success.

> *You*: How do you align instructional leadership with systems thinking?

They Prioritize Collaboration

For these leaders, it's not lonely at the top. Collaboration is for the system and for themselves. They actively lead decision-making and improvement with others, and they learn through professional networks with colleagues.

Kyle structures his organization to be flat, inviting all voices in decisions and solutions. Learning is deeper when more people are involved in the work. He credits his own growth to insights gained through peer networks.

Melanie leads from a place of relationship. She centers people and connection through a heart-forward approach. She listens and uses input to inform decisions. Staying involved in professional organizations enhances her leadership with fresh perspectives.

Shawn knows every employee by name. He fosters two-way communication so that district leadership and school teams work together seamlessly. He's active in regional networks, refining his leadership through shared learning and collaboration.

> *You*: How do you foster collaboration within and beyond your system?

As we move forward, Kyle, Melanie, and Shawn will continue to walk alongside us, sharing how they navigate real challenges, try out strategies, and stay anchored to their purpose through the ups and downs of improvement leadership. They remind us that this work is complex and deeply human, but also very possible!

❓ REFLECTION QUESTIONS

1. Core Values in Action: What did you notice about the way Kyle, Melanie, and Shawn naturally wove their core values into their personal leadership stories?
2. Leadership Characteristics: Kyle, Melanie, and Shawn shared five common leadership characteristics:
   - Leadership as an Opportunity to Transform Culture
   - Equity-Driven Leadership
   - Leading with Vulnerability and Reflection
   - Instructional Leadership and Systems Thinking
   - Prioritizing Collaboration

   In what ways do these characteristics reflect your leadership style? What impact might these characteristics have on school systems? How do these traits contribute to sustained improvement efforts?
3. Your Leadership Story: Educational leaders often introduce themselves in various contexts. How would you briefly tell the story of who you are as a leader, including your core values? (For an extended activity, see the "Try This" below.)

CHAPTER 2 TRY THIS: IDENTIFY YOUR LEADERSHIP VALUES

Step 1: Reflect on the Importance of Core Values

Why does identifying and leading with your core values matter?

Some reasons may include:

- You model them in every decision, word, and action.
- They build trust by ensuring alignment between beliefs, words, and actions.
- They drive what you celebrate, measure, and confront.
- They define your moral compass, shaping expectations and resource allocation.
- They provide clarity and courage in difficult situations.

Step 2: Identify and Prioritize Your Core Values

1. List 10 core values that resonate most with you. (Looking at various core values lists can help spark ideas.)
2. Narrow your list down to your top five values.
3. Rank the five values in order of priority.
4. Rate yourself (0–10) on how well you embody each value.

Step 3: Conduct an Integrity Inventory

To me, integrity is the alignment between what you *believe*, *say*, and *do*.

For each core value, complete the following:

- Believe: What does this value mean to you?
- Say: What language and phrases reinforce this value? What language and phrases contradict it?
- Do: What actions align with this value? What actions undermine it?

(Optional: Complete this exercise with a partner for deeper insights.)

▶ EXTENSION: SHARE YOUR VALUES AND LEADERSHIP STORY

- Develop Your Leadership Introduction: In many settings, leaders introduce themselves. Craft a brief introduction that shares your leadership story. Embed your values, so those you serve understand who you are.
- Make Your Values Visible: Share your values and leadership story with your school board, leadership team, staff, and community in your meetings, newsletters, and decision-making.
- Embed Your Values in Your Work: Regularly refer to your values in your decisions, conversations, and strategic actions.

By engaging in this process, you align your leadership with your core values, fostering authenticity, trust, and a strong foundation for a shared improvement culture.

▶ EXTENSION: WHAT WOULD YOUR TEAM SAY?

When you are ready to engage your team, ask them to identify their values. Knowing your personal values is half the battle. Identifying (then reinforcing) *shared* values and purpose is the other half.

Reflect on:

- How can you create space for your staff and community to explore their own core values?
- How can you facilitate connections between individual values and collective school/department/district values and goals?
- What steps can you take to ensure shared values are actively and explicitly shaping your school/department/district culture, strategies, and decisions?

▶ LEADERSHIP EXAMPLE: GUESS THE LEADER'S CORE VALUES

Strong leaders talk about their values and explicitly live them. One of the most powerful moments in my superintendent experience happened during a leadership retreat with my cabinet and school administrators. I brought in a consultant to lead a session, and (to my surprise) he ended up facilitating an activity testing how visible my values were in my leadership.

The facilitator started by asking me to privately write down my top three to five core values. I quickly jotted them down, expecting others would be asked to do the same. But then he turned to the group and said, "Now, each of you write down what you believe are Marci's core values."

There was no hesitation. "We think we can do that." My team got to work writing their individual lists, then comparing notes. It became a game of leadership Boggle—some values appeared on nearly every list, while others sparked conversation.

"I have equity," one person said.

"Same here!" others chimed in.

"That's a good one. I should have written that," someone else added.

Once the group landed on a shared list of what they thought were my core values, the facilitator asked me to reveal my list. To everyone's surprise, including mine, the two lists were nearly identical.

There have certainly been leadership moments when my team surfaced blind spots I needed to address. Those moments were hard (and needed). But this one was different. It was an affirming moment of leadership. My team could *see* my values.

We closed the activity with a group reflection.

- What actions made my values visible?
- Where might there be gaps between what I say I value and how I lead?
- How can I strengthen alignment between my leadership and my core values?
- How do we, as leaders, demonstrate our core values?

This activity reinforced the importance of leading with authenticity and ensuring that the values we claim are evident in how we show up each day.

But it doesn't stop with personal values. As a leadership team, we regularly refined and revisited our shared values, norms, and collective commitments. Below is an example of what we developed, and more importantly, how we used it as an anchor for our culture, guide for our work, and filter for our decisions.

Our Leadership Team Commitments

In everything we do, we will…

- Focus on learning, collaboration, results, and continuous improvement
- Ensure data-driven decisions using meaningful measurements
- Provide equity of opportunities and resources
- Communicate with and engage students, families, staff, and community

Our Norms:

- Do I use evidence to support my thinking and press others to do the same?
- Do I demonstrate a growth mindset by expecting and accepting the discomfort that comes with non-closure, change, and learning while committing to a deeper understanding at the individual and group level?
- Do I practice clear and positive communication by going directly to a team member with concerns or issues and listening to truly understand?
- Do I encourage and promote equitable contributions, risk-taking, and respect for divergent thinking by asking questions and sharing ideas that challenge my and others' thinking and understanding?
- Do I support and celebrate student, staff, school, district accomplishments?

Our Collective Commitments:

- Prioritize our focus on teaching and learning
- Leverage collaborative teams in support of student learning and growth
- Ensure frequent analysis of meaningful data, including by-student, by-standard
- Provide leadership development, support, and collaboration
- Own and respond to results to promote improvement through reflection, monitoring, and adjustment

Our Decision-Making Model:

- We will determine and communicate if the decision is command, advisory, or consensus, then use the following decision-making filters:
    - How will this decision impact and/or support student and staff learning, results, and wellness?
    - To what extent does the decision align with our mission, vision, values, collective commitments, and goals?
    - How will quantitative and qualitative data be used to inform and evaluate the effectiveness of this decision?
    - What are the non-negotiables related to this decision that must be considered?
    - What impact will this decision have on our stakeholders, and how are they involved in the decision-making?
    - What commitments are needed to achieve the desired results?
    - What resources are necessary to support this decision?

As a team, we didn't just write these statements. We shared them publicly, consistently anchored back to them, and explicitly attached our actions to them so they lived beyond words on a page. They became who we were and how we led together.

Part II

The What: Theories, Principles, and Leadership Paradigm Shifts

Chapters 3, 4, and 5
  Equity-Focused Improvement Leadership

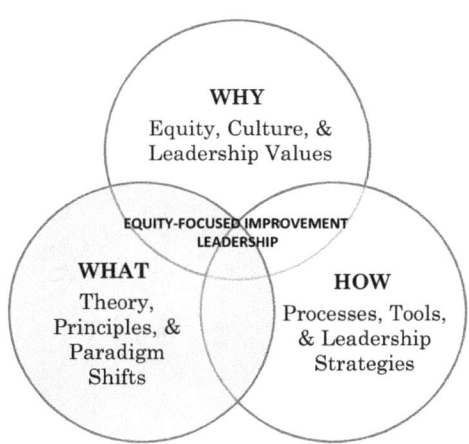

Figure PII.1 Part II—The What.

We've established that equity (Preface), culture (Chapter 1), and leadership values (Chapter 2) are foundational for meaningful improvement. Now it's time to answer the question: What theories and principles actually support this kind of improvement leadership?

This part explores the key theories and research-based concepts of improvement science, helping leaders move beyond a compliance-driven checklist to a growth-oriented and human-centered culture.

- Chapter 3 reviews the theory behind improvement science, including the system-level thinking of W. Edwards Deming and others who shaped the field.
- Chapter 4 introduces six core principles that frame successful improvement, giving you a framework for leading with clarity and intention.
- Chapter 5 synthesizes six key paradigm shifts that separate improvement leadership from traditional leadership.

By the end of this second part, you'll have a deeper understanding of the mindsets and models that support equity-focused leadership. Then, in Part III, we'll turn this theory into action with concrete tools and strategies to lead improvement at scale.

Chapter 3

Theory behind Improvement Science

LEARNING TARGET

I can analyze the theory behind improvement science and evaluate how it can be used to transform leaders and systems.

Success Criteria

- Explain why traditional reform efforts often fail and how improvement science provides a more effective approach.
- Make connections between Deming's models and modern system-wide transformation.
- Evaluate the implications of improvement theory for school systems and educational leaders.
- Apply the principles of improvement science to building collaborative, team-based improvement efforts.

RELEVANT NELP STANDARDS

- NELP Standard 1: Mission, Vision, and Improvement (System Improvement and Improvement Science)
- NELP Standard 2: Ethics and Professional Norms (Failed Reform Efforts, A Transformed Leader, Collaborative Teams)
- NELP Standard 5: Community and External Leadership (Networked Improvement Communities)
- NELP Standard 6: Operations and Management (Systems-thinking)
- NELP Standard 7 (Building-Level): Building Professional Capacity (Job-Embedded Training, Evaluations)
- NELP Standard 7 (District-Level): Policy, Governance, and Advocacy (System of Profound Knowledge; Quality Management)

ICEBREAKER: CRASH AND BURN (AND LEARN)

Think of a time you were part of an initiative that failed or didn't stick.

- What contributed to that failure?
- What leadership lessons can you learn from the experience?

(See Appendix 1 for the Icebreaker Group Activity Facilitation Guide)

CASE VIGNETTE: THE DEPARTMENTS THAT PUT DEMING TO WORK

Background

High Peak School District wasn't in crisis, but it wasn't improving either. Each department had its own goals and projects. Human Resources was introducing a new substitute management system. Technology was tackling AI policies. Special Services was building a Multi-Tiered System of

Support. Curriculum was launching a new Science of Reading program. Despite all the motion, however, it felt like being pulled in different directions. People were working hard, but the work felt fragmented, and results weren't changing.

Turning Point

During a leadership retreat, Assistant Superintendent Garcia shared what she learned at a recent conference session about systems thinking and Deming's System of Profound Knowledge. For the first time, she saw the district's challenge differently. She realized this wasn't about individual department issues but a system issue. Everyone was paddling, but not in sync.

Garcia brought that mindset back to the team and helped leaders connect the dots across departments. They started mapping out how various initiatives overlapped—or didn't. They asked new questions.

- What problem are we trying to solve?
- Who's impacted?
- What's causing it?

As more staff from across the system were invited into the conversation, something felt different. Staff began to feel more invested. Leaders realized how a team's actions in one area ripple into others. Curriculum decisions were discussed alongside technology efforts.

It didn't happen overnight, but, for the first time, it felt like everyone was pulling in the same direction.

Bottom Line

Change ≠ Improvement. Improvement happens when we transform systems instead of stacking on new "solutions." When we zoom out to see the system, we stop chasing symptoms and start creating real, connected progress.

Educational leaders are facing complex challenges that can't be solved by a spattering of initiatives thrown at them, chasing quick fixes, or relying on top-down mandates. What we need to focus on are processes that provide a structured, inquiry-based approach that helps us diagnose root causes, learn as we go, and scale what actually works.

Improvement science answers that call. It's a framework based on theory (research-based) and practice (evidence-based). It offers a disciplined way to identify problems, test solutions, learn from failure, and build sustainable change—change that is actually improvement.

In this chapter, we'll build shared understanding of the theoretical foundations of improvement science, as well as leadership mindsets and practices necessary for being an improvement leader.

Ever wonder why so many well-intentioned and researched reform efforts fall short? Without the right tools to effectively support and scale change, leaders are left trying to push improvement through systems that aren't designed for it (Bryk et al., 2015).

Bryk et al. (2015) put it plainly: "As a field, we undervalue the importance of systematic and organized methods of learning to improve" (p. 468). Too often, we implement changes too fast while learning too slowly. That mismatch is at the crux of failed reforms.

Under pressure to act quickly, districts apply rapid-fix solutions without fully diagnosing the root cause. Then, when the results we hoped to see do not happen, the program is abandoned, and a new one takes its place. This cycle creates initiative fatigue, and, over time, staff disengage. The intent to improve is there, but the system isn't built to support it.

Fullan and Quinn's (2015) research confirms what educators are telling us. Their biggest struggles are: too many ad hoc projects with no clear purpose, top-down mandates disconnected from classroom realities, bureaucratic policies focused on compliance over improvement, fragmentation/silos/lack of collaboration, and distrust and demoralization. Instead of addressing the cause underlying these conditions, we often double down on the wrong things.

Fullan (2011) argues that leaders often respond to these struggles with four *wrong drivers* that actually hinder system reform:

1. Accountability over capacity building—Focusing on monitoring and compliance rather than developing educators' skills

2. Individual quality over group quality—Prioritizing teacher evaluation systems instead of strengthening collective expertise
3. Technology over instruction—Adopting digital tools without a clear instructional purpose
4. Fragments over systems—Launching multiple disconnected initiatives rather than building coherence

These drivers are well-intentioned, but cause more harm than good. They create movement, but not improvement.

So what works? The good news is that Fullan (2011) offers solutions—four *right drivers* that enhance system-wide improvement. "The right drivers are effective because they work directly on changing the culture" (Fullan & Quinn, 2015, p. 4).

1. Focusing direction—Setting crystal-clear strategic priorities to guide system improvement
2. Cultivating collaborative cultures—Building trust, teamwork, and shared leadership across schools and districts
3. Deepening learning—Making professional development meaningful, immediately applicable, and student-centered
4. Securing accountability—Shifting from compliance-based accountability to shared responsibility

None of these happen by accident. Fullan and Quinn (2015) assert that leadership is the key to activating these drivers. This means moving beyond big talk to creating the conditions that actually help people succeed.

▶ SYSTEM IMPROVEMENT THROUGH IMPROVEMENT SCIENCE

Improvement science offers a practical way to bridge the culture we seek and the right drivers that actually move systems forward. It brings together values, process, and strategy in a way that leaders can act on. In fact, Fullan and Quinn (2015) make this connection clear. They link their research on effective system improvement drivers to improvement science, making it a tangible way to build workplace culture through clarity, learning, and collaboration.

Bryk et al. (2015) adds to this, highlighting two big barriers we face in education: system complexity and performance variability. Improvement science helps cut through the noise. When leaders apply the principles of improvement, we can stop the merry-go-round of passing disconnected initiatives and disappointing outcomes and start building systems that support coherent and consistent growth. Improvement science builds knowledge.

Here's where Deming's foundational work comes in. Improvement science is forging new connections between knowledge and practical change in our schools (Langley et al., 2009). It leans on two essential kinds of knowledge needed for system improvement.

1. Content knowledge. This is the *what* of improvement work. It covers your expertise in leadership, instruction, and management (Li, 2024).
2. Profound Knowledge. This is the *how* of improvement work. It comes from Deming's System of Profound Knowledge (Deming, 1994), which covers four key areas:
   - An appreciation for the system
   - An understanding of variation
   - The theory of knowledge
   - Insights into human behavior (Deming, 1994)

This *system* gives leaders principles that we can apply to our own unique organization at any level, whether we are connecting a single department to an entire district or a teacher team to a whole school (Lewis, 2015). By blending these two types of knowledge—content knowledge and profound knowledge—leaders can tackle systemic challenges more effectively (Li, 2024).

Most research emphasizes technical or content knowledge. But that's incomplete. Few studies focus on *how* leaders actually learn and apply new ideas through improvement processes (Lewis, 2015). In fact, Goldsmith et al. (2014) found that many studies overlook process details altogether in favor of jumping right to final results.

We will be slowing down to unpack the *how*, showing how educational leaders can use improvement science to build a positive workplace culture that ultimately produces gap-closing results.

Deming (1982, 1994) didn't just want to tweak old systems. He wanted to transform them. Instead of overemphasizing outcomes, he believed that when we create better processes, better results would follow. It's about creating systems that work better (and keep getting better), not just harder.

Educational leaders are surrounded by interconnected systems of classrooms, schools, departments, and districts. These systems are all shaped by instructional, managerial, and relational processes (Anderson et al., 2024).

Sustainable improvement starts with small, meaningful changes and expands over time. To achieve this, Deming gives us several transformational theories:

- The System of Profound Knowledge
- The 14 Points for the Transformation of Management
- The Seven Deadly Diseases of Management
- The Plan–Do–Study–Act (PDSA) Cycle

In the following sections, we will explore each of these theories more closely.

First, let's start with a key theory behind improvement science—the System of Profound Knowledge. Bear with me. This theory may sound lofty, but it sets the stage for practical leadership application in your schools and district.

▶ DEMING'S SYSTEM OF PROFOUND KNOWLEDGE

When schools and departments struggle, it's tempting to respond with more programs, demanding more complex work, implementing merit systems, tightening accountability, offering incentives, imposing strict standards, or using motivational techniques. But Deming (Deming, 1982, 1994) reminds us that these approaches miss the mark. They don't improve quality. They merely shift responsibility *away* from leadership. Real change starts with us. Deming emphasized that leaders are the ones who must own quality improvement. It's not something leaders can delegate.

That's a bold shift! And it runs counter to many of the prevalent management styles we see today that breed destructive competition among individuals on the same team, teams in the same school, and schools or departments in the same district. Deming pushes back on this mindset. He argues that everyone should work together as a unified system, collaborating rather than competing.

Collaboration is easy to say and hard to lead. We must build deep trust *between* leaders and staff, and *among* staff. That trust is founded on a clear purpose and shared values. In our complex educational systems, principals and superintendents are the ones responsible for setting the tone and shaping the system's direction (Macht, 2016). And that starts by transforming how we lead. This is where Deming's concept of profound knowledge comes in.

Deming's (1994) System of Profound Knowledge includes four interdependent ideas that shape how leaders approach system-level transformation.

1. Appreciation of a System—Understanding how different parts of an organization interact and influence one another
2. Knowledge of Variation—Identifying patterns, inconsistencies, and differences to uncover improvement opportunities
3. Theory of Knowledge—Testing assumptions and learning based on evidence gathered through inquiry
4. Psychology of Change—Recognizing human motivation, collaboration, fear, and the dynamics of change

Hang on to your hat. This work starts with us! Before we can transform the system, we must first transform ourselves (Deming, 1994). (This is an anchor point we will continue to revisit.)

When you internalize the ideas in this system of profound knowledge, you begin to see new meaning in your life, work, data, and interactions with colleagues (Deming, 1994). When you fully grasp these principles, Deming says you apply them to every relationship and decision, providing a solid foundation to transform your organization. According to Deming, a transformed leader will:

- Set an inspiring example
- Listen actively without compromising core values
- Continuously mentor and teach others
- Help staff let go of outdated practices and embrace new ones without feeling guilty about the past (pp. 92–93)

So, let's delve into each one of the four principles that help leaders lead from a place of profound knowledge.

Principle 1: Appreciation of a System

Understanding systems—how interconnected parts work together to achieve a common purpose—is the foundation. Deming (1994) defines a system as "a network of interdependent components that work together to try to accomplish the aim of the system" (p. 50). A system is about more than all the programs and people; it's about how everything connects.

Scholtes (1998) expands on the critical characteristics of a system:

- A system is a whole made up of many interdependent parts
- Each part has a defined purpose and affects other parts, making them interconnected
- You can't understand the systems by analyzing individual parts in isolation; you have to examine how the parts interact to create overall outcomes
- Organizations function as both social and technical systems, requiring leaders to avoid applying oversimplified solutions to complex challenges

In this book, I often refer to *your systems* in the context of your educational leadership. This may be your teams, schools, departments, district, or education organizations, encompassing instructional, operational, and relational processes.

As a leader, you have a key role in creating and communicating your system's purpose. Not all organizations operate as systems. An organization can only become a system when it has a clearly defined purpose or aim (Deming, 1982). You help create, communicate, and align the entire organization toward this purpose. Deming (1994) says that we, as leaders, need to make sure the aim benefits everyone involved—employees, students, families, stakeholders, and the community. He explains: "The aim proposed here for any organization is for everybody to gain—stockholders, employees, suppliers, customers, community, the environment—over the long term" (p. 51). Long-term success requires a culture of learning, where improvement is a continuous, shared responsibility. If that aim is missing, different parts of the system will work in isolation, leading to inefficiencies and conflicting priorities.

That's why leaders must lead with a systems lens. We need to be able to understand and communicate how different internal and external factors influence one another. We need to be able to share insights and predictions with stakeholders. We need to be able to show how changes in one part of the system affect others (Deming, 1994). When people understand their role within the larger system and see the impact of their contributions, they find greater purpose and joy in their work!

Importantly, leaders need to solve problems at the system level. A common leadership mistake is blaming individuals for problems that are actually caused by the system. In fact, Deming (1994) argues that most problems stem from the system itself, not from individuals. In *Out of Crisis* (Deming, 1982), he estimates:

- 94% of problems are systemic and fall under management's responsibility.
- Only 6% of problems are due to individual employees or special causes. (p. 315)

This means we need to stop pointing fingers at staff, students, or others and start improving the design of the systems we lead.

Doing so lays the groundwork for an environment of trust, engagement, and shared responsibility for improvement.

Principle 2: Knowledge of Variation

Variation is everywhere. It is in outcomes across time, locations, and circumstances. Unless we understand why variation exists, we risk making poor decisions. We need to help teams use data to answer critical questions such as, *Why did something go wrong?* or *How can we replicate this success?* When we recognize, analyze, and learn from variation, we can make informed decisions that lead to sustained improvement (Deming, 1994).

Deming (1994) identifies two types of variation that leaders must pay attention to:

1. Special Cause Variation—These are unique, often external events that disrupt the system. We usually see them as one-time disruptions or anomalies. They have a place. We need to analyze these variations immediately, while the details are still fresh, to determine what worked well and what went wrong. This will help us handle the situation better next time or avoid it altogether. (For example, a sharp drop in student attendance during COVID quarantines.)
2. Common Cause Variation—These variations occur naturally within a system and result from multiple influences. These can often fly under the radar and not demand our attention in the same way that special cause variation does. They are built-in, predictable fluctuations in a stable system (Deming, 1994). Because they stem from deep-rooted issues, they require system-wide improvements rather than isolated fixes (Scholtes, 1998). (For example, persistent student attendance decline long after COVID protocols were lifted.)

I often told my leadership team that when problems arise, we approach them from two angles. One, we need to be reactive, responding to the immediate problem. Two, we need to be proactive, zooming out to fix what caused it. In a way, when problems occur, they surface issues that help us improve our system.

Beware! A leadership trap is lurking here. We often overfocus or overreact to special causes while underestimating or ignoring the common causes. We often get pulled into living in the tyranny of the urgent rather than focusing on what is truly important. Put another way, we fix what's loud and miss what's quietly embedded in the system. Don't get me wrong—the urgent matters must be addressed. This cautionary note is a reminder that common cause variations don't smack you in the face like special cause variations. They are also harder to detect. Since common cause variation is often baked into the system itself, we must pause and be intentional about uncovering and addressing underlying structures and processes (Deming, 1994).

We can fall into another trap. Assuming that unexpected events (special causes) are isolated, failing to recognize how consistent, system-wide factors (common cause) influence the seemingly one-time event.

For example, let's say a high school sees a spike in student absenteeism. The principal immediately implements a stricter attendance policy. While this seemed like a reasonable reaction to the data, it was an example of over-focusing on a special cause, a temporary increase in absences, rather than addressing the common cause variations that contributed to ongoing absenteeism in the school.

Upon further investigation, the principal identified deeper, systemic issues: student disengagement. Rather than focusing solely on punishment for missed days, teams developed solutions such as strengthening their tier-one positive behavior system to emphasize relationships and belonging, and expanding the use of student talk protocols to increase relationships and engagement in classrooms. By addressing the root causes of absenteeism rather than reacting to a temporary fluctuation, the school made lasting improvements.

The moral of the story is we learn from variation. However, we need to be careful not to get sucked into the vortex of reacting to special cause variation rather than doing the less sexy but needed work of responding to common cause variation.

However, as my colleague Dr. Carlos Sandoval shared in a recent conversation, special cause and common cause variation aren't discrete entities. They are relative and contextual. A special cause is only *special* in light of what the system considers *common*. A data point or event becomes noteworthy because it deviates from the patterns that those looking at the variation expect. So, what's seen as common in one district may be special in another. Carlos expanded my thinking when he pointed out that even within the same system, one team might view something as special cause while another sees it as just part of the normal pattern. This is because the way we make meaning of variation is shaped by our mental models, including our perspective, experience, and assumptions. So, whether the team determines something is a common or special cause, Carlos encourages us to stay curious about *what* is labeled common or special as well as *why* they see it that way (personal communication, July 21, 2025).

Another cautionary note is for leaders to be aware of the consequences of mismanaging variation. When we misread variation, we:

- See trends where none exist (overreacting to random fluctuations)
- Miss actual trends (ignoring long-term patterns that signal system failure)
- Misplace blame or credit (holding individuals accountable for outcomes beyond their control)
- Fail to use past performance data to predict future trends (losing key insights for decision-making)
- Make reactive, short-term fixes instead of addressing system flaws (Scholtes, 1998)

Instead, we need to approach variation with curiosity by using data to uncover patterns that help us address deeper systems issues.

Principle 3: Theory of Knowledge

We can determine whether our responses to variations are effective by applying Deming's Theory of Knowledge (Deming, 1994), which examines how people think and act based on what they believe to be true. The challenge is that humans often seek out and hold onto information that confirms their existing beliefs while disregarding contradictory evidence. To overcome this confirmation bias, we have to test our inferences, hypotheses, and decisions using evidence rather than relying on assumptions (Scholtes, 1998). So when we see variation in data, whether it be bright spots or gaps, we develop local knowledge to spread what works or improve what isn't working. To accomplish this, leaders need to see themselves as both experimenters and facilitators of learning (Scholtes, 1998). By testing our theories, we can

- Make predictions using evidence
- Surface hidden beliefs and assumptions
- Understand root causes
- Build a culture of learning for both individuals and the organization

We can't eliminate every mistake, but we can build a culture that learns from them and develops resilience by embedding "forgiveness and adaptability" into our work (Scholtes, 1998, p. 34). The key is not to avoid failure, but to build knowledge from every iteration, allowing the system to continuously evolve and improve. How do you eat an elephant of complex change? One bite at a time.

Principle 4: Psychology of Change

Systems don't change unless people do. Perhaps it's obvious, but leading systems requires leading people! Deming (1994) emphasizes that leaders and staff are the driving force behind any transformation. People, not policies or initiatives, create continuous improvement and long-term success. Even more (and more fun), we get to be the ones who create conditions for engagement and joy in the work. Yes, joy! Deming claims that joy in the work is not a privilege, but a fundamental right of our employees.

Deming (1994) consistently reminds us that human nature plays a critical role in organizational success. Employees perform at their best when they feel valued, empowered, and engaged. As leaders, we can maximize our people's potential by providing:

- A sense of pride in their contributions
- Opportunities for innovation and creativity
- The tools and support they need to be effective
- Processes that encourage learning, collaboration, and continuous improvement

Of course, joy and fear are fierce competitors. Part of our job in shaping a workplace culture conducive to improvement is building trust to overcome fear. This involves how we treat staff as partners in improvement rather than manipulating them through extrinsic rewards or fear-based strategies. Unfortunately, many traditional management approaches undermine trust instead of building it. Strategies like incentives, monetary rewards, and ranking systems often create fear rather than motivation (Deming, 1994). Fear stifles the very qualities that are necessary for improvement, such as questioning assumptions, experimenting with new ideas, learning from failure, collaborating, and innovating.

Another aspect of attending to the psychology of leadership is our role in removing barriers. This next point may sound shocking at first: It is not a leader's job to motivate employees (Deming, 1994). What?! Here's why: Deming says that people are naturally motivated by meaningful work, not by the leader. Rather than trying to motivate employees, we are to engage them in meaningful work, and *that* motivates them.

That sounds easy enough, but systemic barriers often prevent staff from feeling engaged. Instead of trying to impose motivation, Deming challenges us to remove the barriers that block motivation by:

- Prioritizing workplace culture as much as productivity
- Fostering respect, collaboration, and trust within the system
- Ensuring people have autonomy, support, and a voice in improvement efforts

When we do that, joy in work naturally follows (Deming, 1994; Scholtes, 1998) and work becomes a place where employees are more than just productive; they are fulfilled, engaged, and inspired to contribute to making it better.

This brings us full circle to the big takeaway from Deming's System of Profound Knowledge. To change the system, as leaders, we have to change ourselves. In the next section, we learn how to do just that.

▶ DEMING'S 14 POINTS FOR THE TRANSFORMATION OF MANAGEMENT

If we want real change in our school systems, we can't just push people to work more or harder. We need to lead differently (Deming, 1982). Deming's 14 Points for the Transformation of Management offers a leadership roadmap that helps us move beyond being compliance officers or micromanagers to being agents of change. Below, I synthesize Deming's 14 Points, translated into the language of school and district leadership.

1. Create constancy of purpose for improving quality—Set a long-term vision and align all efforts across the system toward shared goals that prioritize learning and equity.
2. Adopt the new philosophy of quality improvement—Improvement starts with a leadership mindset shift. We need to model new ways of thinking instead of just setting new expectations for others.
3. Stop depending on inspection to achieve quality—Instead of catching mistakes or evaluating after the fact, build quality into the system processes from the start.
4. Move beyond cost-driven decisions—Build long-term relationships based on trust and reliability rather than on short-term financial or operational constraints.
5. Constantly improve processes and systems—Improvement is not a one-time event. It's an ongoing effort. Embed it in the structures and routines of teaching, leading, and learning.
6. Provide job-embedded training for all employees—Professional learning should be ongoing, relevant, and job-embedded, with ongoing feedback and support, rather than one-and-done workshops.
7. Emphasize leadership, not supervision—Support, empower, and partner with your teams. Don't just manage, monitor, or evaluate.

8. Remove fear from the workplace—Trust is the cornerstone of commitment and innovation. Compliance-driven management undermines engagement.
9. Encourage collaboration across employee groups—Break down silos. Strengthen system improvement and deepen collaboration between and among leaders and staff.
10. Eliminate reliance on slogans—Posters and mandates don't repair broken systems. Use root causes to understand and fix the system, not the individuals *in* the system.
11. Remove quantity-based goals and management by numbers—Numbers alone don't tell the whole story. Include qualitative measures to analyze quality and impact.
12. Remove barriers that rob employees of pride in their work—Swap misusing competition and ranking people with building shared purpose, ownership, and joy in what they do.
13. Invest in ongoing education and self-improvement—Continuous learning applies to people (including leaders) as much as it does to processes. When we grow, our systems grow.
14. Engage everyone in the organization in the transformation—Improvement isn't just leadership work. It's everyone's work. Ownership must be shared.

Although Deming's 14 Points were initially created for industry managers, they clearly pertain to traditional management habits that are still alive in education. As school and district leaders, however, we have the opportunity (and responsibility) to use them to transform the way we lead in service of our systems and the experiences of the people within them.

▶ DEMING'S SEVEN DEADLY DISEASES OF MANAGEMENT

Now that we've explored what educational leadership *should* look like through Deming's 14 Points, we ask ourselves what gets in the way of leaders enacting this kind of transformed leadership? According to Deming (1982), "Seven Deadly Diseases" often block progress. These systemic leadership barriers undermine continuous improvement, damage staff morale, and distract leaders from building healthy, high-functioning systems. If we want to lead a culture of growth and success, we should recognize and actively remove these obstacles.

Here's a look at Deming's Seven Deadly Diseases and their implications for educational leaders.

1. Lack of constancy of purpose—Sustainable improvement requires long-term thinking and a clear and steady purpose. Without it, progress becomes fragmented, innovation slows, and professional learning loses priority. The leader needs to make sure that everyone consistently understands, connects to, and contributes to the vision.
2. Short-term thinking over long-term thinking—The pressure for quick wins can push leaders to cut professional learning or stall strategic actions that matter for the long haul. But short-term gains often come at the cost of long-term stability. Sustainable progress requires consistent investment in people, systems, and structures—even when it's not flashy.
3. Performance evaluations and merit-based ratings—Traditional evaluation models might try to motivate staff. But this often backfires, fostering competition, anxiety, and the illusion of improvement. Deming (1982) cautioned that focusing on individual performance without addressing systemic issues leads to superficial improvement efforts. As he put it: "The idea of a merit rating is alluring… The effect is exactly the opposite of what the words promise" (p. 101). Instead, leadership should shift the focus to collaboration over competition and ensure that improvement efforts concentrate on systems rather than individuals.
4. Frequent turnover in leadership—Leadership churn disrupts progress. When leaders move on too quickly, they don't have a deep understanding of system dynamics. This makes them more likely to focus on short-term accomplishments rather than long-term transformation. Stable leadership matters.
5. Overreliance on measurable data—Yes, data matters. But leaders shouldn't overlook key qualitative factors such as

staff morale, culture, and trust. Deming (1994) disagrees with the idea that "if you can't measure it, you can't manage it" (p. 35). Balanced leadership considers hard data as well as human insight.

6. Excessive employee healthcare costs—Rising healthcare costs can squeeze budgets, limiting what's available for instructional resources, professional growth, and improvement. In our district, we tackled this by having a cross-role healthcare committee. Each month, we reviewed healthcare and prescription data with classified, certified, and administrative staff at the same table. Working together, we found creative, cost-saving solutions like expanding telehealth and helping employees find affordable prescription options. I must admit that I'm passionate about leaders taking excellent care of their people. The charge here is to do so in an effective, supportive, proactive, creative way without losing sight of fiscal responsibility. We must attend to both. When we do, we build trust and well-being that breathe life into long-term improvement.

7. Excessive costs of liability and compliance—When time, energy, and funds are consumed by legal concerns or bureaucratic red tape, it drains focus from the real work of improvement. Spending more time on defensive decision-making than on addressing root causes creates a culture of caution and compliance instead of a culture of learning and growth. Accountability structures should protect and support rather than paralyze growth. Yes, leaders will inevitably deal with legal matters. But we can't allow them to derail our priorities. We must stay rooted in our long-term purpose, even while navigating complexity and competing priorities.

While Deming's Seven Deadly Diseases were originally written for industry managers, they ring true for educational leaders. They reveal the systemic barriers that too often get in the way of sustainable improvement. The takeaway from Deming's Deadly Diseases is that we can't lead transformation using traditional models. We need to think long-term and build stability in leadership and purpose.

Now that we've looked at the vision for leadership qualities (Deming's 14 Points) and the barriers that can derail them (Seven Deadly Diseases), it's time to ask, *What is the antidote to these diseases? What do transformed leaders actually do?* One answer lies in the process that reflects this new way of leading: Deming's Plan–Do–Study–Act (PDSA) cycle.

▶ DEMING'S PLAN-DO-STUDY-ACT (PDSA) CYCLE: A STRUCTURED APPROACH TO SYSTEM IMPROVEMENT

PDSA cycles offer a process for how to lead differently. They embody transformational leadership and facilitate system improvement through inquiry and continuous learning. While Chapter 6 walks through how educational leaders use PDSA cycles in schools and districts, this section focuses on their theoretical foundation, which is how PDSA originated from Deming's work and became a cornerstone of improvement science.

In the 1950s, Deming developed PDSA cycles as a scientific method for system-level problem-solving. He first applied it in industry. Deming (1982) emphasized the importance of testing changes before full implementation, stating: "Any step [of system improvement] may need the guidance of statistical methodology for economy, speed, and protection from faulty conclusions from failure to test and measure the effects of the interactions" (p. 88). In other words, don't leap before you learn!

Over time, PDSA emerged as a foundational strategy in improvement science (Moen & Norman, 2010). The PDSA cycle is a routine designed to be repeated over and over to refine strategy (Deming, 1994). There are four steps:

1. Plan—Clearly define the problem or area for improvement. Set specific objectives, pose guiding questions, and predict potential outcomes. Decide who will be involved, where and when the test will occur, and how progress will be measured.
2. Do—Carry out the planned change on a small scale. Document what happens, noting any surprising or unexpected challenges. Begin collecting data to assess what is and isn't working.

3. Study—Analyze the results and compare them to what you predicted. Look for patterns, successes, and areas that need to be refined. Summarize key insights to inform future decisions.
4. Act—Use what you learned to decide the next step. If the change worked, consider expanding it. If it didn't work, refine the approach and run another cycle, or abandon the strategy altogether.

Deming's PDSA cycle may have started in industry, but it's relevant for educational leaders today. The cycle allows schools and districts to move away from large-scale, untested, high-stakes rollouts. The cycle empowers staff and leader teams to engage in inquiry based on the most local evidence before gradually scaling changes by testing the strategy in their various contexts. By using the PDSA cycle, we reduce risk, enhance decision-making, and cultivate a culture of continuous learning. This helps our school systems evolve in ways that genuinely benefit our own students, staff, and communities, since we know that not all change is improvement.

▶ PROCESS-DRIVEN AND TEAM-BASED

Now we will apply Deming's work to PK-12 education, specifically looking at how improvement science brings it to life. School systems are inherently complex. That complexity can't be addressed with isolated solutions or quick fixes. Bryk et al. (2010, 2015) and colleagues built on Deming's work to create a structured approach for continuous improvement tailored for education. By adapting Deming's work from industry and healthcare, school and district leaders can shift their focus from chasing outcome measures to improving the systems and processes that make a difference for students.

Let's begin with what we can learn from Deming's idea of shifting from outcome-based to process-driven improvement. Traditionally, education has been outcome-driven, emphasizing things like test scores, graduation rates, and attendance. While being outcome-aware is necessary, Deming's (1982, 1994) quality management approach conflicts with overreliance on final results. True quality is built into the processes instead of being inspected at the end (Holt, 1994). That means leaders need to shift their approach by leading in a collaborative way and helping their teams understand that it's the journey that matters, not just the destination. This means that improvement happens throughout the work, rather than at the end when final outcomes are measured.

In contrast, outcome-based education (OBE) imposes rigid performance targets without addressing the systems behind those outcomes. This pressure to hit metrics rather than to improve can lead to a culture of fear, compliance, and one-size-fits-all requirements that disregard the unique needs of different schools (Holt, 1994).

Being outcome-aware is different than being outcome-based (Holt, 1994). We need to be outcome-aware. But being outcome-based tends to remove human judgment and professional expertise from decision-making. While schools and districts must use outcomes, we need to use them to inform and inspire improvement, not control it.

One of the most powerful ways we weave Deming's theory into the fabric of school systems is through the use of teams. Deming (1994) proposed a process-over-policy approach where educators continuously study and refine their practices. Instead of dictating change, improvement comes from empowering those closest to the work to identify challenges and develop solutions using relevant, local data. This is accomplished through PDSA cycles. It is teams, called Networked Improvement Communities (NICs), that engage in the cycles. NICs are where Deming's leadership characteristics and processes come to life in real-world school challenges, helping improvement science go from theoretical to actionable.

NICs are more than collaboration teams. They are intentionally structured groups designed to tackle specific high-priority problems using shared learning and disciplined inquiry. Each NIC is assembled purposefully, bringing together staff, leaders, and experts who are working on similar challenges. This makes the team diverse as well as purpose-driven. By engaging those closest to the work, NICs honor the complexity of our challenges while building shared ownership for the solutions. They leverage collective expertise, creativity, and local data to drive meaningful, context-specific improvement (Bryk et al., 2010, 2015).

NICs exist to collaboratively problem-solve. This is in contrast to the traditional culture of autonomy in education, where classrooms, schools, and districts often function independently. However, Bryk et al. (2015) points out that this approach has reached its limits since the challenges facing education today are too complex for isolated efforts. NICs are designed to work across boundaries. They use data to understand both the problem and the system producing it, developing a theory of improvement that defines an aim, identifies key drivers, and generates change ideas. Through PDSA cycles, they test, refine, and scale improvements based on local, real-world evidence.

A powerful aspect of NICs is that they network. They share team learning, which accelerates system learning. Each team doesn't have to reinvent the wheel. When different teams work on similar problems, they can learn from each other, spread what works, and avoid duplicating efforts. They build on each other's progress. This creates a more efficient, scalable, and faster improvement (Bryk et al., 2010; Bryk et al., 2015; LeMahieu et al., 2017).

Finally, NICs are proven effective. They have demonstrated remarkable success in improving educational outcomes. For example, a Carnegie Foundation study found that a NIC designed to support struggling college math students tripled success rates in half the time (Carnegie Foundation for the Advancement of Teaching, 2017). This kind of progress happens when systems move away from being reactive to being proactively disciplined and collaborative. NICs provide a structure for systems to build in collaboration, share strategies, and scale solutions more effectively (Bryk, 2015; Bryk et al., 2010; Bryk et al., 2015). In doing so, they operationalize the theory of quality improvement (Deming) and the framework of improvement science (Bryk).

Next, we will explore the six core principles that turn these theories into filters that leaders can use to shape improvement efforts.

❓ REFLECTION QUESTIONS

1. How do Deming's theories—such as Total Quality Management, Systems of Profound Knowledge, the 14 Points for the Transformation of Management, Seven Deadly Diseases, and the PDSA cycle—connect with leadership dispositions you value? Where do you see overlaps between Deming's work and contemporary leadership styles and practices you hold in high regard?
2. Which of Deming's principles do you see as most relevant to your role right now? How might you begin to apply that principle in tangible ways to improve your team, school, or district?

CHAPTER 3 TRY THIS: APPLY DEMING'S PDSA CYCLE TO YOUR OWN LEADERSHIP PRACTICE

It is helpful to try something yourself before you lead others in doing it. This tool is designed to help school and district leaders apply the Plan–Do–Study–Act (PDSA) cycle to improve a specific, personal leadership practice.

Step 1: Identify a Small Leadership Problem of Practice

Choose a minor but meaningful challenge in your leadership practice that could benefit from structured improvement. (Examples: Morning routines, using learning targets in staff meetings, regularly visiting classrooms and departments, reviewing weekly student attendance data, providing timely feedback)

- Problem Statement:
  _____
  _____
  _____

- What is contributing to this problem? (Examples: Gather information by talking to people, looking at data, observing)

  _____
  _____
  _____

Step 2: Plan

- Define the Change Idea: What is one small change you could make to address this leadership problem?

  _____
  _____
  _____

- What outcome do you expect from this change? (Your prediction)

  _____
  _____
  _____

- Who will be involved in implementing this change? (Examples: Students, staff members, leaders, parent group)

  _____
  _____
  _____

- What data or feedback will you collect to measure improvement? (Examples: Observation, feedback)

  _____
  _____
  _____

Timeline for Testing the Change: Start Date: _____
End Date: _____

Step 3: Do

- Implement the Change: Carry out the small test as planned.
- Document Observations:
  - What went well?
  _____

  - What challenges arose?
  _____

  - Any unexpected reactions from stakeholders?
  _____

Step 4: Study

- Review and Analyze Data: Did the change lead to leadership improvement? Why or why not? How do you know?
  _____
  _____
  _____

- Compare Actual Results to Your Prediction: Was the outcome what you expected? What surprised you?
  _____
  _____
  _____

Step 5: Act

Decide on Next Steps:

- Adopt: The change worked well! Implement it on a larger scale.
- Adapt: The change had some success, but adjustments are needed before expanding or making it permanent.
- Abandon: The change did not work as expected. Try a different approach.

What modifications or next steps will you take?
_____
_____
_____

Step 6: Reflection and Next Steps

- What did you learn about leading change from experiencing this PDSA cycle in your own leadership practice?
_____
_____
_____

- How does it inform your planning to engage staff in applying the PDSA cycle to their own improvement efforts?
_____
_____
_____

Commit to running another PDSA cycle on the same or a new leadership challenge!

▶ LEADERSHIP EXAMPLE: SUPERINTENDENT'S CABINET AS A NETWORKED IMPROVEMENT COMMUNITY (NIC)

Before leading our district in using improvement science for continuous improvement, I introduced improvement science to my Superintendent's Cabinet, called the Superintendent's Aligned Leadership Team (SALT). We were intentional about learning the process ourselves first, testing it within our own leadership work before guiding school leaders and the rest of the system in applying it.

One of our first opportunities to use the improvement process came during a SALT meeting focused on staffing decisions for the upcoming school year. In recent budget meetings, principals had requested certificated teachers to serve as library media specialists, in addition to the current aide-based model. This request was important, with significant instructional, financial, and cultural implications. As we began discussing the request, we instinctively started jumping into brainstorming solutions to support the request and implement the change.

Then, one of the Executive Directors interrupted.

"Wait! We're slipping into being solutionists! Shouldn't we be using the improvement process to make this decision?"

This was a facepalm moment for me. I hadn't thought of that myself. But we all immediately saw the opportunity.

"Of course! Duh! Let's apply the improvement process to this decision!"

We started by naming and learning about the problem. We took a step back and started with the basics: "What is the problem we are trying to solve?"

Was it about improving library programs? Increasing instructional support? Aligning our staffing to district priorities? It quickly became clear that before we could find the right solution, we needed a shared understanding of the problem. So, we divided up learning tasks. We posted our ideas on the green sticky note shown in Figure 3.1, where we tracked our progress through the process.

Each leader took responsibility for a different piece of the puzzle, so our decisions were based on evidence, not assumptions. We agreed to bring our findings back before moving forward. For example:

- Empathy Interviews: Our Executive Director of HR committed to interviewing current library aides and teachers to gather firsthand insights.
- Fiscal Impact Analysis: The Finance Director ran budget projections to assess sustained financial feasibility.
- Schedule Review: The Executive Director of Teaching and Learning (a former secondary principal) analyzed master schedules across schools to see how library staffing fit into the instructional load.

We learned a lesson. Practicing the improvement process in our own leadership work was invaluable. It forced us to slow down, resist the urge to rush to solutions, and understand the needs of

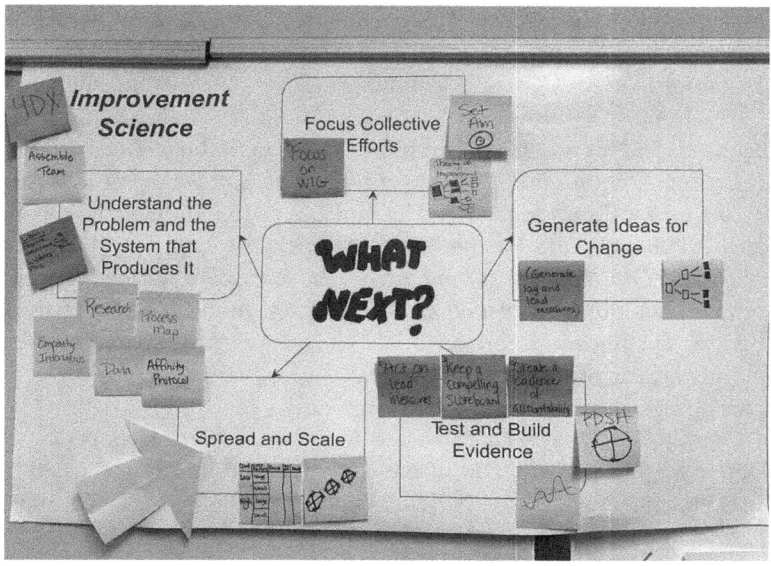

Figure 3.1 What's Next? 5 Phases of an Improvement Process.
(The Carnegie Foundation for the Advancement of Teaching, 2018). Used with permission.

the system. We built the credibility and confidence needed to lead school leaders and teams in applying inquiry cycles to their own challenges. If we expect schools to use inquiry-based decision-making, we must do the same.

References

Anderson, E., Cunningham, K. M. W., & Richardson, J. W. (2024). Framework for implementing improvement science in a school district to support institutionalized improvement. *Education Sciences*, *14*(7), 770.

Bryk, A. S. (2015). 2014 AERA distinguished lecture: Accelerating how we learn to improve. *Educational Researcher*, *44*(9), 467–477.

Bryk, A. S., Gomez, L. M., & Gunrow, A. (2010). *Getting ideas into action: Building networked improvement communities in education.* Stanford, CA: Carnegie Foundation for the Advancement of Teaching.

Bryk, A. S., Gomez, L. M., Gunrow, A., & LeMahieu, P. G. (2015). *Learning to improve: How America's schools can get better and getting better.* Cambridge, MA: Harvard Education Publishing.

Carnegie Foundation for the Advancement of Teaching. (2017). *Networked improvement communities: The discipline of improvement meets the power of networks* (Pathways Vignette No. 1). https://www.carnegiefoundation.org/wp-content/uploads/2017/01/pathways_vignette_01-13-17.pdf

Carnegie Foundation for the Advancement of Teaching. (2018). *Introduction to improvement science: A learning-by-doing simulation.*

Deming, W. E. (1982). *Out of the crisis* (2nd ed.). Cambridge, MA: Massachusetts Institute of Technology, Center for Advanced Engineering Study.

Deming, W. E. (1994). *The new economics for industry, government, education* (2nd ed.). Cambridge, MA: Massachusetts Institute of Technology, Center for Advanced Engineering Study.

Fullan, M. (2011). *Choosing the wrong drivers for whole system reform.* East Melbourne, VIC: Centre for Strategic Education.

Fullan, M., & Quinn, J. (2015). *Coherence: The right drivers in action for schools, districts, and systems.* Ontario: Corwin Press and the Ontario Principals' Council.

Goldsmith, L. T., Doerr, H. M., & Lewis, C. C. (2014). Mathematics teachers' learning: A conceptual framework and synthesis of research. *Journal of Mathematics Teacher Education, 17*(5), 5–36.

Holt, M. (1994). Why Deming and OBE don't mix. *Educational Leadership, 52*(1), 85–86.

How a networked improvement community improved success rates for struggling college math students. (2017). Stanford, CA: Carnegie Foundation for the Advancement of Teaching.

Langley, G. J., Moen, R. D., Nolan, K. M., Nolan, T. W., Norman, C. L., & Provost, L. P. (2009). *The improvement guide* (2nd ed.). San Francisco, CA: Jossey-Bass.

LeMahieu, P. G., Grunow, A., Baker, L., Nordstrum, L. E., & Gomez, L. M. (2017). Networked improvement communities: The discipline of improvement science meets the power of networks. *Quality Assurance in Education: An International Perspective, 25*(1), 5–25.

Lewis, C. (2015). What is improvement science? Do we need it in education? *Educational Researcher, 44*(1), 54–61.

Li (李军), J. (2024). Educational improvement science: The art of the improving organization. *ECNU Review of Education, 7*(3), 714–737.

Macht, J. (2016). The management thinker we should have never forgotten. *Harvard Business Review Digital Articles*, 2–6.

Moen, R. D., & Norman, C. L. (2010). Circling back: Clearing up myths about the Deming cycle and seeing how it keeps evolving. *Quality Progress, 43*(11), 22–28.

Scholtes, P. R. (1998). *The leader's handbook: A guide to inspiring your people and managing the daily workflow.* New York: McGraw Hill.

Chapter 4
Principles of Improvement

LEARNING TARGET

I can apply the Six Principles of Improvement to my own leadership and improvement efforts.

Success Criteria

- Describe each of the Six Principles of Improvement and their role in influencing meaningful change.
- Analyze how the three featured educational leaders define and apply improvement in their leadership.
- Reflect on how the Six Principles align with my own leadership and improvement efforts.

RELEVANT NELP STANDARDS

- NELP Standard 1: Mission, Vision, and Improvement (Problem-Specific, Disciplined Inquiry to Drive Improvement)
- NELP Standard 2: Ethics and Professional Norms (User-Centered, NICs)

- NELP Standard 4: Learning and Instruction (Variation in Performance, Practical, Real-Time Measures)
- NELP Standard 5: Community and External Leadership (Networked Improvement Communities)
- NELP Standard 6: Operations and Management (See the System)
- NELP Standard 7 (District-Level: Policy, Governance and Advocacy (System Leadership and Governance Using Principles of Improvement)

ICEBREAKER: THE BLUEPRINT FOR SUCCESS

Think back to a time when you were part of a curriculum adoption process. Before reviewing curriculum options, your team likely spent time getting grounded in key information, such as learning about state standards, instructional best practices, or educational research (e.g., the science of reading before selecting a reading curriculum).

- Why was it important to get grounded in the foundational work before reviewing and selecting a curriculum?
- Why might it be equally important to understand the foundational principles of improvement before jumping into an improvement cycle?

(*See Appendix 1 for the Icebreaker Group Activity Facilitation Guide*)

CASE VIGNETTE: BEYOND THE DATA WALL

Background

At Falcon Bluffs Middle School, data meetings were a weekly ritual. Every Friday, teams gathered around spreadsheets, data dashboards, and color-coded charts. They tracked test scores, highlighted achievement gaps, and reviewed goal sheets. But despite all this, teachers were overwhelmed and unsure how to move from numbers to meaningful action.

Turning Point

Principal Lloyd noticed the fatigue. He heard it in the way teachers described the meetings:

"We look at data, but what are we doing with it?"

He decided to make a shift. Rather than keeping up with analyzing lots of different data, he asked teams to try something different.

"What if we tested one small change in instruction and used real-time student feedback to measure impact?"

Teachers started experimenting with bite-sized strategies, such as a different way to frame a question or a new routine to boost participation. They looked at exit tickets, quick checks, and student reflections. They came back to the next meeting with stories that supplemented their data.

"This worked."

"That didn't."

"Let's try this next."

Over time, the tone of meetings changed. They were no longer about tracking numbers but about solving problems. Data became a tool for learning. Teachers felt more connected to the purpose behind the numbers and more empowered to act.

Bottom Line

Data alone doesn't drive improvement. Focused inquiry and action do. Ask good questions. Try making small changes. Learn from what happens.

Go small or go home!

We don't get to opt in or opt out of continuous improvement. It's a non-negotiable. Anything worth doing is worth doing well. In this chapter, we explore the six core principles of improvement so that we don't just have improvement, but we lead *quality* improvement.

In Chapter 3, we learned the theory behind improvement science. Now, we turn to how these principles guide leadership and decision-making. As Bryk et al. (2015) explain: "These principles represent the foundational elements for improvement science carried out in networked communities" (p. 12).

While each principle is presented individually, they do not stand alone. They work interdependently. They reinforce each other and work best when applied collectively. Here is an overview of the Six Principles of Improvement (Bryk et al., 2015):

1. Make the Work Problem-Specific and User-Centered
   - Start with real problems facing educators and students (problem-specific).
   - Involve those most affected by the problem in identifying and refining solutions (user-centered).
2. Focus on Variation in Performance
   - Ask: What works, for whom, and under what conditions?
   - Recognize and respond to contextual differences across classrooms, schools, departments, and districts.
3. See the System That Produces the Current Outcomes
   - Identify root causes instead of just treating symptoms.
   - Keep equity at the center of improvement efforts.
4. Use Disciplined Inquiry to Drive Improvement
   - Apply Plan–Do–Study–Act (PDSA) cycles to test and refine change ideas.
   - Move beyond static implementation to dynamic, iterative learning.
5. Measure Improvement Using Practical, Real-Time Metrics
   - Use meaningful, leading, process-focused measures instead of only lagging indicators or outcome measures.
   - Ask: Is this change actually an improvement?
6. Accelerate Learning Through Networked Improvement Communities (NICs)
   - Collaborate across teams, schools, departments, and districts.
   - Share insight and promising practices through structured learning networks.

When we use these principles together, improvement is more focused, inclusive, targeted, data-driven, and collaborative, ultimately leading to sustainable transformation in schools and districts (Bryk et al., 2015).

▶ PRINCIPLE 1: MAKE THE WORK PROBLEM-SPECIFIC AND USER-CENTERED

Let's start by focusing on what *problem-specific* means. One of the most critical questions leaders must ask is: What specifically is the problem we are trying to solve? Jumping to solutions before understanding the real issue and before assembling the right team is tempting (and quite natural). However, effective improvement starts by deeply understanding the problem and engaging those closest to it to ensure changes are both effective and respectful of their expertise (Bryk et al., 2015).

That's where being *user-centered* comes in. Traditional improvement often focuses on averages. But there is no average student, school, or district. Each context is unique and requires tailored interventions. The best people to solve a problem are the people who are close to it, meaning they experience it, understand it, and work directly with it. When the people doing the work help design the solutions, changes are more likely to meet real needs rather than assumptions (Bryk, 2017). Involving the people directly impacted leads to better results while also building a more positive culture by valuing and respecting staff insights.

▶ PRINCIPLE 2: FOCUS ON VARIATION IN PERFORMANCE

The key question in improvement isn't just *What works?* It's *What works, for whom, and under what conditions?* Variation exists across students, classrooms, schools, and districts. Learning from those differences helps leaders adapt strategies to fit diverse needs across contexts.

Variation also creates opportunities to learn from success. When some individuals or teams outperform others under similar circumstances, we call that *positive deviance* (Bryk et al., 2015). Studying those successful outliers, or bright spots, helps us find practices worth spreading.

▶ PRINCIPLE 3: SEE THE SYSTEM THAT PRODUCES THE CURRENT OUTCOMES

Outcomes in education are rarely the result of one decision or action. They are shaped by many complex, interwoven factors. Leaders must develop the ability to see those systems and not blame individuals for failures resulting from the system. As Deming (1994) emphasized, most problems stem from how work is organized, not from individual competence.

Improvement requires us to think upstream. As Bryk (2017) explains: "Upstream problems... eventually become our downstream failures. Improvement research directs us to hike upstream, see where problems first emerge, and fix them there before they expand in size and become much harder to solve" (Bryk, 2017, p. 12). In other words, identify and address issues at their source. Early intervention allows us to focus on preventing recurring failures rather than reacting to crises. Deming (1982) reinforces this point: "Improvement of the system, downstream and upstream, is the responsibility of management to perceive and act on" (p. 371).

This also means that we need to be mindful of how past reforms impact new work. When disconnected initiatives are layered on top of existing work without coherence, they overload staff and erode focus. To avoid repeating past reform missteps, equity-focused leadership requires seeing the system in ways that help predict where new efforts might fail or where breakdowns are likely to occur (Bryk, 2017). That means leaders don't have the luxury of focusing on the new work or just their own piece of the puzzle. We need to consider how all the parts interact and contribute to the larger whole.

▶ PRINCIPLE 4: USE DISCIPLINED INQUIRY TO DRIVE IMPROVEMENT

Improvement science uses a structured approach to testing and learning. That's where the five-phase process (in Chapter 6) and PDSA cycles come in. Deming (1994) and Bryk et al. (2015) emphasize using these cycles to *fail early and fast* on small-scale testing to prevent large-scale failure.

The *discipline* part of disciplined inquiry refers to the structured approach. This slows down our tendency to make rushed decisions by attending to each step: identifying and understanding the problem, generating and testing solutions, analyzing data, refining strategies, and sharing what was learned. The learning from these tests, especially bright spots that the team found when they attended to variability, is then shared to accelerate system-wide learning. In doing so, we are building both individual and system capacity.

▶ PRINCIPLE 5: WE CANNOT IMPROVE AT SCALE WHAT WE CANNOT MEASURE

Measurement in improvement science is about learning, not labeling. It's for guiding action, not accountability. We need to track two kinds of measures: outcomes and processes. Outcome measures assess whether changes lead to desired results (are we achieving our goals?), while process measures track how improvement efforts are being implemented (are we doing what we said we would do?). Leaders use both to determine if the changes are actually an improvement.

Just as importantly, teams also need to anticipate and monitor unintended consequences. We want to be vigilant to make sure that new strategies don't create new problems (Bryk et al., 2015). Unlike traditional accountability metrics, improvement science prompts leaders to use data as a tool for learning rather than punishment. I once heard a colleague refer to using data as "a light, not heat."

▶ PRINCIPLE 6: ACCELERATE LEARNING THROUGH NETWORKED IMPROVEMENT COMMUNITIES (NICS)

No one should be asked to get better on their own. But in many systems, that's exactly what happens. Individuals or teams work in isolation. That means they end up duplicating efforts and have little opportunity to learn from each other.

Fortunately, the structure of NICs combats this. NICs bring staff together to share insights, refine strategies, and spread effective practices (Bryk et al., 2015). They break down silos by fostering collaborative learning across teams, schools, and even districts. This collective wisdom and crowdsourcing accelerates learning. As promising practices spread, so does confidence, a culture of problem-solving, and empowerment.

▶ EDUCATIONAL LEADERS DEFINE PRINCIPLES OF IMPROVEMENT IN PRACTICE

These six principles are grounded in theory, but they come alive in practice. To illustrate this, we turn to our three educational leaders—Kyle, Melanie, and Shawn—who share how they define principles of improvement and share how the principles live in their leadership and school systems. Their insights reveal how these principles influence leadership mindsets to transform system improvement.

Kyle shares how the principles of improvement bring precision to identify and solve problems.

> Improvement science is a process to examine something going wrong in your system. You know it is going wrong, but you are not exactly sure why. It gives you a coherent process to address problems. For me, it is like a can opener. We have this can, and we have looked at it for a long time, but we were never able to get to inside. But now, with improvement of science, I have a tool to open it, and that gets us into really working on it and fixing it. Before, we were lucky if we knew what the problem was, but we never really had precision in applying the change ideas. Now, we have a process to truly solve problems. That is what I see in improvement science.

Kyle sees improvement science as a structured process for diagnosing and addressing systemic issues. Rather than making assumptions or implementing vague fixes, he values the precision that improvement science provides, helping leaders pinpoint problems and apply the right change ideas for targeted solutions.

Melanie shares how the principles of improvement are a commitment to incremental growth.

> For me, improvement science is about growth. I tell people, "It's okay to be where we are today. It's not okay to be in the same place next year." I am not asking you to change everything overnight, but we need to take incremental, layered steps to grow and move forward.

Melanie views improvement as a mindset of continuous progress. Rather than expecting instant, sweeping changes, she leads steady, layered steps that build toward intentional growth. Her perspective aligns with the core principle of disciplined inquiry, where leaders test ideas in cycles, learn what works, and build momentum from small wins over time.

Shawn shares how the principles of improvement are more than a set of tools, but a leadership mindset.

> To me, improvement science means being very clear on the problem you are trying to solve and then using cycles of inquiry to learn and test things in a lower-stakes environment before you scale it up. I believe it is a philosophy and not just a set of tools. For me, it is a way of thinking. The tools help, but I have learned they are really scaffolds to get you into a different way of thinking. So, I hesitate to call it a program. For me, it is a way of leading, and it's a way of thinking that has shaped how I lead.

Shawn highlights the deeper shift that improvement science makes. It changes how leaders think. It's not about a compliance-driven model or a checklist of strategies. It's a leadership stance—one of learning and inquiry. His experience shows us how focusing on structured inquiry allows for better decision-making and builds a stronger foundation for sustainable improvement.

> What spoke to me was knowing that most improvement efforts fail. And I had been a part of several of those. There were really good, well-intentioned people involved, but we were trying to do too much. I had to ask myself: If we're going to spend 20% of our time on something, what should it be, and how do we know that time is going to be

impactful? What does the process look like, and how do we ensure that we will get improvement out of that time? For me, the light bulb went on when I realized we needed to shift our mindset on what improvement is and what it looks like.

Shawn's breakthrough moment came when he realized that improvement efforts often fail, not because of bad intent, but because they lack a structured, effective process. Now he narrows focus, makes time for what truly matters, uses structured inquiry to keep getting better, and leads with greater clarity and impact.

These Six Principles of Improvement are more than a framework. They are a guide. They serve as filters for the way we lead, engage, and make decisions. Now that we have explored the theory of quality improvement (Chapter 3) and the principles of improvement (Chapter 4), we turn our focus to how we adopt improvement as leadership dispositions (Chapter 5). Six research-based paradigm shifts emerged from my synthesis of improvement science literature. These approaches are essential for transformational leaders who strive to foster a system-wide improvement culture.

> **REFLECTION QUESTIONS**
>
> 1. How does your current approach to improvement align with the Six Principles of Improvement? Consider where your leadership practices already reflect these principles and where there may be room to grow.
>   - Make the work problem-specific and user-centered
>   - Focus on variation in performance
>   - See the system that produces the current outcomes
>   - Use disciplined inquiry to drive improvement
>   - We cannot improve at scale what we cannot measure
>   - Accelerate learning through Networked Improvement Communities
> 2. Reflect on an improvement or inquiry process you've led or participated in. To what extent did that process reflect the Six Principles of Improvement? Which principles were missing or underdeveloped, and what impact did that have on the outcomes?

CHAPTER 4 TRY THIS: APPLY THE SIX PRINCIPLES OF IMPROVEMENT

This tool helps school and district leaders assess, reflect, and align their current improvement efforts with the Six Principles of Improvement to drive meaningful, sustainable change.

What school-wide or district-wide issue are you working on or would you like to improve?

___

Directions: Assess how well your current approach to improvement aligns with the Six Principles of Improvement. For each prompt below, write a brief response. What are you currently doing? What's missing?

Make the Work Problem-Specific and User-Centered

Does this improvement effort address a real problem identified by those closest to the work?

___
___
___

Focus on Variation in Performance

Are you analyzing differences in outcomes across students, staff, schools, or departments to identify patterns?

___
___
___

See the System That Produces the Current Outcomes

Are you identifying root causes and system-wide factors rather than placing responsibility or blame on individuals?

___
___
___

Copyright material from Marci Shepard (2026), *Where the Science of Improvement Meets the Heart of Leadership*, Routledge

Use Disciplined Inquiry to Drive Improvement

Are you testing small changes through PDSA cycles rather than jumping to large-scale initiatives?

_____
_____
_____

Measure Improvement with Practical Metrics

Are staff using real-time, meaningful data to track progress, rather than relying solely on state-level or benchmark assessments?

_____
_____
_____

Accelerate Learning Through Networked Communities

Are teams collaborating across schools/departments to share what's working and refine strategies together?

_____
_____
_____

▶ REFLECTION

What is one leadership move you could make to better align your work with these six principles of improvement?

_____
_____
_____

What is your next action step to apply this move?

_____
_____
_____

▶ LEADERSHIP EXAMPLE: BRINGING IMPROVEMENT PRINCIPLES TO LIFE

After introducing the Six Principles of Improvement to my leadership team, I knew that understanding the theory wasn't enough. We needed to connect it to our actual leadership practices. Otherwise, it would remain just another concept. Interesting, but not used.

Our admin team (central office and school leaders) began by revisiting our own leadership foundation: our mission, vision, values, norms, and decision-making model (see Chapter 2's Leadership Example). These were the guiding documents that defined who we aspired to be as leaders. We started all meetings getting re-grounded in our shared norms. For this meeting, the question was: *Are we actually leading in ways that align with these principles of improvement?*

In teaching and leading, we often introduce new ideas by making connections to our current understanding or work. That's just what we did. To shift from theory to practice, we started with two critical reflection questions:

1. How do these Six Principles of Improvement align with the ways we have traditionally approached leading improvement?
2. How are they different?

To make this more than just a conversation, I provided highlighters and asked my team to actively engage with our own system's guiding documents (see Figure 4.1). The task:

- Highlight any connections between our existing values, norms, collective commitments, and decision-making filters and the Six Principles of Improvement.
- Identify areas where our stated commitments and our actual leadership moves were and were not fully aligned.

This wasn't an academic exercise. The activity prompted us to reflect on our leadership integrity—the alignment between what we believe, say, and do (see Chapter 2's Try This).

Principles of Improvement 81

How We Engage with Each Other and Our Work to Achieve Our Mission

Theory of Action: We align the people in our system to engage in continuous improvement and support the learning of all students.

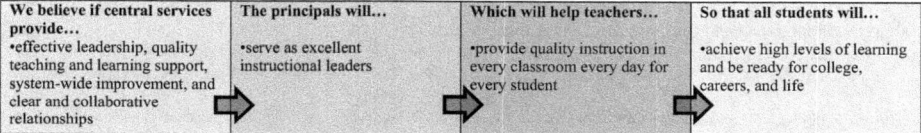

We believe if central services provide...	The principals will...	Which will help teachers...	So that all students will...
•effective leadership, quality teaching and learning support, system-wide improvement, and clear and collaborative relationships	•serve as excellent instructional leaders	•provide quality instruction in every classroom every day for every student	•achieve high levels of learning and be ready for college, careers, and life

In everything we do, we will...
- Focus on learning, collaboration, results, and continuous improvement
- Ensure data-driven decisions
- Provide equity of opportunities and resources
- Communicate with and engage students, families, staff, and community

Critical questions that guide our work
- What do all students need to learn?
- How will we know they are learning it?
- What will we do when they haven't learned it?
- What will we do when they already learned it?

Norms
- Do I use evidence to support my thinking and press others to do the same?
- Do I demonstrate a growth mindset by expecting and accepting the discomfort that comes with non-closure, change and learning while committing to a deeper understanding at the individual and group level?
- Do I practice clear and positive communication by going to the right team member with concerns or issues and listening to truly understand?
- Do I encourage and promote equitable contributions, risk taking, and respect for divergent thinking by asking questions and sharing ideas that challenge my own and others' thinking and understanding?
- Do I support and celebrate student, staff, and district accomplishments?

Collective Commitments
- Prioritize our focus on teaching and learning
- Leverage Professional Learning Communities (PLCs) in support of student learning and growth
- Ensure frequent analysis of student performance data by student, by standard
- Provide leadership development, support, and collaboration
- Own and respond to results to promote reflection, monitoring, and adjustment

Figure 4.1 Values, Norms, and Decision-Making Filters.

our HOW

Decision-Making Model	Decision-Making Filters
<u>Command Decision</u>: Made by one person or group without input from others • When decisions need to be made quickly or are time-sensitive • Personnel issues or issues that require security or privacy • When consensus breaks down or cannot be reached (ultimately, the buck stops at the leader's desk)	• How will this decision impact and/or support student learning and results? • To what extent does the decision align with our mission, vision, values, and collective commitments?
<u>Advisory Decision</u>: Made by one person or a group after input from others • When decisions only affect a few people • When input is needed from everyone, but the timeline is short • When other factors/parameters out of the team's control affect the final decision	• How will data be used to inform and evaluate the effectiveness of this decision? • What are the non-negotiables related to this decision that must be considered?
<u>Consensus Decision</u>: A shared decision made by a team when high levels of support are needed • Made by the whole group or a representative group; a shared decision • When there is ample time for discussion and group decision-making *Definition of Consensus:* *Consensus is a decision that has been reached when most members of a team agree on a clear option, and the few who oppose it have had a reasonable opportunity to influence that choice. All team members agree to support the decision.* From Connie Hoffman, *Putting Sense into Consensus*, Vista Associates, 1998	• What impact will this decision have on our stakeholders, and how are they involved in the decision-making, when possible? • What commitments are needed to achieve the desired results? • What resources are necessary to support this decision?

Inquiry

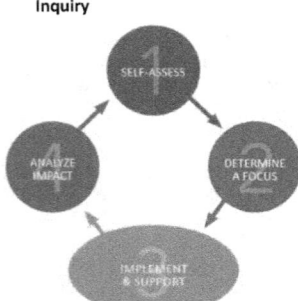

• ASSESS to identify student learning, instructional, and/or leadership problems of practice
• DETERMINE A FOCUS through analyzing evidence and developing a theory of action; ensure alignment and set goals and evidence that will determine meeting the goals
• IMPLEMENT AND SUPPORT by engaging in study, learning, and feedback cycles around the area of focus
• ANALYZE IMPACT through examining results and reflecting on how practice impacts student outcomes; determine whether to continue the same inquiry or identify a new area of focus
(Teacher Inquiry Cycle, 2015)

Figure 4.1 (Continued)

During the activity, we had some lightbulb moments. As leaders highlighted and discussed patterns, we found several areas of alignment.

- ✓ Our commitment to inquiry and shared leadership aligned with the principle of disciplined inquiry to drive improvement.
- ✓ Our decision-making filters emphasized systems thinking, connecting with the principle of seeing the system that produces the current outcomes.

Our focus on meaningful data was a step toward measuring improvement with practical metrics rather than compliance-driven reporting.

However, we also noticed clear misalignments.

- Even though we had a structure and process for collaborative teams, we often focused on district-wide initiatives. This clashed with the principle of making the work problem-specific and user-centered.
- We weren't always studying variation in performance. While we used data and disaggregated it for different groups *within* teams, we didn't capitalize on sharing the data and insight *across* teams.

These realizations led to an important takeaway. Aligning our leadership practices with the Six Principles of Improvement wasn't about adding new work. We sought to be more intentional improvement leaders, getting better at weaving quality improvement into the culture we had already built. This activity helped us examine whether we were truly living our commitments. By using this close-reading strategy and concretely connecting Six Principles of Improvement to our existing leadership commitments, we became more aware of where they already showed up so we could name them, use them with more intention, and expand their impact in our daily practice.

References

Bryk, A. S. (2017). *Redressing inequities: An aspiration in search of a method.* Paper presented at the Fourth Annual Carnegie Foundation Summit on Improvement in Education, San Francisco, CA.

Bryk, A. S., Gomez, L. M., Gunrow, A., & LeMahieu, P. G. (2015). *Learning to improve: How America's schools can get better and getting better.* Cambridge, MA: Harvard Education Publishing.

Deming, W. E. (1982). *Out of the crisis* (2nd ed.). Cambridge, MA: Massachusetts Institute of Technology, Center for Advanced Engineering Study.

Deming, W. E. (1994). *The new economics for industry, government, education* (2nd ed.). Cambridge, MA: Massachusetts Institute of Technology, Center for Advanced Engineering Study.

Teacher Inquiry Cycle. (2015). Seattle: Center for Educational Leadership, University of Washington. https://k-12leadership.org/blog/4-steps-of-inquiry-that-help-principals-improve-instruction/

Chapter 5

Six Paradigm Shifts for Leading Continuous School System Improvement

🎯 LEARNING TARGET

I can analyze leadership paradigm shifts and evaluate implications for my own leadership approach.

Success Criteria

- Synthesize each of the six paradigm shifts and their significance in leading continuous improvement.
- Analyze how our three featured educational leaders exemplify these shifts in their leadership practices.
- Evaluate how these paradigm shifts align with my own leadership dispositions.

RELEVANT NELP STANDARDS

- NELP Standard 1: Mission, Vision, and Improvement (Staff are Knowledge Creators)
- NELP Standard 2: Ethics and Professional Norms (Collaborative, Learn from Failure, Culture)

- NELP Standard 4: Learning and Instruction (Share Knowledge, Meaningful Data)
- NELP Standard 5: Community and External Leadership (Team Effort)
- NELP Standard 6 (Building-Level): Building Professional Capacity (Knowledge-Creators, Learn from Failure, Collaborative Professional Culture)
- NELP Standard 7 (District-Level): Policy, Governance and Advocacy (System Leadership and Governance Using Paradigm Shifts)

ICEBREAKER: SHIFT HAPPENS

Think of a time when you experienced a shift in your leadership mindset.

- What caused the shift? (e.g., new experience, feedback, a challenge, a mentor, professional learning)
- How did your thinking or approach change as a result?
- What impact did this shift have on your leadership, team, or organization?

(See Appendix 1 for the Icebreaker Group Activity Facilitation Guide)

CASE VIGNETTE: THE TEACHER WHO DIDN'T WANT TO CHANGE

Background

Mountain View High School had been pushing for more student-centered practices, but change came slowly, especially in Room 212. Ms. Long was a veteran English teacher known for her structured lessons and calm control of the classroom. She had seen plenty of new ideas come and go and wasn't shy about her skepticism. "I've been doing this for 27 years," she said, "My way is working."

When the leadership team introduced a new strategy encouraging student-led discussions, Ms. Long was polite but not convinced. She quietly opted out of the optional training and stuck with what she knew. Others on the staff followed her lead.

Turning Point

Instead of pressuring Ms. Long, the principal asked, "Would you be open to trying just one change in one class for one period?" Somewhat reluctantly, Ms. Long agreed to let her students lead a discussion on a short story the following week. She gave up control—but just a little.

To her surprise, the students rose to the occasion. The room began to buzz. It wasn't perfect, but Ms. Long thought of a way to make it better by adding a prompt that ensured students referenced the text, responded to each other, and stayed engaged from start to finish. By the third time she used the strategy, when the bell rang, a few students lingered, still talking about the story.

That small moment shifted something for Ms. Long. She wasn't all-in overnight, but she started asking questions and attending planning sessions. Before long, she was trying other practices such as peer feedback protocols. She even joined the teacher professional learning community focused on student discourse and shared what she was learning. Eventually, she began mentoring other teachers through their own changes.

Bottom Line

Mindset shifts rarely happen all at once. But when people see success in something they helped create, they become more open, and even eager, to lead the change themselves. Seeing is believing.

If we want meaningful, lasting change in our schools, we can't rely on the same leadership playbook that got us where we are. Through extensive research on improvement science, I've identified six key paradigm shifts that help leaders create the conditions for learning and innovation.

This chapter builds on the theory foundation (Chapter 3) and principles of improvement (Chapter 4), synthesizing a greater body of improvement science research into six mindset shifts for educational leaders. These shifts challenge outdated leadership models and represent a fundamental rethinking (or transformation) of how we lead improvement. By embracing these six shifts, we can move beyond leadership that leaves staff feeling confused, frustrated, overwhelmed, and disengaged. We can move forward with leadership that improves equitable outcomes while improving culture.

First, let me explain why I call these *shifts*. Moving from a traditional knowledge-based approach to a System of Profound Knowledge represents a fundamental leadership mindset change. Bryk et al. (2015, p. 186) contrast outdated, compliance-driven methods with more collaborative, adaptive, and evidence-based approaches that foster continuous learning and system-wide improvement. Unfortunately, most educational reform efforts do not naturally encourage these ways of thinking.

So, I distilled these six shifts to help leaders anchor to the values and dispositions that support transformative improvement. You'll also hear from our three educational leaders—Kyle, Melanie, and Shawn—whose stories bring these shifts to life. Their real-world experiences reveal the challenges, adaptations, and insights that come with leading in new ways.

Here's a preview of the six research-based paradigm shifts we will explore. Each one is intentionally structured in a *do this–not that* format, representing the shift:

1. Staff Are Knowledge Creators, Not Just Implementers—Staff are the content and context experts. They should help define and design the work that makes the system smarter, rather than carry out decisions made by someone else.
2. Improvement is a Team Effort, Not an Individual Act—Learning is social. Improvement happens when teams co-construct knowledge and solutions, rather than work in isolation.
3. Failure is a Learning Opportunity, Not a Setback—Failures are valuable data. They help us refine strategies, build resilience, and uncover system issues, rather than being treated as obstacles or embarrassments.
4. Knowledge Must Be Shared to Accelerate System Learning, Not Just Individual Learning—Promising practices spread when teams, schools, departments, and districts share what works with each other, rather than keeping learning confined to their own team.

5. Meaningful Data Should Drive Learning, Not Just Accountability—Data should inform, not punish. We need timely, local, leading indicators that are close to the staff using them, rather than primarily serving the needs of a higher authority.
6. Improvement is Shaped by Culture, Not Just Strategy—Lasting change requires trust, belonging, and psychological safety, rather than relying primarily on strategic plans or technical solutions.

Now, let's take a closer look at what each of these shifts means, how they show up in real leadership practice, and why they may matter more than ever.

▶ PARADIGM SHIFT 1: STAFF ARE KNOWLEDGE CREATORS, NOT JUST IMPLEMENTERS

A fundamental shift from the literature on improvement science redefines the role of educators from being passive implementers of top-down initiatives to being active researchers and problem-solvers. Staff themselves are sources of knowledge who engage in active research through inquiry that improves their work.

In traditional initiative-driven models, improvement is believed to come from strict fidelity to programs, as if the knowledge resides in the program itself. Traditional experimental science and top-down reforms assume expertise is embedded in programs instead of in the educators implementing them. This has led to curricula marketed as *teacher-proof*, implying that educators only need to follow prescribed steps. Also, scaling up initiatives in traditional models requires strict adherence to a prescribed process, with little room for local adaptation. Fidelity is the emphasis.

However, improvement science flips this idea on its head, recognizing that knowledge also resides in the people and systems implementing the work (Lewis, 2015). Implementation itself is a learning process as staff use local knowledge-building systems to refine and adapt programs in real-world contexts (Lewis, 2015). Here, implementation is not the end goal; it's a vehicle for building profound knowledge (Deming, 1994). This is important because programs must be refined through real-world use. As teams engage in continuous improvement cycles, they modify and adapt strategies to make them more effective in their specific settings.

For too long, educators have been passive recipients of policies and initiatives. However, Bryk (2017) asserts that true system improvement only happens when those doing the work actively improve how their work gets done.

By engaging and honoring educators as knowledge creators, leaders empower them to make meaningful change. When staff are knowledge creators, schools and districts move from *problem-solving projects* to *problem-solving cultures*. Bryk differentiates between a *project mindset* (where teams tackle temporary initiatives) and a *problem-solving culture* (where teams continuously learn, refine, and improve their work as part of daily practice). When schools shift to a problem-solving culture, they tap into the collective expertise of educators and accelerate improvement.

Research from the Menomonee Falls School District demonstrates five key attributes of a continuously improving organization (Bryk, 2018):

1. Investing in developing all staff—ensuring educators grow as problem-solvers.
2. Embedding improvement into everyday work—providing time, resources, and support for continuous learning.
3. Training principals and teacher leaders as improvement coaches—so they facilitate rather than direct change.
4. Viewing everyone in the system as an improver—with all leadership roles also functioning as coaches of improvement.
5. Promoting improvement experts from within—rewarding those who demonstrate deep engagement in the improvement process.

This shift in how schools approach leadership and learning through positioning staff as knowledge creators ensures that improvement is more local, relevant, and sustainable. What a great way to honor the experts already among us.

Leader Connections to Paradigm Shift 1

Each of our three educational leaders—Kyle, Melanie, and Shawn—apply this shift of staff as knowledge creators in their leadership, helping staff take ownership of improvement rather than simply implementing mandates.

Kyle demonstrates how he empowers and actively guides staff in identifying and understanding real problems, ensuring that those closest to the work are driving the improvement process:

> Improvement science gave me that lens so that every problem I see now I think, 'Have they looked at the problem? Do they really know what it is?'

Rather than pre-determining solutions, he supports teams in identifying problems they care about, which increases engagement and motivation:

> There's an opportunity for teams to move something near and dear to their heart. People are going to be excited to do something when they get to pick what they are going to do.

He emphasizes that real change comes from improving processes in addition to outcomes:

> We can change the system if we change the process. When you talk about process, you are talking about the way you do the work. Teams themselves immediately saw the problems, came up with change ideas, changed the process, and measured the results.

However, he acknowledges that embedding improvement science takes time and intentional effort:

> It is hard for teams to learn and use the whole process. It takes a long time. And it takes a lot of deliberate effort.

Melanie shows how she ensures that staff have the tools and support needed for ownership of continuous improvement. She introduced rubrics to help teachers and principals reflect on where they are in the process and determine their next steps:

> We have rubrics for implementation, so principals have their teachers reflect on where they are at, and then here's the next step on the rubric around the key components for them to move forward.

Her system is not about judgment but about supporting educators through their learning journey:

> There is no judgment about where you are at on the rubric. You are where you are, and we will support you so that your staff continues to progress. It gives us a mechanism to monitor for consistency and fidelity of implementation while empowering principals to lead the journey themselves.

She ensures that educators are both guided and empowered, providing a clear roadmap while allowing flexibility for staff expertise as knowledge creators:

> We hired you to know your kids and staff. Here are the things we will do to support you, but you have the skills and expertise to do the work. And if you get stuck, we build in supports to help.

Shawn shares how he shifted to a culture of inquiry and staff-led problem-solving, guiding his team in deeply understanding problems before rushing to solutions:

> All my principals now will tell you that one of the questions I ask them most often when they have a dilemma is, 'What's the problem you're trying to solve?'

He acknowledges that improvement science requires a mindset shift, especially for leaders who are wired to jump quickly to large-scale implementation:

> There is a cadence around improvement science that doesn't necessarily fit with most people's leadership styles. The temptation is always to go to scale quickly. You must change your approach and give yourself and your leaders permission to do that.

Through this shift, his team has become more thoughtful and precise in problem-solving and in their role as knowledge creators:

> People are much more thoughtful about how they try to provide solutions to problems. We don't rush to solve a problem if we don't have to. If it's not a life-threatening issue, we should take time to really think about it from multiple perspectives before deciding what solution to try.

His role as a leader has shifted from being a problem-solver to being a facilitator of improvement, empowering staff:

> At first, I was heavily involved in inquiry. But if I want to improve a process for third-grade readers, I cannot improve that process. The people who are living and doing the work have to solve that. My role is to provide space and tools to help them do that work.

Additionally, he has learned that staff, as the knowledge creators, should be empowered to use improvement tools flexibly, based on the needs of the team:

> There is not a rigid, linear approach to this. The tools can show up at different places in the process. Improvement science is a philosophy and a way of thinking, and the tools should be used as they make sense in context.

There were common themes across our three leaders in Paradigm Shift 1. These shifts empower staff to be knowledge creators. What can we learn from them collectively?

1. Identifying and understanding the problem first—Kyle and Shawn consistently ask, "What problem are we trying to solve?" while Melanie provides structured reflection tools to guide staff.
2. Engaging staff closest to the work—Each leader ensures that those who work directly with students lead improvement efforts, using a user-centered approach. They are the experts.

3. Providing tools and structures to support inquiry—All three leaders equip staff with structured tools (e.g., rubrics, reflection protocols, and guided questions) to empower them in knowledge-creation improvement work.

In conclusion, Paradigm Shift 1 is about shifting to a culture of knowledge-producing improvement. This requires moving from a top-down model of reform to one where educators are active researchers, engaging in problem-solving and owning the improvement process. By making this shift, leaders transform individuals into learning leaders and school systems into learning organizations.

▶ PARADIGM SHIFT 2: IMPROVEMENT IS A TEAM EFFORT, NOT AN INDIVIDUAL ACT

Learning is inherently social. This shift builds on Paradigm Shift 1. If staff are knowledge creators and not just implementors, then the place where this knowledge-building happens is in teams. This profound knowledge is co-constructed through teamwork as staff engage in structured inquiry cycles, testing and refining their practice to get better at getting better.

This team-focused shift thrives on the synergy of innovation and ownership. Innovation rarely happens in a vacuum. Rather than relying on individuals or individual teams working in isolation, educators need to be supported in learning with and from each other.

As teams begin to see the impact of their work, their belief in their ability to make a difference grows. This sense of *collective efficacy* becomes a powerful force because when teams believe they can make a difference, they're more likely to do so. As the saying goes: *Whether you think you can or think you can't, you're right*. In fact, Hattie (2023) found that collective efficacy is the most influential factor on student achievement, far outperforming other high-impact strategies.

This means leadership must shift. Instead of directing change, leaders connect people to each other. They build capacity, find and protect collaboration time, provide tools, and build trust, facilitate the process—and sometimes even cheerlead. Improvement is a team sport.

Leader Connections to Paradigm Shift 2

Each of our three educational leaders—Kyle, Melanie, and Shawn—embraces this shift by engaging staff in collaborative knowledge-building processes that drive real and lasting improvement.

Kyle has seen a cultural shift where more teams are taking ownership of identifying and solving their problems:

> One of the things I see more of is teamwork. I see more people taking ownership of the process and being involved in the system, be it through empathy interviews or other strategies. It takes adaptive leadership. Improvement science invites people in. There is a structured process you walk through, and they feel a part of the solution.

He shared specific examples of system-wide knowledge-building through teams:

- HR Hiring Process: Originally, hiring took 90 days. By engaging staff in diagnosing the bottlenecks, the team was able to redesign the process for efficiency, improving the timeliness of hiring and staff experience.
- Budgeting System: Staff initially struggled with a budgeting tool designed by leadership. Through collaborative problem-solving, the team identified a lack of training and unclear workflows, leading to improved training and a clarified process.

Kyle emphasized that team-driven problem-solving must be built into routines and meaningful:

> It [teamwork] really must be completely job-embedded. It cannot be some esoteric thing you're working on. It must be work that makes a difference in their lives.

Melanie reiterates that improvement is a team sport, but one that plays within clear lines. She balances team-driven knowledge-building while ensuring alignment with the district's vision:

> I am mindful when I am out talking to parents, visiting schools, or in a leadership team meeting—are we somewhere in that journey that feels like it's in alignment with that big vision that I've cast? And if we start to get outside of it, how do I leverage people back into play?

She uses a powerful metaphor about teams having freedom while staying within boundaries:

> If you guys are on this field, we're good. But if you start to get off track, we are going to get you back to where I think we need to be. The finesse of leadership is empowering the people closest to kids while still maintaining broader alignment.

Her leadership illustrates the balance between empowering teams to innovate while moving the system forward together.

Shawn celebrates teams solving problems and scaling knowledge across the school through a powerful example of a teacher team identifying a problem, developing a solution, and scaling their learning across the district.

> An eighth-grade ELA team initially thought their students were just disengaged. Through empathy interviews and data analysis, they realized the real issue was comprehension of informational text.
>
> The teachers tested different instructional strategies, refining them through PDSA cycles each week. The final product ended up being a three-step annotation process. This ultimately scaled up to become a building-wide model for informational text instruction.

Shawn emphasized that traditional professional learning teams often focus too much on reviewing data rather than engaging in structured improvement cycles:

> I've really tried to shift our team time to improvement science thinking—letting teams grapple with the problem they're trying to solve rather than just coming back with data every week.

His leadership reinforces the importance of teams engaging in all parts of an inquiry cycle.

There were common themes across all our leaders in Paradigm Shift 2. What can we learn from the three of them collectively regarding the importance of teams?

1. Staff are the experts and co-creators of knowledge—Teams need to be empowered to own the improvement process.
2. Knowledge-building must be meaningful and job-embedded—Teams solve real problems they face every day, ensuring improvement efforts are practical and relevant.
3. Leaders provide structure and support without micromanaging—Teams need autonomy to explore solutions, but leaders ensure coherence and alignment across the system.
4. Knowledge is scaled through teamwork—Solutions developed in one team or school are shared across the school or district so learning spreads efficiently.

In conclusion, Paradigm Shift 2 leverages collaborative improvement. Leaders go beyond simply putting people in teams to building a culture of teaming and using the learning of teams to influence school and district improvement.

▶ PARADIGM SHIFT 3: FAILURE IS A LEARNING OPPORTUNITY, NOT A SETBACK

Too often, educational systems view failure as a negative outcome rather than a natural part of the learning process. Shifting this mindset is essential. Failure should be seen as a tool for learning, refining strategies, and encouraging innovation.

Traditional research studies are often designed to determine whether or not an intervention works, but they rarely specify how to take that learning and make it effective for diverse students, staff, and contexts (Bryk, 2015). As a result, schools focus more on proving effectiveness than on learning from implementation and variability in results.

This concept of *variation* is important. Variation is the difference in outcomes within a system. School systems are complex, so, naturally, performance varies. We've all seen a bell curve distribution where some individuals or teams perform at an average level, some struggle, and a few excel. The goal of improvement science is to shift the entire curve to the right, ensuring that high-quality outcomes are achieved by all students in all contexts (Bryk, 2015), elevating performance across the system.

So often, we tend to focus on students on the left side of average on the bell curve—those struggling—and ask what we can do to bump up their performance. However, it's important that we also identify positive deviances, which are those who succeed despite challenges. Then, we study what drives their success rather than just fixing what isn't working. Finally, we scale these successful practices so that effective strategies become the norm rather than the exception.

Another key aspect of Paradigm Shift 3 is using variation to point to the real problem rather than its symptoms. This is where improvement science brings unique value, as it focuses on problems of practice, using variability in outcomes to uncover root causes and inform system-level improvements (Hinnant-Crawford & Anderson, 2022). By doing so, we can examine what in the system is contributing to the problem.

After all, a system is perfectly designed to get the results it currently gets (Deming, 1994). (Read that again. And again.) So, if inequities persist, the system is designed—intentionally or unintentionally—to produce them. Thus, the system itself must be examined and adjusted. Understanding and responding to variation in outcomes disrupts the status quo, shifting improvement efforts from quick fixes to deep root cause analysis.

Another important facet of this shift is using variation as a learning tool. That means we need to get curious. As staff implement change ideas to solve root problems, they continue to learn from what works and what doesn't. Staff *failure* is not an endpoint (or, more often, a stopping point). We can use failure as an opportunity to learn and refine the change strategy. It's time to stop weaponizing data and variation.

As the saying goes: *You win some, and you learn some!*

In addition to learning from variation, we also need to learn from repeated patterns. Bryk (2017) emphasizes that predictable failures must move from the margins to the middle of improvement work:

> If we truly care about addressing inequities in educational outcomes, then we should be haunted by these predictable failures. We need to pull them from the periphery to the center of our improvement efforts.
>
> (p. 10)

However, traditional school reform models work against this mindset. They focus on implementing programs with fidelity, meaning variation is treated as a problem rather than a natural part of learning. Equally problematic is scaling interventions with a focus solely on reducing variation, missing opportunities to study it to understand how different factors influence implementation. Improvement science seeks to reduce high-stakes failure by building system-wide capacity to understand variation, learn from it, and refine change ideas before scaling (Bryk et al., 2010; Lewis, 2015; Langley et al., 2009). We need to be patient, since learning in cycles of testing, refining, and retesting takes time. Although it may not be immediate, every iteration of learning from failure (and success) leads to smarter and more effective change ideas (Bryk, 2015).

As leaders, we must navigate this tension of urgently working to reduce variation for the sake of equity while also leveraging variation as a powerful learning tool. Often, the biggest insights emerge when change ideas fail or produce unintended consequences. These moments challenge our assumptions.

By embracing learning from variation, leaders help move from unpredictable results to consistent, high-quality outcomes that support equity and success for everyone.

Leader Connections to Paradigm Shift 3

Each of our three leaders—Kyle, Melanie, and Shawn—recognizes that creating a culture where failure is seen as a learning opportunity is essential to continuous improvement. They emphasize modeling vulnerability, fostering trust, and structuring reflective practices to help staff feel safe taking risks and refining their strategies.

Kyle models vulnerability and encourages risk-taking. He sees the leader's role as setting the tone for a culture that embraces failure as part of learning.

> You need to show others when you do not know and then learn beside them. Teachers feel vulnerable all the time when you're looking at practice, but if they see you taking a risk, saying, "Ah, I really don't know. I have never done this. I'm going to try it," then they feel safe to do the same.

He underscores the need for staff to feel secure in trying new strategies without fear of negative consequences:

> Staff need to have that feeling that they're going to be safe. We all make mistakes. We are all learning. The culture of risk-taking and learning is important.

Through risk-taking, Kyle helps staff see failure as an essential part of improvement.

Melanie intentionally builds a culture that supports vulnerability and growth. She highlights the importance of safety:

> There must be a culture of safety to have a level of vulnerability and collaboration if you are going to make real change.

She emphasizes that growth can only happen when educators feel comfortable bringing their challenges forward:

> I need to show up with my kids' data, whatever it is, and be willing to talk about it and be vulnerable about the places where it's my responsibility to move that needle.

For Melanie, the key to sustaining this shift is long-term commitment:

> Relationships are messy, and being vulnerable about missing the mark is messy. But you have to stay the course.

She acknowledges that improvement work is complex, emotional, and deeply personal and that leaders must be committed to creating environments where learning from failure is normalized.

Shawn shares how he leads with transparency, reflection, and structured time for learning. He prioritizes modeling vulnerability by admitting mistakes, reflecting openly, and making adjustments.

> We need to be transparent and vulnerable enough so staff can see that you're human, that you make mistakes, and that you learn from them. So you think aloud for them, modeling the process that you are going through when you make a mistake.

He sets the expectation that leaders must acknowledge mistakes and proactively address them.

> We are going to be the first ones to step out, say what we did, how we're going to fix it, and never sweep anything under the rug.

Shawn also emphasizes the need for dedicated reflection time:

> There is a culture of risk-taking—a culture where it is okay to try things, fail at them, improve them, and try again. Teachers have this innate need to teach, teach, teach, and not stop to reflect.

His most successful teams are those that commit to structured time for reflection and adjustment as part of their collective inquiry.

> The most success I have had with teams is when they dedicate that weekly time, at least, to get together. If you are going to do disciplined inquiry cycles, you must get back together and figure out what you have learned and how you are going to adjust.

There were common themes across our three leaders in Paradigm Shift 3 regarding learning from failure. What can we learn from them?

1. Modeling vulnerability—Leaders demonstrate their own willingness to take risks, acknowledge they do not have all the answers, and show staff that failure is a valuable part of learning.
2. Creating psychological safety—Staff must feel safe experimenting and sharing challenges without fear of judgment, reinforcing a relational and trust-based culture.
3. Structuring time for reflection and learning—Intentional time for teams to analyze what worked and what did not. That reflection needs to be built into inquiry cycles.

To conclude, Paradigm Shift 3 is about moving from a culture of blame or shame to a culture of learning. Instead of expecting perfection, leaders recognize that real growth happens when both bright spots and unexpected challenges lead to deeper understanding and better solutions. As leaders, we need to normalize failure as part of the learning process to foster a culture of innovation, adaptation, reflection, and growth.

▶ PARADIGM SHIFT 4: KNOWLEDGE MUST BE SHARED TO ACCELERATE SYSTEM LEARNING, NOT JUST TEAM LEARNING

Improvement rarely happens in silos. After teams own their learning, engage in cycles of improvement, and refine their practices, the next step is to share the knowledge created beyond individual teams. Effective systems ensure that learning spreads across teams, schools, departments, and districts. Thus, a culture of collaboration and transparency are essential.

By fostering cross-team collaboration, improvement science enables:

- Faster learning across a system—Teams don't have to reinvent the wheel but rather build on each other's work.
- The application of insights across different contexts—Teams learn and customize what works, for whom, and under what conditions (Lewis, 2015).
- The potential for fresh perspectives—Ideas from different teams, schools, or districts can inspire breakthrough innovations.

Leader Connections to Paradigm Shift 4

Each of our three leaders—Kyle, Melanie, and Shawn—recognizes the value of knowledge-sharing across teams, schools, and districts. They believe collaboration helps individual team learning and also helps system learning.

Kyle shares about using Educational Service Districts (ESDs) as hubs for shared learning. He believes ESDs are perfectly positioned to facilitate cross-district learning:

> As an ESD Superintendent, I saw the power of a NIC (Networked Improvement Community) and that ESDs are truly the hub. It's a perfect fit for us. We should be pulling districts in around problems they are having and running improvement science processes.

He envisions collaborative networks where districts work together on common challenges rather than each district tackling problems in isolation:

> We could be tackling attendance, re-engagement, or ESL learner support—any big challenge our region is having. That would be a perfect way to bring people in and work on it together.

He believes that when districts come together, they can learn faster and more effectively:

> How do we find solutions together? Because you can't do it alone.

Shawn also discusses the importance of breaking down silos to create a culture of collaboration. He worked to shift his district away from a siloed culture toward a more collaborative, system-wide approach:

> When I started in teaching and learning, one of the things that frustrated me as a principal was how siloed we were as a district. We had pockets of excellence, but little collaboration among leaders and no systemic improvement.

He acknowledges that while autonomy has benefits, it also creates isolation:

> We all just kind of did our thing. And there's part of me that liked that as a principal because I had a ton of freedom. But I also didn't know if what I was doing was right. I could have used the eyes and ears of my colleagues, and they could have used mine.

Shawn worked to create a culture where collaboration was the norm:

> That was my first real attempt at changing the culture—breaking down silos and creating K-12 systems of collaboration that still remain today.

There were common themes across our three leaders in Paradigm Shift 4. What can we learn from them?

1. Teams working on the same problem benefit from collaboration—When teams working on similar challenges share what works and what doesn't, everyone gets better faster. Even when teams are working on different problems,

sharing what they are learning about the improvement process helps everyone get better at getting better.
2. Breaking down silos is difficult, but necessary—It can be a struggle to get people to engage in cross-team or cross-district collaboration, even when they are working on similar challenges.
3. Leadership must create systems that foster collaboration—Teams need structures, time, and routines that make cross-team learning possible.

In conclusion, Paradigm Shift 4 is about moving from isolation to cross-team collaboration and knowledge-sharing structures to accelerate systemic learning. This shift challenges the traditional culture of education, where schools and districts often work in isolation, even when addressing the same problems.

▶ PARADIGM SHIFT 5: MEANINGFUL DATA SHOULD DRIVE LEARNING, NOT JUST ACCOUNTABILITY

Too often, data is used for accountability. Schools monitor progress and collect data around benchmarks, which is often shared with the district office. Districts collect data around state and national assessments, which are often shared with external stakeholders. In other words, our data gathering often serves someone *above* us. This makes data collection feel like a compliance task and a tool for judgment. In either case, these broad, summative measures do not capture the nuances of day-to-day instructional practice, leaving educators to feel like data serves someone else rather than being useful for directly improving their own practice (Bryk, 2015).

Improvement science shifts measurement from external compliance to practice-based evidence. Data should be a tool for learning. When teams generate and use their own data, they define the measurements, making them relevant and practical. Data collection is embedded into everyday practice, rather than being an additional burden (Bryk et al., 2010). This is because teams put the practical measurements to use when assessments are small, timely, and specific (Lewis, 2015). In doing so, change ideas are tested without disrupting daily operations (Yeager et al., 2013). As a result, measurement is more formative than summative. Rapid cycles enable teams to use data to adjust and refine strategies immediately, since they don't have to wait for the timing or results of external measures. This shift empowers educators to use data as a tool for learning.

Leader Connections to Paradigm Shift 5

Each of our three leaders—Kyle, Melanie, and Shawn—recognizes the importance of changing how measurement is used to support learning and reflection. They believe data should be timely, practical, and embedded in the work.

Kyle notes that people want to know whether improvement efforts are working:

> Everybody wants to know whether they made an improvement or not, but no one really knows how to measure it.

Rather than overreliance on outcome data, Kyle encourages teams to use qualitative methods such as fishbone diagrams, process mapping, observations, and other tools to identify root causes and determine if changes are having their intended impact.

> Even a fishbone diagram or empathy interview tool on its own in someone's hands can be so valuable.
>
> If the budgeting process actually gets easier and more manageable for the directors, then I know it's working. We will go through the process map again: Did these things help? If not, what else could we adjust? Then we go back and refine it again.

Kyle stresses that improvement should be visible and happening in real practice.

> If you go into classrooms and you do not see it happening, then it's not happening. I do not care what they say to me until I see something in action.

Kyle's insights reflect the belief that measures should come from the work itself and should help educators really see and improve their practice.

Melanie shares insight on balancing system-wide and micro-level measures. Her district has a growth monitoring framework that breaks down large-scale goals into smaller measures:

> Each of our buildings has targets and stretch targets around certain data indicators.

She helps teams use data to prompt reflection and inquiry. She approaches data with curiosity:

> At a high level, we know if the data are moving. Are more third graders reading on level? We know if the answer is yes or no. But we haven't had a good system for answering with specificity: 'Why is that happening?'

She also encourages practice-based data that emerges from professional learning teams:

> Some of our principals are identifying high-yield strategies. Teachers are saying, "Hey, here are some strategies that we are going to use together and learn from together."

Melanie recognizes that measurements should illuminate teaching and learning, which are too complex to be reduced to a single measure or variable.

> There are so many variables. How do you really know what made the difference in outcomes? It is not like you only have two variables - turn up the heat and the water boils. It's much more complex.

She remains committed to finding more precise ways to make sense of the complexities where multiple variables interact:

> A weakness in my leadership is I have not untangled data use in a way that makes sense of our super sophisticated system.

Shawn believes in shifting from a focus on lagging measures (outcomes reported after they occurred) to leading measures (actions tracked in real-time that influence those outcomes).

> The high school and I have talked about this a lot. They have great systems for supporting kids after they fail. But let's think about how to prevent failure in the first place.
>
> Change ideas are basically leading measures. But you do need a way to measure those, and it doesn't have to be quantifiable. It can be more experiential or observationally based.

There were common themes across all our leaders in Paradigm Shift 5 about using meaningful measures for learning. What can we learn from the three of them collectively?

1. Data should serve the people doing the work rather than for accountability or external compliance.
2. Measures are meaningful when they are embedded in practice.
3. Qualitative measures, such as observations, interviews, and feedback, are key data sources that add to the insights we get from numbers alone.
4. Measuring improvement is complex and ongoing. No leader has fully figured out the most authentic ways to use data and track progress, but they continue to refine their approaches.

To conclude, Paradigm Shift 5 focuses on moving from *data for accountability* to *data for improvement*. It's up to us to create a data-literate culture where measures are truly meaningful and support learning.

▶ PARADIGM SHIFT 6: IMPROVEMENT IS SHAPED BY CULTURE, NOT JUST STRATEGY

This shift may seem obvious considering the emphasis on workplace culture in Chapter 1. But the idea that culture, not just strategy, shapes improvement belongs in this list of six paradigm shifts for leaders for two main reasons. First, this theme emerged when I surveyed existing research and listened to experienced leaders. Second, a list of paradigm shifts necessary for equity-focused improvement leadership would be incomplete without including the cultural transformation that underpins the other five shifts.

In traditional systems, extrinsic motivators such as incentives and consequences are often used to prod staff to follow implementation expectations. Yet, these do more harm than good to workplace culture (Deming, 1994; Lewis, 2015). In contrast, improvement science assumes that staff are intrinsically motivated to grow when leaders build trusting relationships with and among their teams and engage staff in meaningful work (Deming, 1982; Scholtes, 1998).

This human-centered approach to systems thinking highlights three elements:

- Leaders engage with staff as respected experts, colleagues, and collaborators.
- The workplace is relational, fostering trust, belonging, and shared purpose.
- Work is intrinsically motivating because it's meaningful and fulfilling.

This shift from transactional to transformational, human-centered systems thinking is the secret sauce for improvement. It is where culture and strategy come together. This is the *heart* work.

Leader Connections to Paradigm Shift 6

Each of our three leaders—Kyle, Melanie, and Shawn—is actively working to foster cultures of trust, ownership, and joy.

Kyle demonstrates how he is focusing on a culture of trust and shared leadership. He is embedding improvement into the culture:

> We started improvement science, then I used it as a superintendent. I really wanted to make sure we were using these tools in our own agency so that we learned them more and exercised our muscles.

Kyle emphasizes the importance of trust when introducing processes:

> There must be some trust when you bring something new to people. They need to think, "Kyle knows what he's doing, so I'm going to invest my chips to learn and try this."

He also ensures that staff feel valued and connected to a greater purpose:

> People need to know that I value them. You are here because you chose to be here. The ESD is all about people. Our mission is to make everybody successful, and people buy into that. They feel that, and it is exciting.

His vision for how improvement science becomes embedded in culture follows a progression:

1. Learn the tools—Staff develop foundational skills and language.
2. Apply the tools—Staff actively use them in improvement efforts.
3. Change the culture—Staff shift mindsets and beliefs, embedding improvement science into daily work.
4. Culture drives the work—Staff naturally integrate improvement science into decision-making without needing direction.

Kyle believes this final stage is when improvement science becomes part of the organization's identity.

Melanie shares how she emphasizes moving from compliance to commitment and voice. She wants staff to feel engaged of improvement efforts:

> It's important that people see themselves in the work and feel like, "I can buy into this and participate."

She differentiates between compliance-driven participation and authentic engagement:

There's a difference between someone who is coming in every day to meet a quota—checking off a box—and someone who is saying, "I am leaning into this because I have a heart connection to our goal."

Her vision is for teachers to own improvement along with the principals:

My ultimate hope would be that when central office leaders show up to the student-school review every year, the principal sits in the back while teachers own the work.

She also prioritizes modeling presence, listening, and relationship-building:

I don't expect anything from anyone else that I am not willing to do myself. I'm in buildings all the time. I am present where people are. I model my expectations of how we treat each other and what we prioritize.

Melanie has worked to break down old workplace norms that discourage collaboration and vulnerability:

Some people were all-in right away, but others were hesitant. It took some people a while to trust that we were really going to function this way. The old culture was one where you were assigned work, brought it back, and were typically criticized. After a while, people just stopped bringing the work.

She recognizes that changing workplace culture is not linear:

In the beginning, there was excitement but also skepticism. Then, in the middle, it got clunky—some fits and starts. But now, this is how we function most of the time.

Her vision is for staff to feel joy and connection in their work:

> I want every person to jump out of bed and be like, "I'm going to work today! Even when it's hard, I'm showing up because I know I will be supported."

She compares staff culture to student culture, emphasizing that adults need the same sense of belonging, support, and clarity that we provide for students.

Shawn emphasizes creating a culture of inquiry, inclusion, and fun. He prioritizes visibility and engagement to build relationships:

> Being in transportation, nutrition services, classrooms—you really get a pulse on district culture when you are in all those places.

He tracks belonging data to make sure everyone feels valued:

> We track belonging data for staff, students, and families. We ask: "Who doesn't feel like they belong, and what can we do to change that?"

He also believes fun is an essential part of leadership:

> Every Monday morning, our leadership team starts with a hilarious connection question like, "What was your most embarrassing fashion choice?" It's 10–15 minutes of laughter before we do a strategic check-in. That atmosphere matters.

For Shawn, joy is a leadership strategy:

> I always try to have fun. I enjoy being with these people, and we have a good time together. As a leader, you must be the catalyst for that.

There were common themes across all our leaders in Paradigm Shift 6, which focuses on culture. What can we learn from the three of them?

1. They have seen workplace culture shift positively—From early resistance to growing acceptance, they see progress toward greater engagement.
2. Building relationships is central to leadership—Being present, listening, and making personal connections are key to fostering trust and ownership.
3. Joy and fun matter—A positive culture fuels continuous improvement.

In conclusion, Paradigm Shift 6 is about moving from compliance to an authentic workplace culture. This looks like leaders who are in close proximity to their staff, who use that proximity to build relationships, and who lean into relationships to celebrate and nudge improvement. This shifts the focus from doing improvement to making it part of the way we do life and work together.

▶ SHIFTING LEADERSHIP MINDSETS

Across industries, the negative consequences of rigid standardization and surface-level change are clear. Education is no exception. When leaders chase quick fixes or mandates over meaningful change, the toll is felt across culture, morale, and, ultimately, student outcomes (Deming, 1982, 1994). We become reactive rather than proactive, and we create burnout and resistance.

The six paradigm shifts for leading improvement are ways of thinking and approaching our work. If we are serious about closing equity gaps and ensuring that schools regularly produce better outcomes for all students across all contexts, then these shifts are a moral imperative.

Part II helped us understand the theories, principles, and paradigm shifts of improvement science. In Part III—The How, we'll turn our attention to the processes, tools, and leadership strategies that operationalize these concepts. It's time to move from learning about improvement to leading it.

> **REFLECTION QUESTIONS**
>
> 1. Connecting Strengths to Shifts: How do the six paradigm shifts resonate with your leadership strengths? How might you harness them to lead continuous improvement in your school or district?
>   - Staff Are Knowledge Creators, Not Just Implementers
>   - Improvement is a Team Effort, Not an Individual Act
>   - Failure is a Learning Opportunity, Not a Setback
>   - Knowledge Must Be Shared to Accelerate System Learning
>   - Meaningful Data Should Drive Learning, Not Just Accountability
>   - Improvement is Shaped by Culture, Not Just Strategy
> 2. Growth Opportunities: Which paradigm shift presents the greatest leadership challenge for you? What mindsets, habits, or strategies might help you enhance this aspect of your leadership to better support continuous improvement?
> 3. Learning from Leaders: Which specific experiences shared by Kyle, Melanie, and Shawn sparked new ideas or inspired insights for you? What ideas or practices might you bring into your own leadership work as a result?

CHAPTER 5 TRY THIS: APPLY THE SIX LEADERSHIP PARADIGM SHIFTS

Use this tool to reflect on your leadership mental models and develop actionable steps for using the six paradigm shifts to frame your work. For each shift, consider how the mindset is reflected in your practice, identify barriers, and plan a next step to move the disposition forward.

Paradigm Shift 1: Staff Are Knowledge Creators, Not Just Implementers

Reflection: How often do staff in your organization engage in creating local knowledge through inquiry?

_____
_____
_____

Copyright material from Marci Shepard (2026), Where the Science of Improvement Meets the Heart of Leadership, Routledge

Current Reality: How are staff seen and treated as the creators of change ideas?
_____
_____

Barriers: What gets in the way of staff engaging in action research and inquiry?
_____
_____

Next Step: What is one concrete action you can take to empower staff as knowledge creators?
_____
_____

Paradigm Shift 2: Improvement Is a Team Effort, Not an Individual Act

Reflection: Does collaboration in your school or district extend beyond surface-level cooperation into true team-driven learning?
_____
_____

Current Reality: How do teams currently engage in joint problem-solving and sharing?
_____
_____

Barriers: What conditions or mindsets prevent deep team-based learning and collaboration?
_____
_____

Next Step: How can you strengthen team structures and routines to foster collaborative teamwork?

_____
_____
_____

Paradigm Shift 3: Failure Is a Learning Opportunity, Not a Setback

Reflection: Is failure seen as a necessary part of learning, or is something to be avoided?

_____
_____
_____

Current Reality: How does your system respond to setbacks or when improvement efforts don't go as planned?

_____
_____
_____

Barriers: What cultural or structural factors make staff hesitant to experiment or take risks?

_____
_____
_____

Next Step: What leadership move can you take to model or normalize failure as part of the learning process?

_____
_____
_____

Paradigm Shift 4: Knowledge Must Be Shared to Accelerate System Learning, Not Just Individual Learning

Reflection: How does learning get shared across teams, schools, or departments in your system?
___
___

Current Reality: What structures exist for staff to share insights, successful practices, and lessons learned?
___
___

Barriers: What limits knowledge-sharing across teams, schools, or departments?
___
___

Next Step: What is one way you can create or strengthen structures for sharing learning?
___
___

Paradigm Shift 5: Meaningful Data Should Drive Learning, Not Just Accountability

Reflection: Do staff view data as a tool for their own learning or for compliance?
___
___

Current Reality: What types of data are most valued, and how are they used in decision-making?
___
___

Barriers: What makes it difficult for staff to access or act on data that informs their practice in a timely way?
_____
_____

Next Step: What is one way you can ensure data is used at the most local level for meaningful improvement?
_____
_____

Paradigm Shift 6: Improvement is Shaped by Culture, Not Just Strategy

Reflection: Does your workplace culture encourage trust, collaboration, and open communication?
_____
_____

Current Reality: How would you describe the current workplace culture in your school or district?
_____
_____

Barriers: What challenges are getting in the way of creating a culture of trust, joy, and shared purpose?
_____
_____

Next Step: What leadership move could strengthen a more positive improvement culture?
_____
_____

Action Planning: Moving Forward

After reflecting on the six shifts, identify one area where you want to take immediate action:

- Which paradigm shift do you want to focus on first?
- What is one specific leadership move you will make in the next month?
- How will you measure progress and impact?

Note: What would your team say? This tool can be used as a team discussion tool in leadership meetings.

▶ LEADERSHIP EXAMPLE: LEADING BY DOING— IMPLEMENTING IMPROVEMENT SCIENCE THROUGH MTSS

After our Superintendent's Cabinet—called Superintendent's Aligned Leadership Team (SALT)—deepened its understanding of improvement science, we made a collective commitment to put our learning into action by demonstrating the same paradigm shifts we hoped to see system-wide.

Since we already operated within a Multi-Tiered Systems of Support (MTSS) framework, we aligned our approach to it. Just as we differentiated support for students, we differentiated leadership support to help embed improvement principles and paradigm shifts at all levels of the organization.

▶ TIER 1: WHOLE TEAM (SALT)—BUILDING A SHARED CULTURE OF IMPROVEMENT

In SALT meetings, we dedicated intentional time to focus on a "What's next?" step of the improvement cycle (Carnegie Foundation for the Advancement of Teaching, 2018). As a Cabinet, we:

- Identified a shared problem and used improvement tools to address them so we could practice the same processes we expected others to use.

- Shared insights from our own improvement work, fostering transparency and collaboration.
- Created feedback loops to reflect on and refine our own leadership practices and strengthen system-wide support.

Growth was fundamental to how we led and embedded in the habits of how our system improves at all levels.

▶ TIER 2: TARGETED GROUPS—FACILITATING IMPROVEMENT WITH TEAMS

We then extended improvement work to the departments and teams we each led. Instead of directing teams to implement change, SALT members:

- Facilitated improvement cycles alongside their teams, co-owning the learning process.
- Provided structure, guidance, and tools while allowing teams to define their own problems and test solutions.
- Brought key learnings back to SALT, so team insights could inform cohesive, system-wide strategies as well as leadership growth.

This reinforced our belief that improvement is a collective effort.

▶ TIER 3: INDIVIDUAL LEADERS—PERSONALIZING SUPPORT FOR GROWTH

Recognizing that leaders are at different stages in their improvement journey, we provided personalized support to SALT members at the individual level based on their needs:

- Improvement science processes and protocols were integrated into joint, collaborative work between the superintendent and each central office leader.
- During our regularly scheduled one-on-one meetings between the superintendent and each central office leader

I checked in and engaged in coaching, support, or thought partnership (as needed) to help lead improvement work with their teams.
- We embedded inquiry cycles into leadership evaluations so that it was not an add-on but rather core to leadership growth and work.

This individualized approach created a culture (and expectation with support) where every leader is a *learner* of improvement in addition to being a *leader* of improvement.

By modeling improvement science at the leadership level, facilitating it with our teams, and customizing support for individual leaders, we created a three-tiered improvement system of supports. We learned it and practiced it so we could lead it.

References

Bryk, A. S. (2015). 2014 AERA distinguished lecture: Accelerating how we learn to improve. *Educational Researcher, 44*(9), 467–477.

Bryk, A. S. (2017). *Redressing inequities: An aspiration in search of a method.* Paper presented at the Fourth Annual Carnegie Foundation Summit on Improvement in Education, San Francisco, CA.

Bryk, A. S. (2018). *Advancing quality in continuous improvement.* Paper presented at the Carnegie Summit, Stanford, CA.

Bryk, A. S., Gomez, L. M., & Gunrow, A. (2010). *Getting ideas into action: Building networked improvement communities in education.* Stanford, CA: Carnegie Foundation for the Advancement of Teaching.

Bryk, A. S., Gomez, L. M., Gunrow, A., & LeMahieu, P. G. (2015). *Learning to improve: How America's schools can get better and getting better.* Cambridge, MA: Harvard Education Publishing.

Carnegie Foundation for the Advancement of Teaching. (2018). *Introduction to improvement science: A learning-by-doing simulation.*

Deming, W. E. (1982). *Out of the crisis* (2nd ed.). Cambridge, MA: Massachusetts Institute of Technology, Center for Advanced Engineering Study.

Deming, W. E. (1994). *The new economics for industry, government, education* (2nd ed.). Cambridge, MA: Massachusetts Institute of Technology, Center for Advanced Engineering Study.

Hattie, J. (2023). *Visible learning, the sequel: A synthesis of over 2,100 meta-analyses relating to achievement* (1st ed.). Routledge. London.

Hinnant-Crawford, B. N., & Anderson, E. (2022). 5S framework for defining problems addressed through improvement research in education. In *The foundational handbook on improvement research in education* (pp. 297–324). Rowman & Littlefield Publishers. New York.

Langley, G. J., Moen, R. D., Nolan, K. M., Nolan, T. W., Norman, C. L., & Provost, L. P. (2009). *The improvement guide* (2nd ed.). San Francisco, CA: Jossey-Bass.

Lewis, C. (2015). What is improvement science? Do we need it in education? *Educational Researcher, 44*(1), 54–61.

Scholtes, P. R. (1998). *The leader's handbook: A guide to inspiring your people and managing the daily workflow.* New York: McGraw Hill.

Yeager, D., Bryk, A., Muhuch, J., Hausman, H., & Morales, L. (2013). *Improvement research carried out through networked communities; Accelerating learning about practices that support more productive student mindsets.* Paper presented at the White House Meeting on Excellence in Education: The Importance of Academic Mindsets, Washington, DC.

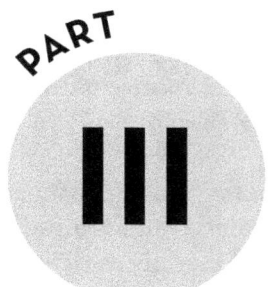

Part III

The How: Structured Processes, Tools, and Leadership Strategies

Chapters 6, 7, 8, 9 and 10
  Equity-Focused Improvement Leadership

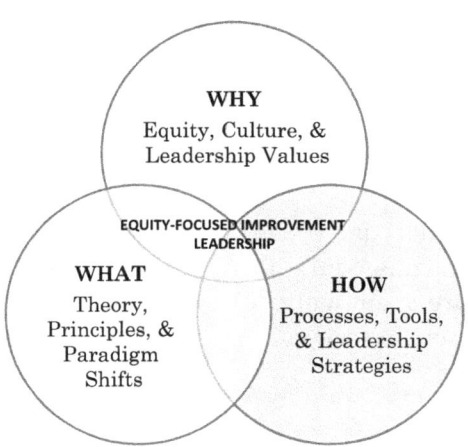

Figure PIII.1 Part III: The How.

Now that we've explored *why* improvement matters (Part I) and *what* the theory supports (Part II), we turn to the *how*—the practical processes, tools, and leadership strategies that turn vision into action.

This part answers the most pressing question for leaders: How do we actually make it happen? These chapters help leaders navigate some of the most common—and most challenging—barriers that make or break real improvement.

- Chapter 6 provides a structured process and set of tools that support disciplined inquiry, helping teams through data-informed iteration tailored to the real needs of students and staff.
- Chapter 7 explains why a positive workplace culture is the foundation of all improvement, how culture supports or sabotages improvement, and what leaders can do to bridge the gap between leadership vision and staff experience.
- Chapter 8 addresses leadership challenges and strategies for increasing staff ownership of improvement, empowering them to solve their own challenges and lead change.
- Chapter 9 focuses on how leaders confront common challenges by creating an environment of psychological safety that encourages risk-taking and public learning essential for authentic improvement.
- Chapter 10 outlines ways leaders can build improvement into the system, leading a true systemic improvement culture.

By the end of this part, you'll have a clear, actionable roadmap for operationalizing equity-focused inquiry, strategies for fostering a culture of authentic learning, and systems for sustaining improvement at scale.

Chapter 6

Processes and Tools for Leading through Disciplined Inquiry

 LEARNING TARGET

I can apply structured processes and appropriate tools to lead disciplined inquiry for continuous improvement.

Success Criteria

- Define the characteristics of disciplined inquiry and why it's essential for effective improvement.
- Apply a five-phase process for leading disciplined inquiry in an educational setting.
- Select and use the appropriate tools to support each phase of the inquiry process.

RELEVANT NELP STANDARDS

- NELP Standard 1: Mission, Vision, and Improvement (Improvement Process, Focus Collective Efforts, PDSA)
- NELP Standard 2: Ethics and Professional Norms (Understand the Problem and the System, Collaboration)

- NELP Standard 3: Equity, Inclusiveness, and Cultural Responsiveness (Inclusive Inquiry Processes, Root Cause Analysis for Equity, See the System)
- NELP Standard 4: Learning and Instruction (Generate Ideas for Change, PDSA)
- NELP Standard 5: Community and External Leadership (Collaborative Inquiry, Understand the Problem)
- NELP Standard 6: Operations and Management (Solving Operational Problems—Generate Ideas for Change, PDSA, Spread and Scale)
- NELP Standard 7 (Building-Level): Building Professional Capacity (Inquiry as Professional Learning)
- NELP Standard 7 (District-Level): Policy, Governance, and Advocacy (Using Disciplined Inquiry at the Superintendent Cabinet and Central Office Level)

ICEBREAKER: INQUIRY IN ACTION

Think of a time when your team engaged in an inquiry process to solve a problem.

- Was the inquiry structured and disciplined, or was it unstructured and loose?
- What worked and what didn't?
- How did the process impact the outcomes?

(See Appendix 1 for the Icebreaker Group Activity Facilitation Guide)

CASE VIGNETTE: IT TAKES (MORE THAN) TIME

Background

Deer Valley Elementary School had finally carved out common planning time for teachers. After years of hearing staff say, "We just need more time to collaborate," the leadership team adjusted the bell schedule and

> protected 60 minutes every Wednesday afternoon. It felt like a win. But months into the new schedule, frustration started bubbling up.
>
> > "We sit together, but things aren't all that different."
> > "I'm not sure what I'm supposed to bring."
> > "Another meeting, another form to fill out."
>
> Principal Mers was puzzled. They had given teachers the time. Why weren't they seeing a bigger impact?
>
> ## Turning Point
>
> The district admin team was trying to solve this very issue. One principal asked, "Is it will, or is it skill?" Maybe the problem wasn't effort or attitude. Maybe leaders were not sure how to facilitate disciplined inquiry. After all, when did they ever get taught that?
>
> Back at school, Mers and the instructional coach decided to treat teacher collaboration the same way they approached classroom instruction—with modeling, scaffolding, and feedback. In the next few meetings, as a staff, they led a full cycle of inquiry to model and provide guided practice: identifying a real problem, reviewing data, forming a prediction, testing a small strategy, and reflecting on results. They didn't just tell teams what to do, they showed them, step by step.
>
> Using a gradual release of responsibility, Principal Mers and the coach had teams run their own cycles at their own pace while they gave feedback and support. The tone shifted. Instead of vague talk or frustration, teams focused their energy. They picked clear problems. They tested small changes. They shared results. Not everything worked, but now there was a structure to learn from what did and didn't work.
>
> ## Bottom Line
>
> Time alone won't change practice. If we want staff to engage in inquiry, we must teach it with the same intention and care we give our students. We can't lead what we don't know.

One reason education is so complex is that each school and district faces unique challenges, making improvement efforts difficult to standardize. What works for one school or district doesn't always work for another. Traditional reform models often fail because they overlook the different needs of schools, districts, and communities.

This is where disciplined inquiry comes in.

Improvement science provides a structured, yet adaptable framework that allows educators to identify challenges, collaborate on solutions, and implement changes in a way that is responsive to their own situation and context. This chapter explores how school and district leaders can apply improvement science processes using practical tools to engage in an articulated five-phase inquiry cycle.

The goal is to improve systems. By focusing on process improvement rather than compliance, educational leaders can create sustainable, equity-driven changes that truly make a difference for students and staff. This is where the heart of educators meets the science of improvement.

As we learned previously, educational systems require continuous learning and adaptation. Improvement science answers the call by helping teams develop, revise, and fine-tune tools, processes, work roles, and relationships (Bryk, 2015). We will now layer on to this learning by adding the actual processes staff can use to test ideas in real-world conditions to see what works, for whom, and under what circumstances.

In Chapter 3, we touched on Networked Improvement Communities (NICs) through the research. In this actionable chapter, we will discuss the role of NICs in the five-step improvement process. As recently as 2015, Bryk noted that no professional infrastructure existed for educators to systematically test and refine change ideas through shared learning (Bryk, 2015). NICs fill this gap by expanding learning across teams, schools, and districts, allowing educators to refine strategies faster and more effectively.

As they apply their profound knowledge in different contexts, NICs develop adaptive, scalable solutions, ensuring that insights are grounded in real-world practice rather than theory alone. Learning-by-doing becomes the driver of change and accelerator of progress.

As we engage teams in the five-phase process, we need to lead with purpose by keeping equity (our why) at the center of our inquiry. While disciplined inquiry provides the structure, equity must remain the north star guiding all decisions and actions (Anderson et al., 2024) so that we create more just and inclusive educational experiences for all students.

▶ THE FIVE-PHASE IMPROVEMENT PROCESS OVERVIEW

Disciplined inquiry follows a structured process designed to guide teams through ongoing cycles of learning. This section walks through an inquiry process that uses five steps (The Carnegie Foundation for the Advancement of Teaching, 2018). Although the steps are presented linearly, the process can be non-linear or recursive.

It may be helpful for teams to envision these steps in a circular format to depict the cycle of inquiry (Figure 6.1), but since the process is not linear, it is important for teams to ask, "What do I need to learn next to advance improvement?" As such, arrows radiate from the inside to each question.

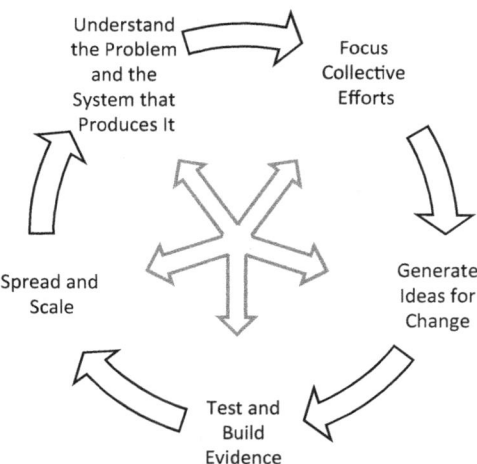

Figure 6.1 5-Step Improvement Process.

(The Carnegie Foundation for the Advancement of Teaching, 2018). Used with permission.

Start by assembling a team. Consider the type and scope of the issue, get the right people at the table to solve the problem, and ensure leadership is actively engaged. A tool to support this step is:

- Assemble a Team Check-In—Helps leaders ensure that the improvement team includes the right mix of roles, perspectives, and proximity to the problem (Appendix 2.1)

Then follow the five steps:

1. Understand the Problem and the System Producing It (Root Causes)
   Improvement begins with a deep understanding of the problem. Too often, teams assume they know the issue when, in reality, they are only seeing symptoms. Leaders must slow down, analyze root causes, and ensure that improvement efforts are equity-centered and informed by those closest to the issue. Tools to support this step are:
   - Identify an Issue Tool—Points teams toward a problem area to explore (Appendix 2.2)
   - Data Analysis Protocol—Leads teams through making sense of data (Appendix 2.3)
   - 5 Whys Protocol—Helps teams drill down to the root cause of a problem (Appendix 2.4)
   - Fishbone Diagram (Cause-and-Effect Analysis)—Visually maps out multiple contributing factors (Appendix 2.5)
   - Process Mapping—Makes workflows visible and identifies inefficiencies or inconsistencies in the system (Appendix 2.6)
   - Empathy Interviews—Gathers first-hand insights from those experiencing the problem, such as students, staff, or families (Appendix 2.7)
   - Research-Based and Evidence-Based Practices—Learns from what has been proven to work (Appendix 2.8)
   - Affinity Protocol—Categorizes related concepts to identify patterns, themes, and root causes (Appendix 2.9)

2. Focus Collective Efforts
   Once the root cause is identified, teams must narrow their focus to a specific, high-leverage problem. Without a clearly defined aim, improvement efforts can become scattered. Tools to support this step are:
   - Setting an Aim Statement—Defines what is improving, for whom, and by when (Appendix 2.10)
   - Driver Diagrams—Identifies key drivers behind a problem and prioritizes areas for change (Appendix 2.11)
3. Generate Ideas for Change
   At this stage, teams brainstorm and develop potential solutions. The goal is not to find a perfect solution immediately but to generate small, targeted change ideas that can be tested quickly. Tools to support this step are:
   - Change Ideas—Determines, organizes, and prioritizes actions that impact the driver and support the improvement aim (Appendix 2.12)
   - Theory of Action Statement—Connects proposed changes to expected outcomes through an if-then statement (Appendix 2.13)
4. Test and Build Evidence Through PDSA Cycles
   Rather than implementing changes at full scale right away, teams use Plan–Do–Study–Act (PDSA) cycles to test ideas on a small scale, measure effectiveness, and refine strategies before expanding. Tools to support this step are:
   - Plan—Defines the change, develops a hypothesis, and decides on measures of success (Appendix 2.14)
   - Do—Implements the change on a small scale (Appendix 2.15)
   - Study—Analyzes the results and compares them to predictions (Appendix 2.16)
   - Act—Decides whether to adopt, adapt, or abandon the change (Appendix 2.17)
5. Spread and Scale What Works
   Once a change has been tested and refined, the next step is to expand it wider and, ultimately, across the system. Scaling should not be rushed, so teams can ensure that solutions are contextually adaptable. Tools to support this step are:

- Spread and Scale Decision-Making Tool—Determines readiness for expansion (Appendix 2.18)
- Networked Improvement Communities (NICs) Shared Learning Tool—Leverages cross-team learning to accelerate improvement and equity (Appendix 2.19)

Now let's go deeper into each of the five steps of the improvement process cycle.

▶ ASSEMBLE A TEAM: LAYING THE FOUNDATION FOR IMPROVEMENT

Previously, we discussed the role NICs play in improvement. Now, we will get to the mechanics of building a team. Using the Assemble a Team Check-In tool will help leaders establish effective teams (Appendix 2.1). The composition of the team should align with the level at which the problem exists, whether it be:

- Grade-level or content teams—For classroom-based instructional challenges
- School-level teams—For broader issues affecting student outcomes, culture, or instructional practices
- District department-level teams—For operational or instructional concerns within a specialized area
- District-level teams—For large-scale issues or initiatives impacting multiple schools

Key considerations for team formation include:

- Involve those closest to the work—Staff, students, and others most affected by the issue should be directly involved in designing and testing solutions.
- Ensure leadership proximity and engagement—Leaders cannot completely delegate improvement efforts; they must be actively engaged.
- Clarify the leader's role—Leaders may serve as facilitators, coach, team members, or champions, depending on the team's needs.

- Champion improvement as a priority—Improvement work should be embedded into existing structures, not treated as an add-on or extra initiative.

Team assembly matters. Putting together a well-structured, diverse team ensures that improvement efforts are informed by multiple perspectives, leading to better solutions. A mix of expertise, authority, and lived experience is an asset. By thoughtfully assembling the right team and ensuring leadership proximity, schools and districts lay a strong foundation for disciplined inquiry.

Putting a team in place is not a one-and-done activity. Teams should revisit their composition throughout the process, such as after they learn about the problem and select change ideas.

(*Use the Assemble a Team Check-In in Appendix 2.1 to reflect on whether your team is inclusive, well-positioned, and equipped to move the work forward*)

With a team assembled, it's time to engage the team in a collective inquiry.

▶ PHASE 1: UNDERSTAND THE PROBLEM AND THE SYSTEM THAT PRODUCES IT

The first phase in disciplined inquiry is to deeply understand the problem before attempting solutions. Teams need to take the time to identify, analyze, and uncover the root cause of the issue they are trying to solve.

Identify an issue. First, teams identify an issue (Appendix 2.2). For a team to be motivated and engaged in improvement, they must first be dissatisfied with the status quo. Teams may find it helpful to ask themselves: What is one inequitable outcome that keeps you up at night? That question often leads to an authentic, uncomfortable, high-impact issue. The problem area should:

- Phrase the issue as a negative—Clearly define the issue as a problem
- Not disguise solutions as problems—Do not say what should be done

- Not place blame—Focus on patterns and systems, not individuals
- Be actionable—Eventually lead to actions that are within the team's control

At this point, the issue is a somewhat broad topic. The team is not yet able to articulate a narrow, specific problem because they need to learn more first. The goal for now is to identify an issue worth exploring.

(Use the Identify an Issue tool in Appendix 2.2 to help your team identify a problem area to explore)

Assess the data. We are educators. Our nature is to want to solve problems. Before narrowing the problem area and moving to solutions, we have to endure the discomfort of sitting with the issue. That means we resist being fixers and instead dig into what's really going on. A first step in understanding the issue is to analyze it. One tool for learning more about the problem area is the use of a Data Analysis Protocol (Appendix 2.3). This gives teams data-driven clarity about the problem before acting.

When we approach a problem without data, we are often going off assumptions, and those tend to be incomplete, biased, or just plain incorrect. A data analysis protocol slows down the process and creates space for shared exploration of what the data is telling us. It helps teams explore, identify patterns, and inform hypotheses about the root causes of issues, so that eventual solutions are based on evidence rather than perception.

There are many processes that can be used to make sense of data. A Data Analysis Protocol (Appendix 2.3) leads teams through understanding the context and what the data represents, engaging in objective noticing, approaching the data with curiosity through wonderings, and then beginning interpretation. This protocol helps teams stay grounded in the data as they build an initial shared understanding of the issue.

(Use the Data Analysis Protocol tool in Appendix 2.3 to lead your team through data analysis)

Find a root cause (5 Whys). Exploring data is only an initial step. Too often, teams look at data and then immediately attempt to fix the problem. However, often the issues we see on the surface are symptoms of a deeper system issue. The team needs to dig deeper into what might be causing the problem. That's where the Five Whys Protocol comes in (Appendix 2.4). This protocol is a simple but powerful strategy for identifying the root cause of a problem by asking "Why?" multiple times.

First, teams state the initial problem. Then they ask, "Why?" five times, digging deeper into the underlying causes. This is where leaders need to be careful with facilitation. Teams are naturally tempted to list *different* reasons, going wider rather than deeper. Instead, teams need to peel back the layers of one line of reasoning. This challenges teams to move beyond symptoms and obvious answers and presses them to reflect on less overt explanations or causes.

The final goal is to clearly name a root cause that is within the team's control. If the team lands on a cause outside its sphere of influence (such as state funding or family dynamics), then the team needs to backtrack and follow another line of reasoning.

Note: While it often takes five *whys* to get to the root cause related to leadership practices, teams should ask as many *whys* as they need to get to the grain size of the problem that can be addressed. As you go, keep checking your responses against your original problem area to make sure the line of reasoning is logical and makes sense.

(*Use the Five Whys Protocol tool in Appendix 2.4 to facilitate root cause analysis*)

Find multiple root causes (fishbone). Another tool to engage in cause-and-effect analysis of the problem is the Fishbone Diagram (Appendix 2.5). Unlike the Five Whys, which follows one line of inquiry, a fishbone diagram helps the team explore multiple possible causes while still asking *why* to uncover deeper root issues for each line of inquiry.

Teams begin by writing the problem statement at the *head* of the fish. They create major *bones* (categories) on the diagram with contributing factors such as processes, policies, resources, training, and student factors. Teams then brainstorm subcauses under each category by asking *Why* multiple times to drill down deeper into contributing factors.

What shows up is a systems picture depicting that there are several factors contributing to the issue, and each factor has underlying causes. When the diagram is complete, teams can step back and identify trends or patterns they see across multiple sources, which root causes are within their control, and which root causes would make the biggest impact. Finally, teams select the most impactful cause(s) to focus on. (Refer to Appendix 2.5 to see a model of a fishbone diagram.)

(*Use the Fish Bone Diagram tool in Appendix 2.5 to guide your team through complex problems that have multiple root causes*)

Map the process. Another tool that supports making systems visible is Process Mapping (Appendix 2.6). This helps teams look beyond the immediate problem and also consider the system that produces it.

Once your team agrees on the process you'll examine, perhaps one that surfaced from your Five Whys or Fishbone Diagram, each person will independently sketch how they *think* the process works. No peeking! It's important that each person create their own flowchart, such as using boxes to represent each step, arrows to show sequence, and labels to clarify actions, timelines, and the person responsible. It might be tempting, but resist the urge to let the team build the process map collaboratively at this stage. It's okay if it feels messy or the process is unclear. This step is designed to surface different perceptions or mental models of the same system. (Even when our team was certain we all knew the process for addressing student absenteeism, using Process Mapping revealed surprising inconsistencies in how each person understood the steps.)

Next, do a gallery walk so each team member can see the process that all the other team members drew. Discuss noticings. For example, did some people include steps that others left out? Are there places of uncertainty, such as where people left question marks or didn't know where the process led to? Did folks with different roles know different parts of the process or perceive the process differently? This often reveals different perspectives or levels of understanding of how people experience the same process.

Finally, the team gets to put the various maps together to build a shared process map—one that includes all the pieces, roles, timelines or durations, and areas to improve, such as breakdowns, bottlenecks, inconsistencies, or pain points. Building the collaborative map using sticky notes is helpful so you can move the boxes around as you figure things out. This is an illuminating way to build a clear and shared understanding of the system and to, quite literally, get on the same page. Process Maps make the invisible system visible.

(*Use the Process Map tool in Appendix 2.6 to help your team "see the system."*)

Talk to the people involved (empathy interviews). Another tool to help the team understand the human experience of the problem and the system that produces it is Empathy Interviews (Appendix 2.7). Empathy interviews help us make solving problems a work of heart. They bring the voices of those who experience, are affected by, or are responsible for solving the problem into the improvement process.

Empathy interviews help us live our core value of equity as the team considers whose voices we need to hear. Then, we create safe environments and ask questions that allow those directly experiencing the system to tell their stories, input, ideas, and emotions. Interviewers capture these conversations using scripting and quotes to preserve the authentic voices of those who share. That way, when the team reviews empathy interview responses, they can look for patterns and variation. In addition to helping the team move past assumptions we can make from data or on charts, these stories from the field motivate the team to act with compassion and remember our *why*.

(*Use the Empathy Interview tool in Appendix 2.7 to facilitate understanding the human experience*)

Review existing research. Another tool to inform Phase 1 is reviewing existing research-based and evidence-based practices (Appendix 2.8). In addition to gathering system data, teams should consult external research and evidence to understand how others have approached similar problems. It is important to expand your team's existing thinking beyond strategies you already know. Two ways to do that are:

- Research-based practices that connect local challenges to proven strategies
- Evidence-based practices that come from what has worked for others who solved problems of practice in their context

Improvement science values both research- and evidence-based practices, and even combines them through active improvement research that tests ideas in real-world contexts and refines them through iterative cycles of learning (Li, 2024). When teams explore their identified issue through fresh lenses, such as research- and evidence-based practices, they can uncover possible blind spots or see the problem and system in new ways.

(*Use the Research-Based and Evidence-Based Practices tool in Appendix 2.8 to guide your team through discovering practices that have been proven to work for others*)

Look for themes (affinity mapping). Phase 1 is not a linear sequence. Teams may need to revisit earlier tools for understanding the problem as new insights emerge. Often, a final part of Phase 1 is moving from understanding the problem to uncovering themes in root causes. Teams will synthesize the multiple data types (e.g., quantitative, qualitative, process, experiential) from Phase 1 and make sense of it all by using an Affinity Protocol tool (Appendix 2.9).

In this process, teams capture each key findings from across the data on a sticky note. This could include things like data points, process map gaps, interview quotes, and insights. Teams begin to group the sticky notes that relate to each other, ultimately naming the categories. This allows teams to shift from data to information, helping them prioritize key insights so they can determine what efforts might make the biggest impact.

(*Use the Affinity Protocol tool in Appendix 2.9 to lead your team in making meaning of data and information from Phase 1*)

Phase 1 of disciplined inquiry helps the team slow down and not rush to solutions before deeply understanding the problem and the system that produces it. This work is the foundation for Phase 2 in the improvement process: Focus Collective Efforts. With root causes identified, teams can narrow their focus from the issue or problem area to a specific, well-defined problem so that efforts are targeted, actionable, and measurable within available resources and time. This also prevents teams from trying to fix everything at once, which would lead to frustration and slower progress.

▶ PHASE 2: FOCUS COLLECTIVE EFFORTS

Using the findings from *Phase 1: Understanding the Problem and the System that Produces It*, it's time for teams to use the insight to set a specific aim and use a driver diagram to prioritize actionable and impactful change ideas. If you don't know what an *aim* or *driver diagram* is, don't worry—these concepts will be explained shortly.

First, let's briefly revisit the team we have in place. Now that we have a clearer understanding of the problem, it's time to ask ourselves: Do we have the right people at the table? The people who helped define the issue may not be the same people who can best solve it. A strong improvement team includes those with subject-matter expertise, front-line experience, and diverse perspectives. Consider:

- Is there someone who works closest to the issue and understands daily challenges?
- Do we need additional voices, such as students, families, or community members?
- Would an expert in the system or process bring valuable insights?

Before moving forward, take a moment to adjust the team and ensure we have the right people in the room to co-create real solutions, and then get the new team members up to speed.

Set a clear aim. With the right team in place to address the problem, using the information you analyzed in Phase 1, the team will develop an aim statement. An aim is one clear, measurable goal that defines what you are trying to accomplish, for whom, and by when.

Several potential improvement aims may have emerged when you explored the problem, but you only need one. Avoid the temptation to make the aim broad enough to fit multiple goals. A narrow, equity-focused aim brings clarity, allows for more precise testing, and increases the positive impact.

The way we go about coming up with an aim statement also matters. When teams co-develop this aim, it builds ownership and shared commitments, strengthening the foundation for successful implementation and follow-through. Naming an aim that really matters to the team and those they serve is motivating.

(*Use the Set an Aim tool in Appendix 2.10 to help your team create a focus and define success*)

Find the drivers. Now that teams have a narrowed focus through an aim statement, they are ready to connect drivers to the aim using a Driver Diagram tool (Appendix 2.11). Teams use primary and secondary drivers to target strategies at the aim. These drivers are designed to disrupt the status quo and improve outcomes.

A Driver Diagram is a map and a thinking organizer that helps teams visualize key elements (drivers) that influence the goal (aim). Each driver is broken down from primary drivers to secondary drivers. (Refer to Appendix 2.11 for a model of a Driver Diagram.) This driver diagram becomes a roadmap for improvement. However, the diagram is metaphorically in pencil. As the team tests and refines various change ideas, the drivers may change to reflect insights.

Driver diagrams have a specific structure (as depicted in Appendix 2.11).

- The Aim—The aim is located on the far left of a driver diagram. This is the specific, measurable outcome the team wants to achieve.

- Primary Drivers—The primary drivers offshoot from the aim. These are the categories that directly impact the aim and are key areas to focus on.
- Secondary Drivers—The secondary drivers offshoot from primary drivers. These are the categories that break down into more specific areas of needed change. In your system (the existing structures, processes, and practices), this is where you should focus your energy to affect the primary driver.
- Change Ideas—Change ideas will be added in Phase 3, but they are located on the far right of the driver diagram. These are the specific actions that teams test and refine to influence drivers and ultimately achieve the aim (Fathima, 2016).

To aid in understanding, let's consider an example of driver diagram components. Imagine a school aiming to increase student attendance by 10% over the next semester.

- Primary drivers could include student engagement, school climate, and family involvement.
- Secondary drivers under the student engagement primary driver might be stronger teacher–student relationships and more engaging classroom instruction.
- Change ideas for the teacher–student relationships secondary driver could include morning check-ins and personalized phone calls for at-risk students.

Lines are used to connect aims to primary drivers, primary drivers to secondary drivers, and secondary drivers to change ideas.

This structured approach helps teams break big challenges into manageable responses. The diagram turns vision into action with a clear path forward, while still leaving room for iterative learning along the way. When teams engage in Phase 3: Generating Ideas for Change, they drill down even further into specific, actionable strategies.

(*Use the Driver Diagram tool in Appendix 2.11 to help your team build a map for improvement*)

▶ PHASE 3: GENERATING IDEAS FOR CHANGE

Develop change ideas. Recall that a system is perfectly designed to get the results it is currently getting (Deming, 1994). This means that improving outcomes requires intentional disruption of existing processes. *Change ideas* are the disruptors. Change ideas are:

- Alternatives to the status quo—designed to produce different results
- Selected by those closest to the work, ensuring relevance and feasibility
- Tested in small, iterative cycles—minimizing risk and maximizing learning

Change ideas can involve new interventions designed from scratch, or they could be modifications and refinements of existing practices. Since no one can predict exactly how a change will play out, improvement science starts small, testing change ideas in controlled situations (Bryk et al., 2015).

But where do change ideas come from? If we solely rely on what we already know, with no new wellspring of fresh ideas, we will likely not see change. After all, if we knew better, we would do better. It's time to stop fishing in the same pond. New ideas that are specific and actionable can come from data, experience, external knowledge, or innovation. Teams should consider:

- Research—What does existing research say about solving this problem?
- Practice—What have other schools or organizations done successfully?
- Design—What new, creative solutions might work in our context? (Carnegie Foundation for the Advancement of Teaching, 2018).

A Change Ideas tool can support teams in putting research, practice, and design ideas into action (Appendix 2.12). Adding change ideas to the Driver Diagram helps teams connect each idea to a specific driver by organizing them under the appropriate drivers on the diagram. Draw arrows to show how the change ideas connect to drivers. One change idea may influence multiple drivers, or one driver may have multiple change ideas. (Refer to Appendix 2.11 to see a model of a Driver Diagram.)

Next, the team selects the first change idea to test. Since not all change ideas can be tested at once, teams should prioritize one high-impact change idea or a *change bundle* to start with. (A change bundle is where more than one change idea is intentionally used together because some interventions are more effective when changes are combined, such as combining parent outreach and student goal-setting to improve attendance.)

Consider the following criteria when you are selecting a change idea or change bundle to test:

- High potential impact—Will it significantly move the needle on the aim?
- Feasibility—Can it be implemented with available resources and time?
- Quick learning potential—Can results be assessed in a short timeframe?

(Use the Change Ideas tool in Appendix 2.12 to guide your team in adding change ideas to their Driver Diagram)

Develop a theory of action. After teams have selected their change idea, it's time to articulate how it connects to the broader plan (drivers and the aim). A *theory of action* is an "if–then" statement that tells how the change will lead to improvement. For example, *If* we implement family attendance calls and student goal-setting with regular check-ins for students who miss two days per month (on track for chronic absenteeism), *then* that will lead to stronger student and family engagement, *which will* impact our aim of reducing chronic absenteeism. A Theory of Action tool can help teams develop a clear theory of action statement (Appendix 2.13).

A theory of action statement is a powerful leadership tool. It connects your *why* (aim), your *how* (drivers), and your *what* (change idea) in one concise, yet compelling statement. This explicit clarity is a valuable leadership talking point when communicating with others. Whether you are kicking off a team meeting, opening a professional development session, updating your school board, creating agendas or newsletters, or engaging your community, a theory of action statement connects today's work or current action to the bigger picture or desired outcome. It helps you keep the improvement actions grounded in a shared vision and aligned to results.

(*Use the Theory of Action tool in Appendix 2.13 to guide your team in connecting strategy to their aim*)

Now that we have a Driver Diagram complete with change ideas, we move from plan to action by pairing the Driver Diagram with structured testing. The next phase is to test the selected change idea or change bundle through Plan–Do–Study–Act (PDSA) cycles (Deming, 1994).

▶ PHASE 4: TEST AND BUILD EVIDENCE

"All improvement is change, but not all change is improvement" (Berwick, 2003, p. 450). To find out if the selected change ideas will actually lead to improvement, teams must test the impact of their theory of action. The Plan–Do–Study–Act (PDSA) cycle, originally developed by Deming (1994), provides a structured way to test changes, analyze results, and refine strategies. Over time, these small tests work together to lead to sustained system-wide improvements (Berwick, 2003; Bryk et al., 2015). PDSA cycles ensure that improvements are evidence-based. Teams can try out a change idea quickly, analyze the impact, and make adjustments.

Effective PDSA cycles are done in teams where shared learning occurs, tests are designed for the specific context to ensure relevance, and tests are kept small and done frequently (rather than larger and slower) because real change requires many repeated tests.

In addition to testing theories, teams use PDSA cycles to build knowledge. These cycles support the shift from basic knowledge to profound knowledge as teams run tests, assess results, and refine strategies, processes, and products that

TABLE 6.1 Connecting Key Questions of Improvement to Driver Diagram Elements (Langley et al., 2009)

Key Questions of Improvement Science	Connections to Driver Diagram
What are we trying to accomplish?	Aim
How will we know that a change is an improvement?	Measures
What changes can we make that will result in improvement?	Change Ideas tested through PDSA cycles

improve both their own practice and the system (Bryk et al., 2015; Deming, 1994). This situates staff as knowledge creators.

Over time, the findings are shared across teams to accelerate system learning and scale what works. NICs can test the change idea simultaneously in different settings to modify the change as needed. Ultimately, small, focused tests add up to improved systems where change is sustained (Berwick, 2003). PDSA cycles help our theory of improvement and driver diagram to live and breathe in our daily work (Langley et al., 2009). Table 6.1 establishes connections between the Driver Diagram components and the PDSA cycle, aligning with key questions of improvement science.

Plan. The first step of the PDSA cycle is *plan* using a Plan tool (Appendix 2.14). This is where we define the change and how it will be measured. The *plan* step ensures the team clearly understands what they are testing, how they will test it, and what they predict will happen.

Key planning steps include:

1. Identify the change idea being tested.
2. Predict what will happen.
3. Determine how results will be measured.
4. Clarify roles: Who will do what, when, and where?

(Use the PDSA Plan tool in Appendix 2.14 to lead your team in getting ready for implementation)

Do. The second step of the PDSA cycle is *do*, where the team implements the test of the change idea on a small scale. The Do tool (Appendix 2.15) can support this step. While this is the moment of execution, it's not about going big, at least not initially. It's about testing the change under real conditions while observing to learn what actually happens on a small scale (e.g., one classroom, one grade level, or one team).

During this *do* step, the members collect two types of data:

- Process measures—Did the change idea happen as intended?
- Outcome measures—Did the change idea improve the aim?

The team also collects any variations, surprises, or unexpected effects that emerge. The key to this step is *doing* the change idea but also paying attention to what happens while you do it.

(*Use the PDSA Do tool in Appendix 2.15 to help your team implement and track your results and observations*)

Study. The third step of the PDSA cycle is *study*, which the Study tool (Appendix 2.16) can support. This phase is where teams pause to analyze outcomes and compare their results to the predictions they made in the *plan* phase. This is an opportunity to consider whether the change idea worked as expected, what insights can be learned from the results, and whether the change led to improvement.

Some key reflection questions to ask in this step are:

- Was the cycle carried out as planned?
- What was surprising or different than expected?
- Did the results match our prediction?
- What did we learn from this test?
- What are our next steps?

(*Use the PDSA Study tool in Appendix 2.16 to guide your team in learning from results*)

Act. The final step of the PDSA cycle is *act*. Teams can use the Act tool (Appendix 2.17) to decide on their next steps based on what they learned. Specifically, teams determine whether to adopt, adapt, or abandon the change idea based on the results (Carnegie Foundation for the Advancement of Teaching, 2018). If they adopt, they scale up and integrate the change permanently. If they adapt, they modify the strategy and run another cycle. If they abandon, they stop testing that change idea and run a test on another change idea. This phase helps teams be intentional about scaling what works, improving what could work, and letting go of what doesn't.

(*Use the PDSA Act tool in Appendix 2.17 to help your team use results and decide on next steps*)

Small-scale iterative testing works. PDSA cycles reduce risk because if a change idea fails, only a small group is affected. Small tests also build confidence because they allow teams to refine strategies using real-time data and engage in quick iterations before full implementation. Finally, they ensure evidence-based decision-making, allowing teams to know that the changes are proven to work in their own context before expanding it.

The next phase helps teams determine how to move from testing to growing what works.

▶ PHASE 5: SPREAD AND SCALE

Scale up ideas that work. Once a change idea has been tested and refined through multiple PDSA cycles, the next step is to determine if and how it should be expanded across the system. *Spread* and *scale* are how leaders help successful changes reach more students, staff, and schools.

Spread means *testing* the change idea in different contexts through additional PDSA cycles to continue adapting and refining it. This increases reach while continuing to learn how the change idea performs in different settings (Greenhalgh & Papoutsi, 2019).

Tracking data is a way teams gather evidence of improvement. Over time or iterations, PDSA cycles give teams the results they need to determine whether a change idea is truly driving improvement, helping teams separate the effects of their actions from external factors (Langley et al., 2009). Data also reveals whether a system remains stable after implementing a change, which is critical for making reliable predictions about future outcomes (Deming, 1982; Langley et al., 2009). With a clear understanding of what works, teams can make informed decisions about when and how to spread and scale successful changes.

Once a change has been proven effective in one or more contexts, leaders strategically expand testing and implementation, spreading the change across teams and sites. This can occur through applying the change to another class, subject area, grade level, or department—or even expanding across multiple schools or departments. This spreading allows the team to test the change with different students or staff to ensure equity.

Deliberate spreading allows teams to adapt the strategies that worked in one setting to different conditions before rolling out full implementation. Testing in different contexts and with different groups builds capacity for scaling and system-wide improvement.

On the other hand, *scale* means *implementing* changes that have already demonstrated success more broadly. Still, local teams may need to tailor the change to their specific situation. For effective scaling, leaders need to consider infrastructure, resources, and support needed (Greenhalgh & Papoutsi, 2019). That might include policies, training, and long-term planning.

Although we teased spread and scale apart to explain them, they work together. Fortunately, we have a tool to support teams in spread and scale decision-making (Appendix 2.18).

To decide when and how to spread and scale, teams determine how confident they are that the change will continue to work in new settings based on its testing history and observed outcomes. As depicted in Table 6.2, a change idea with low confidence has worked once but lacks clear cause-and-effect, so it needs more testing. When an idea has been tested multiple times with moderate success, it falls under some confidence, though more variation still needs to be explored. Finally, a change idea with high confidence has consistently produced improvement across different conditions and is ready for full implementation (Langley et al., 2009).

Testing the change in a variety of contexts becomes important. It ensures a change idea is scalable and sustainable.

TABLE 6.2 Confidence Levels (Langley et al., 2009)

Confidence Level	Description
Low Confidence	Change idea worked once but with unclear cause-and-effect. Additional testing is needed.
Some Confidence	Change idea has been tested multiple times with moderate success, but more variation needs to be tested.
High Confidence	Change idea has consistently produced improvement in different conditions. Ready for full implementation.

TABLE 6.3 Scales of Tests (Langley et al., 2009)

Test Scale	Example
Small-Scale Pilot	Apply the change idea in one classroom, one grade level, or with one group of students.
Follow-Up Test	Repeat the test with modifications (e.g., different teachers, additional support structures).
Wide-Scale Test	Expand to multiple grade levels, subject areas, or schools to see if the impact holds.
Full Implementation	Adopt the change system-wide as part of regular practice.

Although it is not always perfectly linear, the process of spreading and scaling follows phases, as outlined in Table 6.3.

First, a small-scale pilot applies the change in a limited setting, such as one classroom, grade level, or group of students. Then we spread through follow-up tests that repeat the implementation with modifications, such as with different teachers or modifying the strategy. If successful, a more wide-scale test spreads the change to multiple grade levels, subject areas, or schools to determine whether the impact remains consistent. Then, with proven effectiveness, we scale the change into full implementation, so that it becomes a regular part of practice (Langley et al., 2009).

(Use the Spread and Scale Decision-Making Tool in Appendix 2.18 to help your team make decisions)

Monitor implementation. Even after spreading and scaling, leaders and teams need to continue monitoring, learning, and customizing what is working, where, and for whom. The NIC Sharing Learning tool (Appendix 2.19) supports this process. Effective scaling is complex. NICs can function as infrastructure to advance both spread and scale when leaders leverage all aspects of the NIC:

- Networked—Cross-school, cross-department, or cross-district teams test changes in parallel. As teams spread change ideas across new settings, they help each other refine and adapt the changes through intentional collaborative learning structures.
- Improvement—Teams engage in iterative testing and contextual adaptation as they spread change ideas. They gather data, refine change ideas, and serve as knowledge creators. As teams develop confidence in change ideas, they support scaling by sharing what works, for who, and under what conditions, helping to identify the supports needed to implement more broadly.
- Community—Teams collaborate and share what they are learning for the greater good of advancing more equitable outcomes and experiences across the system. This is a community that leverages collective wisdom that extends the reach and depth of the improvement effort. This culture of trust and generosity also strengthens the foundation for meaningful scaling, as NICs can serve in shared leadership.

(Use the Networked Improvement Community (NIC) Sharing Learning Tool in Appendix 2.19 to help your team learn about what works, where, and for whom as your teams spread and scale change ideas.)

Improvement is not a linear process. The five-phase cycle of improvement is presented in a sequence for learning purposes, but because problems, people, and systems are complex the process is often messy and non-linear. And yet, there is beauty in the mess as more adults build capacity, more students experience success, and more aspects of the system improve.

> **❓ REFLECTION QUESTIONS**
>
> 1. Applying Disciplined Inquiry: How might you use the 5-phase improvement process for disciplined inquiry or incorporate its principles and tools to enhance your current inquiry process?
>   ☐ Understand the problem and the system that produces it
>   ☐ Focus collective efforts
>   ☐ Generating ideas for change
>   ☐ Test and build evidence using PDSA cycles
>   ☐ Spread and scale
> 2. Strategic Use of Tools: Which specific tools (Appendix 2.1–2.19) do you see as most beneficial in your current or future improvement efforts? How might you integrate those into your existing practice?

📝 CHAPTER 6 TRY THIS: TOOLS THAT SUPPORT DISCIPLINED INQUIRY

The tools mentioned throughout this chapter to support every phase of the inquiry process are gathered in Appendix 2 for your convenience.

2.1 Assemble a Team Check-In
2.2 Identify an Issue
2.3 Data Analysis Protocol
2.4 5 Whys Protocol
2.5 Fishbone Diagram
2.6 Process Mapping
2.7 Empathy Interviews
2.8 Research and Evidence to Understand the Problem
2.9 Affinity Protocol
2.10 Setting an Aim

Copyright material from Marci Shepard (2026), *Where the Science of Improvement Meets the Heart of Leadership*, Routledge

2.11 Driver Diagram
2.12 Change Ideas
2.13 Theory of Action
2.14 PDSA-Plan
2.15 PDSA-Do
2.16 PDSA-Study
2.17 PDSA-Act
2.18 Spread and Scale Decision-Making Tool
2.19 Networked Improvement Community (NIC) Shared Learning Tool to Support Spreading and Scaling

▶ LEADERSHIP EXAMPLE: LEADING INQUIRY FROM THE TOP

When our Superintendent's Cabinet, SALT, set out to improve district learning and operations, we started with a question: *What is one problem in my department that, if solved, would create meaningful change?*

We wanted to learn the inquiry process ourselves so we could lead by example and through experience. We hung anchor charts in my superintendent's office (our meeting room) to support our learning and implementation, as shown in Figure 6.2.

To begin with, we tackled a collective problem to practice using the inquiry process and tools ourselves. We felt we needed to practice the process to learn it. Then, each leader put that learning into action by applying it to a real, persistent challenge in their own department.

Each problem they chose was also their professional growth goal, tying their improvement efforts directly to their leadership growth and evaluation. This made the work practical, strategic, authentic, and aligned with their role in supporting system-wide improvement.

Depending on their leadership role, some central office leaders focused on curriculum alignment, improving hiring practices, reducing chronic absenteeism, or strengthening emergency response systems. Each leader selected a core area of their work that needed improvement and took ownership of leading an inquiry to address the problem.

Process and Tools for Leading through Disciplined Inquiry 153

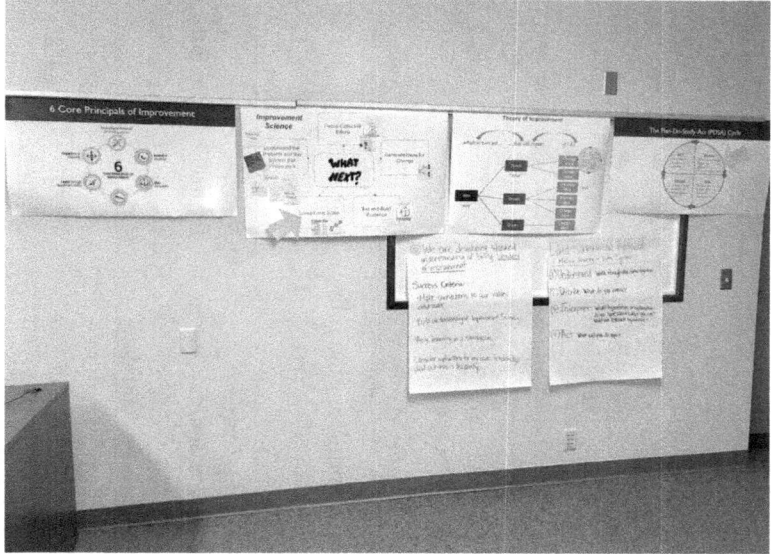

Figure 6.2 Artifacts and Resources Anchor Charts for SALT's Learning and Inquiry.

Table 6.4 highlights how each central office leader identified a problem, mapped out its key drivers, and tested targeted solutions using the PDSA process. It also shows alignment to their evaluation criteria—not because the inquiry was evaluative, but because we wanted to make inquiry part of the way we got better and led better, not just *another thing*.

Our leadership team knew we needed to model the work and lead through shared inquiry. As central office leaders developed their work with their teams and shared it with district leaders, they also modeled the use of tools like Driver Diagrams to guide their improvement efforts. In Figure 6.3, one leader is seen presenting his Theory of Improvement for Technology Integration, using a Driver Diagram to illustrate how key strategies align to impact student learning.

This practice of visualizing improvement work allowed leaders to communicate their strategies clearly and create a shared understanding of why and how changes were being made. These tools became a way to communicate a vision, serve as roadmaps for action, help teams stay focused, measure progress, and support real-time adjustments.

TABLE 6.4 SALT Improvement Focus Areas Connected to Evaluation Framework

Role	Problem Area (Aim)	Key Drivers	Change Idea (PDSA Cycle)	Connection to Leadership Evaluation
Executive Director for Teaching, Learning, and Assessment	Improve consistency in student learning by standard and skill (horizontal and vertical alignment)	- Guaranteed & Viable Curriculum (GVC) - System tools/ processes for GVC development	- Develop a curriculum map template - Build principal leadership capacity to facilitate alignment	2.2 Aligned curriculum & assessment for equitable access 1.2 Distributed leadership
Executive Director for Student Support Services	Reduce chronic absenteeism by addressing root causes	- Excused & unexcused absences - External factors requiring Tier 3 support	- Launch a Community Truancy Board to connect families with resources before legal action	3.1 Effective data use for decision-making
Director of Communications	Strengthen emergency response and preparation	- Crisis Communication Plan - Incident Command System	- Clearly articulate and communicate staff roles in crisis situations	4.3 Engaging community & managing external communication
Executive Director for Human Resources	Hire the best candidates through a fair, equitable process	- Standardized hiring practices - Screening tools & filters	- Ensure shared understanding among supervisors when screening candidates	1.3 Sustained improvement efforts
Assistant Superintendent for Business, Operations, and Safety	Ensure consistent safety procedures under new law	- Secure facility - Locking procedures	- Implement system-wide door-locking protocols	3.3 Policy & program alignment with legal requirements

Process and Tools for Leading through Disciplined Inquiry 155

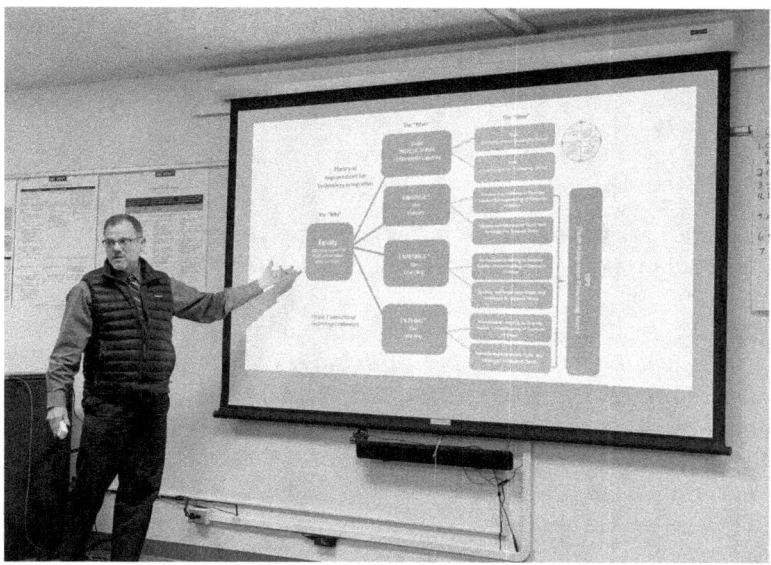

Figure 6.3 Executive Director Steve Rabb Presents a Driver Diagram Focused on Advancing Equity through Technology Leadership.

Our leadership team used inquiry to move from problem to action. We were learning about leading change by engaging in co-inquiry. As we did so, something powerful happened: We practiced and modeled the very work we were asking others to do. Our leaders were out of their offices and in the work analyzing data, testing small changes, and refining strategies based on real results. Their efforts sent a clear message across the system that continuous improvement is for everyone. With a leadership stance of inquiry and continuous learning, we sought to create a culture where improvement is part of *the way we do things around here*.

References

Anderson, E., Cunningham, K. M. W., & Richardson, J. W. (2024). Framework for implementing improvement science in a school district to support institutionalized improvement. *Education Sciences, 14*(7), 770.

Berwick, D. (2003). Improvement, trust, and the healthcare workforce. *Quality and Safety in Health Care, 12*(6), 448–452.

Bryk, A. S. (2015). 2014 AERA distinguished lecture: Accelerating how we learn to improve. *Educational Researcher, 44*(9), 467–477.

Bryk, A. S., Gomez, L. M., Gunrow, A., & LeMahieu, P. G. (2015). *Learning to improve: How America's schools can get better and getting better.* Cambridge, MA: Harvard Education Publishing.

Carnegie Foundation for the Advancement of Teaching. (2018). *Introduction to improvement science: A learning-by-doing simulation.*

Deming, W. E. (1982). *Out of the crisis* (2nd ed.). Cambridge, MA: Massachusetts Institute of Technology, Center for Advanced Engineering Study.

Deming, W. E. (1994). *The new economics for industry, government, education* (2nd ed.). Cambridge, MA: Massachusetts Institute of Technology, Center for Advanced Engineering Study.

Fathima, N. (2016). A quality improvement tool - driver diagram: A model of driver diagram to reduce primary caesarean section rates. *International Journal of Research in Medical Sciences, 4*(5), 1339–1342.

Greenhalgh, T., & Papoutsi, C. (2019). Spreading and scaling up innovation and improvement. *BMJ,* l2068. https://doi.org/10.1136/bmj.l2068

Langley, G. J., Moen, R. D., Nolan, K. M., Nolan, T. W., Norman, C. L., & Provost, L. P. (2009). *The improvement guide* (2nd ed.). San Francisco, CA: Jossey-Bass.

Li (李军), J. (2024). Educational improvement science: The art of the improving organization. *ECNU Review of Education, 7*(3), 714–737.

Chapter 7

Addressing the Vision–Implementation Gap of a Positive Workplace Culture

🎯 LEARNING TARGET

I can analyze the challenges leaders face in fostering a positive workplace culture and apply strategies to close the vision–implementation gap.

Success Criteria

- Justify the role of a positive workplace culture in continuous improvement.
- Analyze how three featured leaders prioritize and cultivate positive workplace cultures.
- Evaluate common leadership challenges in building and maintaining culture.
- Apply targeted strategies to bridge the gap between vision and reality.

RELEVANT NELP STANDARDS

- NELP Standard 1: Mission, Vision, and Improvement (Cast a Clear Vision)
- NELP Standard 2: Ethics and Professional Norms (Positive Workplace Culture, Collaboration, Model the Culture)

- NELP Standard 3: Equity, Inclusiveness, and Cultural Responsiveness (Supportive, Nurturing, Inclusive Culture, Diverse Voices and Perspectives)
- NELP Standard 5: Community and External Leadership (Share Stories)
- NELP Standard 7 (Building-Level): Building Professional Capacity (Healthy, Collaborative, Trusting Professional Culture)
- NELP Standard 7 (District-Level): Policy, Governance, and Advocacy (Addressing Governance Structures—Top-Down and Siloes, Casting a Vision)

ICEBREAKER: VISION VS. REALITY

Think of a time when you worked in an organization that the leader's hope and vision for workplace culture didn't match the actual experience of staff.

- What was the leader's stated vision for the culture?
- What was the reality for employees?
- What do you think contributed to this disconnect?
- Were there any efforts to bridge the gap? If so, what worked or didn't work?

(See Appendix 1 for the Icebreaker Group Activity Facilitation Guide)

CASE VIGNETTE: LISTEN, LEARN, AND LEAD—IN THAT ORDER

Background

Acorn Middle School had been through five principals in eight years. Each new leader arrived with a vision—new programs, new slogans, new expectations. The staff, once vibrant and collaborative, had grown guarded. Teachers showed up, did their job, and kept to themselves. Staff meetings were quiet. Shared leadership structures existed on paper, but no one trusted they would last.

> By the time Principal Harrison arrived, the building was in survival mode. He was met with polite nods and cautious silence. With every good idea he offered, he heard crickets. "We've tried that before," someone would murmur. "We'll see how long this one lasts."
>
> **Turning Point**
>
> Harrison made a choice not to launch anything new. Not at first. For the first several weeks, he simply listened. He scheduled one-on-one check-ins with every staff member. He asked, "What's working? What's getting in the way? What do you need to do your best work?" He roamed the halls, dropped into classrooms, and made space for informal conversations.
>
> Then, slowly, he started rebuilding structures—together. Harrison asked teachers to co-design the focus and format of their collaboration. He invited staff to define what kind of school they wanted to be and how they'd get there.
>
> Trust didn't return overnight, but something shifted. People started speaking up in meetings. They offered ideas and followed through. New staff were welcomed into the fold. Soon, Acorn Middle School was reenergized.
>
> **Bottom Line**
>
> Vision can't take root in soil depleted by mistrust. Slowing down to rebuild relationships is what allows improvement to bloom. Without trust, no improvement initiative will flourish. Leaders must cultivate the conditions of the environment before expecting authentic change.

Improvement is a culture, not a program. While systems need clear, articulated processes (as discussed in Chapter 6), the biggest barriers to effective improvement are rarely technical. They are cultural. If the conditions for improvement aren't right—when people don't feel valued, safe, supported, and empowered—change efforts flounder, no matter how promising the processes. That's why leaders need to look upstream. Beyond the frameworks. Beyond the processes. To the environment that either enables or prevents the work from authentically happening.

Each chapter in this culture-focused sequence assesses the cultural landscape, recognizes common barriers, and provides strategic leadership moves to close the vision-implementation gaps that undermine an improvement culture. Chapter 7 offers an overview, laying the foundation for the next two chapters which explore more specific aspects of culture that consistently emerged through my research: ownership and vulnerability. The good news is that culture is not fixed. Culture is constantly shaped by our shared values and leadership actions.

Research confirms that workplace culture significantly impacts educator retention, job satisfaction, and student outcomes. According to Seppala and Cameron (2015), positive workplace cultures enhance collaboration, innovation, and well-being. However, cultures of fear, compliance, and high-stakes accountability erode morale and inhibit risk-taking.

This challenge is directly connected to a paradigm shift discussed in Chapter 5:

- Paradigm Shift Six—Staff teams function in a positive workplace culture

Systemic change requires a healthy organizational culture, yet attempts to improve culture can fall short when there is a chasm between our leadership vision and the daily experiences of staff.

▶ THE VISION-IMPLEMENTATION GAP: POSITIVE WORKPLACE CULTURE

Educational leaders often articulate bold, equity-inspired visions for their schools and districts, envisioning positive cultures of collaboration and trust that promote continuous learning. However, despite these aspirations, it is difficult to translate this vision into day-to-day staff experiences. This disconnect is what I call the *vision–implementation gap*. The leadership imperative is aligning the vision for a positive culture with tangible actions to address the breakdown between strategy and execution.

This is the vision–implementation gap for workplace culture:

- *Vision*: Leaders envision a purpose-driven, high-trust, collaborative environment where staff feel valued, connected, and energized by the work.
- *Implementation Gap*: Staff often feel disjointed from a lack of focus, overwhelmed, siloed, and focused on compliance.

While the next two chapters drill into the specifics of staff ownership and vulnerability, this chapter addresses two broader cultural challenges in education that actively work against continuous improvement efforts in schools and districts:

1. Top-Down Leadership Structures Limiting Staff Engagement
2. Working in Silos

Each challenge section includes:

- Background and research
- Leadership perspectives (vision)
- Challenges faced by leaders (implementation gap)

After considering these two challenges, we will explore three leadership strategies for closing the vision–implementation gaps connected to a positive workplace culture.

▶ CHALLENGE 1: TOP-DOWN LEADERSHIP STRUCTURES LIMITING STAFF ENGAGEMENT

A culture of continuous improvement often butts up against traditional hierarchical structures. Deming (1994) emphasized that for a system to transform, its leaders must first transform themselves. He argued that leaders must lead by example, be strong listeners, and guide staff through shifts in practice and mindset without inducing guilt over past approaches. According to Deming, leadership is not about control or compliance, but about creating conditions where people feel empowered to contribute to continuous improvement.

Scholtes (1998) reinforces the idea that effective leadership is relational in addition to being operational. He argued that leaders must move beyond traditional, hierarchical leadership models and instead focus on personal relationships, deep listening, and respect. Leaders who invest in one-on-one interactions and actively listen to their staff's experiences foster a workplace culture where teams feel seen, heard, and valued. This sense of belonging strengthens staff engagement and increases commitment to improvement efforts. And yet, in many school systems, traditional hierarchical structures remain the norm.

Vision

Leaders aspire for collaborative cultures. Leaders featured in this book, like many others, are pushing back on these outdated hierarchical norms. They have a different vision for the culture of their systems.

Kyle believes:

> A culture of trust and collaboration is the foundation of improvement.

He builds that culture through an "informal and low-hierarchy" leadership style. He is creating an environment where staff feel valued, empowered, seen, respected, and connected to a larger purpose.

> People here need to know that I value them.

For Kyle, trust is built through fair compensation, professional respect, and workplace flexibility, like remote work options that reinforce trust, showing staff that leadership respects their professionalism and autonomy. This says:

> We trust you. We value you.

Melanie echoes this belief. She describes herself as a "heart-forward leader."

> I lead from a place of relationship.

She conducted a listening tour, actively demonstrating this value in action. By being present and responsive, she shows that leadership is about showing staff they are valued through being seen and heard.

> This is how we do our work—by prioritizing people first.

Shawn believes that culture begins with belonging.

> Making and maintaining strong relationships is one of my core values.

He believes personal connections matter at every level, so much so that he makes it a priority to know the names of all 510 employees in his district.

> That connection is important.

Each of these leaders articulates their belief in collaborative leadership, being relational, and valuing others.

Implementation Gap

Despite these visions, many leaders remain embedded in (or inherit) hierarchical systems that undermine engagement. Decision-making remains centralized, limiting staff voice and creating distance between leadership and those closest to the work. When staff don't feel included or respected, trust erodes, and staff avoid risk-taking or engagement altogether.

To make matters worse, many leaders and staff carry a history of mistrust from past failed initiatives, inconsistencies, or lack of follow-through. This heightens staff hesitancy to engage in new improvement efforts before they even begin.

Let's hear about our leaders' experiences with the challenge of hierarchical structures.

Melanie reflected on this tension.

> Every once in a while, especially when it's a high-stress situation, people revert back to just, "Tell me what you want me to do."

Shawn describes early improvement efforts that unintentionally sent a message that those closest to the work are excluded, reinforcing hierarchical structures.

> I started working with my administrators without the users at the table being a part of the process.

He also shared a persistent tendency toward leader-driven problem-solving:

> We were, in essence, trying to solve problems *for* people instead of solving problems *with* people.

▶ CHALLENGE 2: WORKING IN SILOS

Improvement efforts falter when staff work in silos. Improvement science relies on shared learning and collaborative inquiry. However, when individuals work alone, stay within their own teams, or even confine learning to one school or department, the system loses.

Seppala and Cameron (2015) found that positive workplace cultures are built on trust, respect, and psychological safety. In these environments, people treat each other with care and support, which fosters collaboration rather than competition. Their research highlights that when staff feel valued, they are more likely to engage in problem-solving, take initiative, and contribute to improvement efforts. Leaders play a key role in shaping this environment by modeling positive behaviors, demonstrating empathy, and creating structures that encourage collaboration.

Further, Scholtes (1998) corroborates that when leaders prioritize respect, trust, and collaboration, staff are more likely to embrace improvement efforts. They are also more likely to engage in the deep, meaningful work of system transformation.

Vision

Leaders value breaking down silos by embracing a vision where individual staff members are a part of something bigger than themselves and work together to achieve great things for students.

Kyle ties each individual's role to a broader mission, ensuring that every employee understands their contribution to a shared goal.

> Our mission is to make everybody successful. That really resonates with people. Our job is to make sure that districts, families, and kids in communities are successful. And people buy into that. They feel that, and it's exciting.

By aligning daily work with a clear purpose, Kyle creates a culture where employees feel motivated and engaged.

Melanie builds a work environment where staff feel deeply connected to their work, but also the students they serve, their colleagues, and the district's collective mission—even on the hard days.

> I want every person to jump out of bed and be like, "I am going to work today. Even when it is hard, I'm showing up because I am so connected to my kids and the environment. And I know I am going to get the support and help I need, especially on my hardest days."

Shawn prioritizes presence, recognizing that being in schools and departments is essential for maintaining a strong culture. He wants staff to feel connected to each other and connected to leadership.

> Being with others, involved in the community and schools, and with teachers working together is how we ensure that culture does not drift or deteriorate.

Without consistent leadership presence, cultures can weaken over time.

The next thing you know, you've lost a department or some of the culture has gone sideways somewhere because our presence, vision, and support are what build the culture. And so you can't do that from your office.

To deepen this culture of belonging, Shawn's district conducts hundreds of empathy interviews to hear directly from staff, students, and families.

Implementation Gap

Leaders want a connected culture; yet it is still a struggle to break down silos. Sometimes the barriers are structural, like limited time, tight schedules, or operational demands that crowd out collaboration time. Other times, the barriers are relational, such as a lack of trust. When this is the case, it often feels easier to blame structures than to face the deeper cultural issues at play. Whether the barriers are structural or relational, the result is often the same. Staff revert to isolated work. Even the best vision can't be realized in a fragmented system.

Still, leaders share that silos remain a challenge.

Kyle highlights siloed problem-solving as a persistent cultural norm in education, even when collaboration would be more effective.

> Many districts chose to tackle the same problems on their own rather than collaborate regionally. They default to familiar ways of working within their own systems.

Shawn shares the challenge of shifting from isolated excellence to shared learning as a norm within his district.

> We had great work happening in pockets, but unless we built structures for spreading that learning, improvement efforts stayed isolated.

He also shares how silos prevent leaders from collaborating and understanding the broader landscape across districts.

> We're trying to solve our own leadership problem and develop our own understanding of equity as leaders. But we don't even know what districts in our region are grappling with, why they're stuck, or what they're actually trying to accomplish.

Both quality improvement (Deming, 1994) and improvement science (Bryk et al., 2015) emphasize that a strong workplace culture is essential for system transformation. Leaders who intentionally foster a culture of trust, ownership, and learning can bridge the gap between vision and implementation, ensuring that staff thrive in a place of care, value, and support.

▶ STRATEGIES FOR CLOSING THE VISION-IMPLEMENTATION GAP

Next, we will explore three deliberate, research-backed strategies for closing the vision-implementation gap and laying a strong foundation for a positive culture.

1. Cast a Clear Vision—Define and communicate the culture you want to build.
2. Model the Culture—Demonstrate the behaviors, values, and expectations you want to see in staff.
3. Share Stories of Impact—Reinforce the culture shift by painting a picture using examples within the system.

By implementing these three strategies, school and district leaders can move beyond simply valuing a positive workplace culture to making it an organizational reality of their staff experiences. Each strategy section includes research (theory) and leadership moves (practice) with examples and lessons learned from our three leaders.

▶ STRATEGY 1: CAST A CLEAR VISION

Leaders set the tone for workplace culture; a key step in fostering it is casting a clear, compelling vision that defines the direction, purpose, and aspiration for the organization. Without consistent communication and alignment, workplace culture can become fragmented or misaligned (Macht, 2016).

Deming (1982) emphasized the importance of consistency in leadership vision, warning that a lack of clear purpose can weaken improvement efforts. He argued that leaders must practice long-term thinking and ensure that everyone in the system understands the mission.

When I became superintendent of a new district, I launched a three-phase entry plan: Engage, Vision, Focus. First, I prioritized listening and learning. I built relationships through a listening tour, rode buses to see all corners of the district, visited schools, expanded communication efforts, and met with community leaders and partner organizations. I also created detailed community and district profiles—covering demographics, programs, facilities, finances, and events.

From these conversations, I began asking a central question:

What are your hopes for a graduate?

The responses were powerful. People talked about students developing strong academic and thinking *skills*. They named *character* traits like respect, perseverance, and kindness. They wanted graduates prepared for *success* in life in whatever pathway or location they chose—near or far. Additionally, one theme surfaced in nearly every conversation: educators in our system knew *each student* by name, understood their stories, and did whatever it took to support them.

Out of this process and the voices of our students, staff, and community, our co-created vision emerged: *Each Student: Skills and Character for Success*. This statement added clarity and held shared meaning.

Help Staff See Themselves in the Vision

When staff see how their contributions have a place in your shared vision, they will be more inclined to commit to your mutual goals (Kouzes & Pozner, 2023). But when staff do not see how their roles and day-to-day work connect to the bigger picture, they may disengage or see improvement work as just another thing that leaders put on their plates.

One of my favorite short stories is about an author, Jim Belasco, who was following Dr. Cooley on his rounds one day. On the way to the operating room, Dr. Cooley stopped and talked to a man mopping the floor. Belasco was curious about the nearly 10-minute conversation, so he went up to the man to ask about it. The man with the mop told the author that Dr. Cooley talks to him often. Belasco asked, "What do you do at the hospital?" The man replied, "We save lives." My dad was an elementary school custodian, so this story resounds with me on many levels. As a leader, my hope is that everyone from the board room to the classroom to the lunch room knows our vision, sees us living it, and knows how important they are in making it happen (Belasco, 1990).

I often ask myself and other leaders these two questions:

- If I asked anyone in your system what the shared vision is, what would they say?
- If I asked anyone in your system how their work connects to that vision, what would they say?

To help staff connect to our own *we save lives*, at our beginning-of-the-year district kickoff meeting, we invited students to share short stories about staff who had shaped their experience and helped them build *skills and character for success*. A middle schooler talked about a lunch server who greeted her by name. An elementary student shared about his teacher aide. Others spoke about their bus driver, coach, custodian, and teachers. Each story was a reminder that each staff member is vision-critical, not just teachers and administrators.

The next year, we took it further. Students shared how staff helped them grow in the three specific areas outlined in the vision:

- An elementary student talked about how her teachers built her academic *skills*.
- A middle schooler described how a coach helped him develop *character* traits of perseverance and responsibility.

- A high schooler shared how FFA prepared her for *success* after graduation.

Out of the mouths of babes! These were real voices and stories of students making it clear that *each person* in the system matters in achieving our vision: *Each Student: Skills and Character for Success.*

Embed the Vision into the Daily Work

A vision must be more than words on a page, slide deck, or email signature line. It must be embedded in daily conversations, operations, and decision-making. A well-crafted message helps staff imagine possibilities (Kouzes & Pozner, 2023). It should be written, constantly referred to, and reinforced through leadership actions.

I'll share an example. As superintendent, I knew that a vision would drive change only if it were embedded in the continuous improvement process. So our leadership team was intentional about making the vision a living part of our system, ensuring that every improvement effort was directly tied to it. In fact, we created a graphic that tied each aspect of the vision to our three district priorities.

- *Each Student* (and staff) →Evaluation System: Just as we aimed to understand and support each student's needs, we adopted a differentiated and collaborative evaluation system to personalize adult learning and growth.
- *Skills* → Continuous Improvement: We focused on measurable goals related to Attendance, Behavior and Course performance (the ABCs) through collaboration at the team, school, and district levels.
- *Character* → PBIS: We focused on creating a warm, belonging culture of positive behavior supports and expanded engagement in co- and extracurricular activities.

This way when someone asks, "What is your district working on?" We didn't answer with the strategy (PBIS), but we could start with the purpose (building a positive culture through PBIS).

These weren't new initiatives. They were existing efforts we refocused and named in alignment with the vision to give our work clarity and purpose.

Similarly, we embedded the vision into hiring and onboarding, framing interview questions around it to ensure new staff aligned with our district's core purpose. During new staff orientation, employees connected their personal *why* to our shared vision. In leadership meetings, we built agendas around its key elements. Professional development sessions explicitly connected new learning to the district's vision and color-coded priority that was the focus for the session.

This approach also extended to system-level decisions. Every long-range plan started with the vision, mapping goals to improvement efforts with clear metrics for tracking progress. Budget requests weren't just about funding needs; they were framed around how resources would support progress toward our vision.

Even our governance structures reflected this commitment. School board agendas were coded to vision elements, board reports began with a slide connecting the topic to the vision and strategic priorities, and my weekly updates to board members followed the same structure—organized under *Each Student, Skills,* and *Character,* so that everyone saw the connections.

Make the Vision Visible

Storytelling is a powerful tool for reinforcing the vision and bringing it to life. Whether in meetings, newsletters, or community updates, we shared stories of students and staff to help show how small actions are building toward something bigger. Even in social media, my team used hashtags to explicitly name and connect everyday experiences to the long-term vision and focused priorities. We also used visual tools such as a color-coded graphic that mapped each priority to part of the vision. This became an at-a-glance reference and way to frame and connect our work that added clarity. We weren't *doing* improvement; we were building skills for success. We weren't *doing* PBIIS; we were building character for success. Tangibly putting the vision and the aligned priorities graphic on agendas, slides, newsletters, and other communications, the vision remains front-and-center in every decision, reflection, and next step, turning it into an actionable throughline across our work.

Melanie models this beautifully. She and her team co-created foundational visuals that clearly communicated their district's values and norms. They are used in every meeting and conversation, reinforcing the district's core beliefs. By making these messages simple and memorable, staff can internalize and articulate the shared workplace culture.

> If you don't put it in front of people constantly, it fades into the background. We had to make it part of how we operate.

Leaders must cast a vision that is shared, clear, seen, and referred to in daily operations. Staff need to see themselves as active contributors to the vision. It should live in how we collaborate, hire, budget, evaluate, and celebrate. We need to be consistent and perhaps even feel like we are overcommunicating as we articulate, reinforce, and embody the visionary workplace culture we want to create.

▶ STRATEGY 2: MODEL THE CULTURE YOU WANT

A positive workplace culture does not emerge through words alone; leaders who model trust, openness, and a commitment to continuous learning shape it. Leaders set the tone for the organization, and their behavior directly influences how staff engage within the culture. If a leader's actions do not align with their stated vision, trust erodes and staff become skeptical of the vision.

I'll share an example. As a superintendent, I color-coded my calendar to make sure that my time and priorities aligned with our vision. Each strategic goal was assigned a specific color, helping me visualize where I was dedicating my attention. For example, supporting teaching and learning was purple, since our instructional framework was purple.

It is easy to let urgent matters overshadow important work, and guess what often gets crowded out when unexpected issues arise? Yes, the important work of instructional leadership. But our vision emphasized quality instruction in every classroom every day, so my time had to reflect that priority.

Of course, there were times I had to cancel what was on my calendar to readjust priorities when pressing matters emerged. But my secretary knew that if I couldn't make a purple appointment on my calendar, such as visiting classrooms, we would reschedule it instead of canceling it. Culture is reinforced through daily interactions and decision-making. Our leadership team often said:

> People can see what we value by how we spend our time, what we celebrate, and what we confront.

If we prioritized instructional leadership, professional learning, and relationship-building, then those actions had to be visible in our schedules, behaviors, and decisions. Leaders who demonstrate the values they wish to see by showing up, being present, and engaging authentically reinforce the culture and encourage staff to do the same.

Shawn captured the concept of modeling the desired culture perfectly:

> As I go, so goes the district.

To model a collaborative work environment, leaders must intentionally foster social connections and empathy (Seppala & Cameron, 2015). This includes engaging with staff rather than issuing directives, modeling care for individuals through personal connections, creating safe spaces for staff to share ideas, mistakes, and feedback, and fostering a culture of inquiry where staff feel comfortable taking risks.

In addition to being relational, leaders must also model engagement in improvement efforts. Leaders need to do more than supervise; they must actively participate in inquiry, test new ideas, and refine processes (Scholtes, 1998).

Think: Where are you when learning is happening in your system? Are you standing along the sides or at the back supervising, or are you pulling up a chair alongside a team, engaging and learning with staff? Are you listening and coaching? Are you asking questions and making your own "Ah-ha" moments known?

Deming (1994) highlighted that leaders must model lifelong learning, showing a willingness to adapt, improve, and lead with curiosity. This means engaging with data, openly reflecting on challenges, and modeling learning that reinforces that improvement is not a compliance task but a way of thinking and leading.

Shawn prioritizes visibility, connection, and presence as essential to culture-building:

> I make sure I'm in schools, in classrooms, and talking to staff. You can't lead culture from your office.
>
> People work hard when they feel seen, valued, and connected to the mission. That starts with leadership.

Leaders must model the behaviors they want to see in their teams, and we must go first.

▶ STRATEGY 3: SHARE STORIES OF IMPACT

Sharing stories makes workplace culture tangible, connecting abstract values to real experiences. Leaders should consistently highlight successes. One goal of storytelling is to celebrate wins.

Storytelling can also be used to normalize challenges and learn from failure. Instead of only sharing polished success stories, leaders can model vulnerability by openly discussing mistakes, lessons learned, and adaptations made along the way.

Scholtes (1998) emphasized the need for leaders to "build forgiveness into our work" (p. 34). When something goes wrong, leaders should use it as a learning opportunity rather than a source of blame. By using storytelling to publicly demonstrate a commitment to learning from failure, leaders create a culture where staff feel safe to take risks, reflect on challenges, and embrace continuous improvement.

Deming (1994) also stressed that data variation plays a key role in improvement. Leaders must use data-driven storytelling to help teams analyze and reflect on questions such as: "Why did something go wrong?" and "How can we replicate this success?" By framing failures as opportunities for growth, leaders encourage a culture of resilience and inquiry. Effective leadership includes shaping the narrative that reinforces why the work matters.

I'll share an example. One of the most powerful ways my district sustained momentum in our continuous improvement efforts was through storytelling. I was fortunate to work with a communications director who had an incredible ability to determine which stories should be told in writing and which ones needed a human voice. She recognized that some moments called for a direct message from leadership. At times, people needed to see and hear from me. A memo or email was not the right communication modality; we needed a video clip where my passion, heart, and commitment were visible. A well-placed video allowed us to reinforce our *heart* work and shared purpose.

Just as importantly, she ensured that I wasn't the only one telling stories. Improvement is not a leader-driven initiative; it is a collective effort, and the voices that shape the work must also shape the narrative.

Through written stories, photos, and videos, she captured the experiences of students, staff, and community members, allowing them to share their own perspectives on the progress we were making.

We were intentional in asking ourselves:

> What stories are being told (and retold), whose voices are being amplified, and whose voices are being missed?

By ensuring a diversity of voices and perspectives, we created a culture where storytelling both documented improvement *and* fueled it.

Kyle regularly shares stories of staff successes as well as stories of struggle, adaptation, and growth:

> People move towards success when they see it in others. But we also need to show that failure is part of learning.

The improvement process is complex and sometimes messy, and staff need to see that when we use failure as a necessary part of learning and growth, it is not a mere setback. By sharing stories that highlight both success and struggle, leaders cultivate a culture of continuous learning, ensuring that staff see how they fit in with the culture and are active contributors to it.

▶ CONCLUSION: STRENGTHENING A POSITIVE WORKPLACE CULTURE

To bridge the gap between leadership vision and staff experiences, leaders must intentionally cultivate a workplace culture. This is no easy task since we are up against cultural norms of top-down leadership and working in silos. However, leaders can overcome these barriers through (a) casting a vision, (b) modeling the values they want to see, and (c) sharing stories that celebrate progress and normalize learning from failure. In doing so, leaders create an environment where staff feel valued, engaged, and motivated to contribute to meaningful improvement efforts. Once trust is established, the next challenge is ensuring that staff members truly *own* the improvement process.

REFLECTION QUESTIONS

1. Workplace Culture Challenges: What experiences have you had or observed related to the challenge of fostering a positive workplace culture? How has culture impacted engagement in continuous improvement?
2. Leadership Strategies for Improving Workplace Culture: How might you employ one or more of the following leadership strategies to improve workplace culture?
   - Cast a Vision—Clearly define the shared compelling vision of a preferred future and communicate it consistently.
   - Model the Culture—Demonstrate the values and behaviors you want to see.
   - Share Stories—Use storytelling to reinforce learning, celebrate success, and normalize challenges.

CHAPTER 7 TRY THIS: DEEPEN A POSITIVE IMPROVEMENT CULTURE

This tool is designed to help leaders consider how they might bridge the gap between leadership vision and staff implementation of a positive workplace culture.

1. **Describe Your Current Culture—How Would You Characterize It?**

   _____
   _____
   _____

2. **Identify a Culture Challenge—Where does the vision-implementation gap exist?**

   Reflect on a recent initiative or improvement effort in your school or district. What could have been improved in the culture that would have made the staff experience better?

   _____
   _____
   _____

3. **Implement a Strategy—Choose one leadership move to strengthen workplace culture.**

   Choose one of the strategies below to implement over the next month.
   - Strategy 1: Cast a Vision That Becomes Part of Daily Work
   - Strategy 2: Model the Culture
   - Strategy 3: Collect and Share Stories of Success and Failing Forward

Copyright material from Marci Shepard (2026), *Where the Science of Improvement Meets the Heart of Leadership*, Routledge

4. Create an Action Plan

Write your plan, including the who, what, when, where, and how. Be specific!

_____
_____
_____

Follow-Up and Reflection

Track impact and refine your approach.

After one month, reflect on the impact of your chosen strategy.

Did the change bring improvement? How do you know? What is next?

▶ LEADERSHIP EXAMPLE: FROM VISIBILITY TO ACCESSIBILITY

As a superintendent, I quickly learned that visibility wasn't enough. Being seen in schools, attending events, and making rounds in classrooms had their place, but visibility alone is self-serving—a performative act that checks a box but doesn't build trust. What truly mattered was *accessibility*, which is others-serving. It's being approachable, listening, and letting people know they are valued and supported.

I wanted staff, students, and families to know that I wasn't just around; I was available. I saw them. I saw their work. I saw their contributions. So, I made a conscious decision. Instead of leading from my office, I would lead from their spaces.

I committed to showing up where the work happens. When I needed to meet with department supervisors, I didn't call them into the central office. Instead, I went to them. For example, when I met with our transportation director I headed to the bus garage, walking past rows of yellow buses, checking in with drivers as they wrapped up their morning routes. When I met with our nutrition services supervisor, I sat down in the main kitchen, surrounded by the hum of ovens and the rhythm of meal prep—and often enjoying a school lunch. I met our facilities director on-site at a project, standing next to rolls of fresh field turf just waiting to be played on. (I must admit, I spontaneously stumbled upon some adventures like bus drivers putting me behind the wheel of a bus at the bus rodeo, being in the stands with pep band, sampling the BBQ Club's new recipe, labeling a preserved animal carcass in science class, dancing at prom, and the list goes on.)

These were small, but intentional moves to show that student and staff work and learning mattered. You can't lead what you don't know, and you can't know unless you're willing to be where the work is happening. My visits to schools and departments were about relationships, not supervision. I walked into classrooms to celebrate teaching and learning. I stopped by cafeterias to sit with students. I stood in the bleachers at sports games and arts performances to cheer with families. I joined a table group during professional development to learn with staff. I'd send a quick text to a coach after a game about a moment I noticed, such as a quiet word of encouragement to a struggling athlete or a demonstration of leadership from a student on the team. Before performances, I'd step backstage to wish musicians and actors well, so they knew their superintendent was there cheering them on.

I tried to leverage this time to shine a light on others. Being present allowed me to witness the incredible, often-unseen moments that made our schools special. And when I saw them, I shared them. Social media became a way to highlight staff and students. I posted about teachers trying new instructional strategies, bus drivers who greeted students by name, custodians making floors so shiny you needed sunglasses, the unseen moments of leadership happening in every corner of our system...

This continued at the board level. When we recognized students at board meetings, I'd followed up with handwritten notes—a simple, yet personal way—to let students know that they were seen and special. (Thanks to my own superintendent, Mike Nelson, who modeled this for me.)

This became more than a leadership move—it began to create a shared mission. Sure, some staff were looking over

Figure 7.1 Driving a Bus During the Transportation Team's Bus Rodeo.

Figure 7.2 Coach McKinniss with a Basketball Player During a Game.

Figure 7.3 Visiting a Science Classroom While Students Classify a Specimen.

their shoulder, wondering why I was in their space. Over time, however, I increasingly saw the shift. Staff who once saw the superintendency as distant and out of reach started stopping me in the hallways to share a story, an idea, or invite me to see something cool they were doing with students. Students who had never interacted with a superintendent felt comfortable telling me what was on their minds. Community members who had only known the district through emails and board meetings saw a leader alongside them, not above them. This was not special to me—our whole leadership team embodied this. We believe that leadership isn't about being *seen*; it's about serving and being *with*. Our hope was to contribute to a culture where every person, in every role, knew they were valued as a person and were essential to our shared vision (Figures 7.1, 7.2, and 7.3).

References

Belasco, J. A. (1990). *Teaching the elephant to dance: the manager's guide to empowering change.* New York: Plume.

Bryk, A. S., Gomez, L. M., Gunrow, A., & LeMahieu, P. G. (2015). *Learning to improve: How America's schools can get better and getting better.* Cambridge, MA: Harvard Education Publishing.

Deming, W. E. (1982). *Out of the crisis* (2nd ed.). Cambridge, MA: Massachusetts Institute of Technology, Center for Advanced Engineering Study.

Deming, W. E. (1994). *The new economics for industry, government, education* (2nd ed.). Cambridge, MA: Massachusetts Institute of Technology, Center for Advanced Engineering Study.

Kouzes, J. M., & Pozner, B. Z. (2023). *The leadership challenge: How to make extraordinary things happen in organizations* (7th ed.). Hoboken, NJ: Jossey-Bass.

Macht, J. (2016). The management thinker we should have never forgotten. *Harvard Business Review Digital Articles*, pp. 2–6.

Scholtes, P. R. (1998). *The leader's handbook: A guide to inspiring your people and managing the daily workflow.* New York: McGraw Hill.

Seppala, E., & Cameron, A. (December 1, 2015). Proof that positive work cultures are more productive. *Harvard Business Review.* https://hbr.org/2015/12/proofthat-positive-work-cultures-are-more-productive

Chapter 8

Addressing the Vision–Implementation Gap of Staff Ownership (User-Centered)

 LEARNING TARGET

I can analyze the challenges leaders face in fostering staff ownership and apply strategies to close the vision–implementation gap.

Success Criteria

- Justify the role of staff ownership in sustaining continuous improvement and a positive culture.
- Analyze how the three featured leaders prioritize and cultivate staff ownership in their organizations.
- Evaluate the common challenges leaders face when increasing staff ownership.
- Apply targeted strategies to bridge the gap between a leader's vision for staff ownership and the actual experiences of staff.

RELEVANT NELP STANDARDS

- NELP Standard 1: Mission, Vision, and Improvement (Staff-Driven Inquiry)
- NELP Standard 2: Ethics and Professional Norms (Collaboration)

- NELP Standard 4: Learning and Instruction (Meaningful Measurements)
- NELP Standard 5: Community and External Leadership (NICs, Systematize Collaboration Time)
- NELP Standard 6: Operations and Management (Structures and Supports)
- NELP Standard 7 (Building-Level): Building Professional Capacity (Staff-Led Inquiry, Build Capacity, Distribute Leadership)
- NELP Standard 7 (District-Level): Policy, Governance, and Advocacy (Structures and Supports)

ICEBREAKER: WHO OWNS THE WORK?

Think of a time when you were part of a school or district initiative. Did you feel true ownership over the process, were you following a directive, or were you disengaged?

- What made you feel invested and engaged in the work?
- Or, if you didn't feel ownership, what made it feel like just jumping through another hoop?
- What impact did your level of ownership have on your motivation and the success of the initiative?

(See Appendix 1 for the Icebreaker Group Activity Facilitation Guide)

CASE VIGNETTE: FROM COMPLIANCE TO COMMITMENT

Background

At Pike Lake Elementary, teacher collaboration was technically happening. Grade-level teams met every Thursday, followed the same agenda, and filled out the required planning forms. But it all felt like a routine. The problems teams were working on came from the school improvement plan, not their classrooms. Everyone was on the same step of the inquiry cycle, regardless of their students' needs. The process was orderly, but uninspiring.

Teachers quietly complied but privately vented.

"We're just going through the motions."

"It's a checkbox."

"I miss when team time was actually useful."

Turning Point

After sitting in on several team meetings, Principal Jenkins saw the problem clearly. There was structure, but no ownership. So, she made a bold shift. Instead of mandating one unified goal and keeping teams lock-step in the inquiry process, she invited teams to identify their own problem of practice. They could choose what mattered most in their classrooms—and use the inquiry process to explore it.

The change was immediate. A first-grade team focused on phonemic awareness struggles. The fourth-grade team dug into vocabulary. Special education teachers explored ways to build more inclusive small-group supports. The teams modified the forms so they reflected real thinking instead of what felt like compliance.

Principal Jenkins didn't remove expectations. She added support. She modeled how to define a problem clearly. She helped teams pace their work. And she made space in staff meetings for teams to share what they were learning with each other.

Soon, teachers began following up with one another during door-jamb conversations. Collaboration became purposeful. Ownership returned.

Bottom Line

Authentic improvement happens when teachers have agency over their own learning that is directly connected to the needs of their students. It doesn't come from filling out the right form (although that can help)—it comes from engaging with the right problem. When people feel a sense of ownership and empowerment, the work becomes meaningful.

As we say: Don't make a decision *about* them *without* them.

The First Principle of Improvement, as outlined in Chapter 4, is making the work *user-centered* and *problem-specific*. These two concepts frame the next two chapters.

- Chapter 8 focuses on making the work *user-centered*. Solutions are developed and refined by those closest to the work. What gets in the way of this? Authentic ownership.

- Chapter 9 focuses on being *problem-specific*. Improvement should focus on real, pressing, bold challenges. What gets in the way of this? Authentic vulnerability.

This chapter zeroes in on user-centered improvement through staff ownership, which makes the difference between compliance and commitment. While most leaders believe in the importance of ownership, translating this into everyday practice often remains a significant challenge. This makes improvement efforts feel leader-led rather than staff-driven.

Through my research, it became clear that shifting ownership requires a fundamental change in leadership mindset and practice. This shift is directly connected to three key leadership paradigm shifts discussed in Chapter 5:

- Paradigm Shift One—Staff are knowledge creators
- Paradigm Shift Two—Improvement is a team effort
- Paradigm Shift Five—Meaningful data should drive improvement

Through the experiences of Kyle, Melanie, and Shawn, we get leadership insights into building capacity, distributing leadership, and building the system-wide supports necessary for authentic staff ownership.

▶ VISION-IMPLEMENTATION GAP: OWNERSHIP

Empowering ownership is a leadership imperative. Leaders want their people to feel personally connected to processes and outcomes, knowing they have a stake in the success and a voice in decisions. Even more, leaders want staff to know they are respected as experts and that we trust them to drive inquiry, make decisions, and enact change.

However, the reality is that leaders face challenges in cultivating staff ownership. Staff can feel hesitant to initiate or lead improvement efforts for many reasons, from staff feeling like the work is for compliance, to not fully understanding the process, to not feeling supported to make changes.

This is the vision–implementation gap for increasing staff ownership:

- *Vision*: Leaders want staff to initiate and lead improvement efforts, using inquiry and data as tools for highly relevant continuous learning.
- *Implementation Gap*: Staff often feel that change is done *to* them rather than being done *with* them, causing them to not feel equipped, empowered, or adequately supported to facilitate change.

Two common challenges stand in the way of realizing the vision for staff ownership:

1. Shifting from Leader-Directed to Staff-Driven Inquiry
2. Using Meaningful Measurements

Each challenge section includes:

- Background and research
- Leadership perspectives (vision)
- Challenges faced by leaders (implementation gap)

Stay tuned. After examining these two challenges, we will explore three strategies to bridge the gap between vision and implementation for staff-owned improvement.

▶ CHALLENGE 1: LEADER-DIRECTED INSTEAD OF STAFF-DRIVEN INQUIRY

Many school and district improvement efforts remain leader-driven, with staff expected to implement rather than lead the process. (That's why there has been a historic focus on fidelity.) While staff may engage in continuous improvement cycles, they often do so in response to leader directives rather than initiating problem-solving processes on their own. One reason is that staff may not know where to start. Without a structured approach, staff are not empowered to lead their own inquiry. As a result, they tend to jump to solutions before fully understanding the problem, because they know something must be done.

However, staff really should be the ones to define problems and tailor interventions to their students and communities (Bryk, 2017). This means leaders need to not only ask themselves what problem needs to be solved, but they need to have staff ask themselves and each other that question to progressively shift ownership to staff (Bryk, 2015).

Vision

Leaders have a vision for Challenge 1—shifting from leader-directed to staff-driven inquiry. Each of our leaders shared that this is a value.

Kyle observed a critical shift when staff were allowed to identify the problems they wanted to solve:

> When staff get to pick what they're going to do, they engage at a whole new level. It's their work, not mine.

He saw that staff engagement increases dramatically when they can move forward on something personally meaningful:

> Improvement work should be an opportunity to move something near and dear to your heart because people are going to be excited about doing something when they get to pick what they are going to do.

He hopes that staff use the language and tools of improvement science more naturally:

> If I see people having those conversations and doing it at the team level, I think that's a huge sign of success.
>
> I hope to see it more outside of the work that I do. I'd like to hear people using the jargon and tools naturally like, "Oh yeah, we did empathy interviews with that" or "Where's the process map?"

Melanie echoed this by drawing an analogy from classroom teaching:

> My best days as a teacher were when you hardly heard my voice. That's my hope for our buildings—that we don't primarily hear leader voices.

She envisions teachers leading discussions on their data and improvement efforts.

> My ultimate hope would be that our central office team shows up to the student school review every year, and the principal sits in the back while teachers are owning that work and are able to talk about why their data are moving or not and how they will recalibrate when it isn't improving.

She also emphasizes the need for structured autonomy:

> We gave staff more freedom to lead improvement cycles, but we also provided the tools and supports to guide them through the process.

Shawn sees staff-initiated improvement efforts as a sign of success:

> I want this to not just be me leading. I want teams to feel like it's okay to innovate and take risks in a structured, low-stakes way.

He believes that the best workplace cultures foster curiosity, problem-solving, and shared responsibility:

> There must be a culture of inquiry, of continuous improvement, of ownership. A culture that does not blame, but one that says, "Let's dig in and solve a problem together."

Additionally, staff are identifying their own problem, so this work is user-centered.

He reinforces this by embedding problem definition into his leadership mindset:

> Improvement science gave me that lens so that every problem I see now, I think, "Have they looked at the problem? Do they really know what it is?"

He applies this same approach in his coaching with principals:

> All my principals now will tell you that one of the questions I ask them most often is, "What's the problem you are trying to solve?"

By embedding this question into daily practice, leaders help staff develop the habits of critical thinking and inquiry necessary to own their improvement work.

Shawn also sees his role evolving:

> My role is trying to give them some tools, so I am more of a sponsor/facilitator. They need the training, but less of me doing the work.

Implementation Gap

Even though leaders have a vision for Challenge 1, staff often rely on leaders to direct or guide inquiry rather than initiating improvement efforts independently. Staff do not yet see improvement science as their "go-to" framework for problem-solving.

Kyle shares the challenge of transitioning from leader-led to staff-led inquiry. He initially structured improvement efforts as leader-driven, where teams followed mandates about what to test and track. However, this resulted in passive engagement. Over time, Kyle realized that true ownership required a shift from leaders prescribing the work to staff identifying and solving problems they truly cared about.

> We had to stop asking, "How do we get staff to do improvement science?" and start asking, "How do we make improvement science their work, not ours?"

Addressing the Vision–Implementation Gap of Staff Ownership

Kyle, Melanie, and Shawn all recognize this gap.

Kyle: "It's still not there yet, to be honest. I feel like I'm always the one to say, 'Let us use this precise improvement process for this.'"

Melanie: "Every once in a while, especially when it's a high-stress situation, people revert back to just, 'Tell me what you want me to do.'"

Shawn: "We were, in essence, trying to solve problems for people instead of solving problems with people."

This is a common leadership challenge. Leaders are used to setting direction and driving change, so the transition to staff-led improvement can feel slow and uncomfortable.

Shawn reflected on the early stages of implementing improvement science and realized that leaders often approached the work from a top-down perspective. By taking this approach, leaders unintentionally maintain staff dependency. Even though staff engage in improvement work, they still follow a leader-directed process rather than leading the work themselves.

Shawn moves from quick fixes to deep inquiry.

> If we don't take the time to define the problem correctly, we risk staff disengaging because solutions feel imposed rather than owned.

Over time, Shawn saw the impact of ownership:

> The biggest impacts I have seen have been in those teams that have really been bought in and love the process.

For improvement science to become a staff-initiated and staff-led practice, leaders must actively shift from directing the work to equipping staff with the skills and confidence to lead it themselves.

> **PAUSE TO REFLECT ON CHALLENGE ONE**
>
> - Do your staff naturally ask, "What's the problem we are trying to solve?"
> - How can you create systems that encourage staff-led problem-solving?

▶ CHALLENGE 2: LACK OF MEANINGFUL MEASUREMENTS

Too often, data collection in schools is focused on accountability rather than improvement (Bryk, 2015). Staff view data as a compliance tool, something collected for those *above* them, such as state agencies, school boards, or district administrators. Or they view data as something that is done *to* them rather than a resource that helps them improve their own work or as a tool that directly benefits their students (Bryk, 2015).

For improvement science to be truly effective, educators must engage with close-to-the-classroom and close-to-the-work measurements that help them track progress and refine their strategies in real time. We will refer to these as *meaningful measurements*. This shift from *data for compliance* to *data for learning* remains a major challenge. Improvement science addresses this by emphasizing practice-based evidence—data that is collected, analyzed, and used by educators themselves to drive change (Bryk, 2015).

Vision

Our three leaders—Kyle, Melanie, and Shawn—articulate a clear vision, aspiring for staff to use *meaningful measurements*. They emphasize the importance of shifting from compliance-driven accountability to inquiry-driven improvement. They want staff to use data as a learning tool.

Melanie has worked to align her district measurement systems with strategic goals, but in a way that supports, rather than punishes, educators.

Addressing the Vision–Implementation Gap of Staff Ownership

> There's alignment from our strategic goals into our district strategic plan, to our school improvement plan, to the way our board governs, to our accountability system. And accountability is a little "a," not a big "A." Accountability like a hug—it's coaching, not accountability like a hammer.

She also developed a tool that helps teams track incremental progress.

> We have what we call the Growth Monitoring Framework that breaks those big aspirational goals down into smaller, more manageable chunks of growth from where we are now to where we want to be. Each of our buildings has targets and stretch targets around certain data indicators so that staff can track real progress, not just end-of-year test scores.

Melanie even uses meaningful process measurements to increase ownership among adults. She emphasizes clear expectations paired with autonomy by implementing a self-assessment rubric where principals and teachers track their own progress and determine their next steps together.

> The key was making the work visible without controlling it. Staff needed both clarity and space to take ownership.

Shawn echoed this, emphasizing that data should be approached with curiosity, not blame.

> There has to be a culture of inquiry and continuous improvement. There has to be a certain amount of curiosity. It can't be a culture that blames. It has to be a culture that owns problems, one that is really interested in rolling your sleeves up and digging in and trying to solve a problem.

He also worked to shift how teams talk about data.

> We had to shift the conversation from "Here's your data" to "What is this data telling us about our students and how we teach?"

Despite these strong commitments to meaningful measures and data use, leaders continue to struggle with embedding practical measurement systems that empower teams at all levels.

Implementation Gap

Leaders discuss how challenges persist in embedding meaningful practices at the team level. I must make this clear: This is *not* a fault of staff. This is a system problem of practice that requires thoughtful leadership solutions.

Kyle articulates the issue clearly:

> Everybody wants to know whether they made an improvement or not, but no one really knows how to measure it in a way that's useful to them.

Melanie reflected that, despite the progress her district has made in monitoring growth, there are still gaps in how data is used.

> So, I think what we've learned is that we don't have a phenomenal data system yet.

A leadership issue is that educational measurements often remain at the macro level. Even when leaders value growth-oriented data use, measurement systems often remain high-level, district-driven, and disconnected from daily team practice. Additionally, in many districts, data collection is perceived as punitive, focusing on accountability metrics rather than instructional improvement. Staff often fear data will be used to evaluate them rather than support their growth (Bryk et al., 2015).

Melanie reflected on her district's Growth Monitoring Framework, which breaks aspirational goals into smaller, more manageable benchmarks at the building level. Although this system provides a clear structure for tracking progress, it doesn't always translate into actionable insights for individual teams and teachers.

> At a high level, we know if the data are moving. Are more third graders reading on level? We know the answer is yes or no. But we have not had a good system for asking, "Okay, why is that happening?"

She recognizes that identifying root causes remains a major barrier.

> Part of that is everyone was on a different journey. So, it's like, the third graders' reading didn't move, but they're not using the core curriculum—they're using this other thing. But these other students' reading did move, but they are not using the core curriculum either. So, we have not had a great system for isolating the causes.

Without a structured way to analyze cause-and-effect relationships at the classroom and team level, continuous improvement efforts risk remaining broad and unfocused.

> **PAUSE TO REFLECT ON CHALLENGE TWO**
>
> How can you help teams focus on measures that are team-determined, close to the classroom, and provide data about the problems teams are trying to solve to improve student learning and teacher practice?

▶ STRATEGIES TO CLOSE THE VISION–IMPLEMENTATION GAP OF STAFF OWNERSHIP

The good news is that there are specific leadership strategies aimed at closing the vision–implementation gap in staff ownership. If improvement efforts must be user-centered, meaning that the people closest to the work must own, drive, and use the process themselves (Bryk et al., 2015), then leaders need to foster staff agency so that teams feel empowered to lead change, innovate, and collaborate toward meaningful outcomes.

In the following sections, we explore three actionable, research-based, and evidence-based leadership strategies that help schools and districts address the challenges of increasing staff ownership.

1. Build Capacity: Train staff in using inquiry processes and tools. Sustainable improvement requires investing in the knowledge, skills, and mindsets of educators to enhance their ability to lead and sustain change (Elmore, 2004).

2. **Distribute Leadership**: Develop other leaders of improvement. Schools that distribute leadership among educators create a culture of shared responsibility, which leads to higher levels of engagement and improved student outcomes (Spillane et al., 2004).
3. **Provide Structures and Supports**: Ensure time, tools, and structures are in place. Well-designed structures and supports enable educators to engage in continuous improvement and shared decision-making (Fullan, 2016).

Each strategy section includes research (theory) and leadership moves (practice) with examples and lessons learned from our three leaders.

▶ STRATEGY 1: BUILD CAPACITY

To ensure implementation is truly user-centered, educational leaders must focus on building the capacity of staff to feel empowered and confident in using the principles, processes, and tools of improvement to solve their problems. Administrators are used to being problem-solvers by nature, so we want to jump in and help fix things. However, we must equip staff with the knowledge and skills to lead their own inquiry independently, while we, as leaders, step into a support role.

As Shawn reflects, improvement science challenges this traditional "fix-it" mindset.

> I've talked to a couple of younger superintendents about this over the last couple years and this feeling that they have to be the problem solvers and the ones to do things. Improvement science butts up against that.

To address the challenges of staff ownership, we will focus on three areas of capacity-building: (1) improvement processes and tools, (2) meaningful measures, and (3) capacity-building at all levels.

Build Capacity in Improvement Processes and Tools

Staff need to understand and internalize the principles of inquiry cycles, root cause analysis, and iterative learning. This will equip them with the skills and confidence they need to initiate and engage in improvement science independently. This relates directly to Challenge 1 (Shifting from Leader-Directed to Staff-Driven Inquiry). Good leadership looks like good teaching. When we build capacity, we need to use explicit instruction, moving from modeling to guided practice to independent practice (Archer, 2011).

Rohanna (2022) studied five schools and found that leaders must build capacity in hands-on ways around two things. One is how to work together, including teaching collaborative inquiry skills such as productive questioning and dialogue. Another is what to do during collaboration, such as following a process and using improvement tools (e.g., root cause analysis, driver diagrams, PDSA cycles). Rohanna also reiterates that, in addition to providing professional learning, leaders need to provide ongoing coaching and support by attending team meetings and facilitating collaboration.

We need to ensure staff internalize the tools and principles of improvement so they can use them on their own when needed, allowing them to not be dependent on leadership to drive every improvement effort.

Kyle described his approach:

> The first part of implementing improvement science is really about learning how to use the tools so that [staff] can then think about how to apply the tools later when they need them.

I'll share an example from my district. To provide support for team capacity-building, we started by explicitly teaching the inquiry process. Then, school leaders led teams through a guided process to practice each step. When it was time for teams to run their own inquiry cycles independently, we recognized that while they had learned the process, they still needed a scaffold. At the same time, leaders needed a way to support teams without disrupting their momentum.

To bridge this transition, teams placed a printed version of the inquiry cycle on cardstock in their collaboration workspaces. Some teams used a simple item or arrow to indicate their current phase in the process. Other teams expanded on this idea, adding dates to track their movement through each phase.

This small, but powerful visual helped teams have clarity about which inquiry step they were on and where they were going. It allowed them to stay focused when the principal joined in without having to pause and explain their progress because, at a glace, the principal could see what part of inquiry the team was working on. It enabled principals to provide just-in-time support, being able to jump into conversations as they walked through meetings. What started as a scaffold became something that some teams chose to continue as part of their regular practice.

This was a great reminder for our team that we, as leaders, are still teachers. Capacity-building follows the same principles as effective teaching: Provide direct instruction, guided practice, scaffold independent application, and provide ongoing feedback and support. We know how to build capacity because we are teachers at heart!

Build Capacity for Meaningful Measures

Another aspect of capacity-building is making measurements meaningful. This relates directly to Challenge 2 (Using Meaningful Measurements). *Meaningful measures* refer to data that is teacher-driven, timely, relevant, and directly connected to the work of those using it. If measures are going to be truly meaningful to staff, they must be empowered to select their own measures. Leaders should help teams ask themselves whether their selected measure will enable their team to learn in real time, rather than waiting for long-term results (Lewis, 2015). In addition to being timely, the measure should be close and relevant to the classroom or their immediate work, beyond state, district, or school data that they are required to use.

Thinking back to previous chapters, let's reflect on some of the times that staff use of measurement and data authentically comes up throughout the inquiry process:

- Select and analyze relevant data at the beginning of an inquiry cycle to understand the problem.
- Use data to set and decide how to measure their aim.
- Run PDSA cycles, determining how they will measure the impact of their change idea (Plan), collect data (Do), interpret their data (Study), and use data to make decisions (Act).

- Study impact and refine strategies.
- Inform decisions to spread and scale.

This means leaders need to empower educators as data-literate decision-makers, so they can make sense of data and use it to inform their next moves.

Let's distinguish between two types of data that teams use:

- *Outcome measures* track quantitative results such as student proficiency, graduation rates, number of suspensions, and attendance rates.
- *Process measures* often track qualitative results such as observations, empathy interviews, implementation of strategies, and feedback (Lewis, 2015).

When we are thinking about meaningful measures, some of the data will be outcome data. However, leaders also need to build the capacity of staff to utilize process measures, enabling teams to track various improvements beyond just scores (Lewis, 2015). Process measures often track adult actions that we believe will lead to a positive impact on students. They are typically a lead measure, such as a change idea. Since process measures are observable and actionable, we can monitor them frequently, tracking progress on the work itself. When teams also pay attention to process data, it deepens ownership since they can see how their daily actions make a difference.

To summarize, here's how Kyle, Melanie, and Shawn made deliberate efforts to build capacity for meaningful measures in their contexts:

- *Kyle's* district introduced team-designed measurement tools so that teams could co-create their own benchmarks for success.
- *Melanie's* teams focused on small tests of change rather than solely district-wide data dashboards, ensuring that data remained close to the classroom.
- *Shawn* led his teams in using empathy interviews with students as a primary measurement tool, reinforcing that meaningful data isn't always numerical.

Build Capacity at All Levels

The role of shared leadership in expanding capacity across the system touches both capacity-building (Strategy 1) and distributed leadership (Strategy 2). Deming (1982) emphasized that leaders must provide job-embedded training for *all* staff. This equips them with new skills, and it also intrinsically motivates them toward continuous improvement. Bryk (2018) confirms that districts that invest in developing *all* of their people are the most successful in integrating improvement science effectively into daily practice.

Because one leader alone cannot build the capacity of an entire school or district, leaders must scale their efforts by training others to serve as coaches and facilitators of improvement. Bryk (2018) found that districts that prepare their central office, principals, and teacher leaders as improvement coaches experience greater success in embedding improvement science into school culture. Coaching, in this context, looks like leaders going beyond *telling* or providing direction to engaging in joint work, observing practice, and giving feedback to support learning.

Shawn's approach reflects this principle:

> The way I help staff is through my leadership of principals, so they can directly support their teams. My job is to pour into principal leadership so they can pour into others.

Instead of directly leading every improvement effort, Shawn focuses on equipping principals to build capacity in their own schools. This ensures that improvement science is not solely dependent on district leadership but is empowered at all levels.

To be effective, capacity-building must be differentiated based on role (Anderson et al., 2024).

District-level leaders should:

- Understand and model the improvement process.
- Support the development of structures and routines that enable staff-led inquiry.
- Allocate resources to ensure staff have time and tools for continuous improvement.

- Train and coach principals to build leadership capacity in their schools.

School and department leaders should:

- Provide foundational professional development on improvement for all staff.
- Coach individual teams based on their starting point with inquiry.
- Embed time for collaboration into meetings, professional development, and the master schedule.
- Support staff in using data for learning.

Teacher-leaders should:

- Serve as liaisons on school and district leadership teams.
- Act as internal experts for their grade-level or department teams.
- Support their peers in using improvement processes and tools effectively.
- Make practice public and share learning.

By developing expertise across different leadership levels, leaders can build sustainable capacity. This is how leaders create systems that learn and adapt.

To summarize:

- *Kyle's* ESD taught the improvement process and tools and then embedded collaborative improvement into existing meeting structures, gradually shifting meetings from being leader-led to being increasingly staff-owned.
- *Melanie's* district implemented a gradual release model, where staff moved from guided inquiry to self-directed improvement cycles.
- *Shawn's* district leadership initially provided professional development to staff, but, over time, they shifted responsibility to school leadership and eventually included staff teams in leading the learning.

▶ STRATEGY 2: DISTRIBUTE LEADERSHIP

For improvement science to be fully owned in school and district culture, leadership must be distributed among staff. We'll discuss three ways leaders can be intentional about distributing leadership: (1) identifying key leaders at all levels, (2) gradually releasing leadership responsibility, and (3) building a leadership bench.

Identify Key Leaders at All Levels

All educators, not just formal leaders, must see themselves as leaders of continuous improvement. However, many improvement initiatives still weigh heavily on the shoulders of leaders, causing us to miss the expertise and insights of those who work directly with students or directly support those who do. This relates to Challenge 1 (Shifting from Leader-Directed to Staff-Driven Inquiry).

Studies show that teacher-Directed improvement efforts lead to higher engagement and sustainability (Bryk et al., 2015). To maximize the kind of iterative learning, testing small changes, and scaling effective practices inherent in improvement work, staff must see themselves as co-creators of solutions rather than passive recipients of leadership direction. When educators actively lead their inquiry cycles, they refine their practice, build collective efficacy, and sustain improvements over time (Lewis, 2015).

Deming (1982) argued that transformation requires everyone at all layers of the organization to be engaged in the work. Similarly, Bryk (2018) emphasized that for system reform to take hold, every staff member must see themselves as improvers, and every leader must be a coach of improvement.

One way to build capacity in our systems is to identify and empower key leaders for shared leadership.

Kyle explained that once leaders understand the improvement process, their next job is to build a critical mass of staff who can sustain and expand the work.

> My role is to find leaders within the organization that will take it on. Choose the people that you think will be there immediately to change, want to learn, and will pick it up so that it becomes a critical mass.

He highlighted the importance of strategically selecting early adopters—educators willing to engage with improvement science and can serve as influencers within the system.

> You know who in your organization are influencers and people that want to try it. So, the first thing is to get that cadre of people to try to get to the tipping point or get enough leaders that understand the process that can start implementing it in their own areas. Once you develop that core group of people, they have the same inquiry mindset as the leader does, so they help spread it out.

This critical mass strategy ensures that improvement science does not stay isolated at the top. Instead, leaders create a tipping point, where improvement spreads beyond district leadership and becomes embedded at all levels.

Gradual Release of Leadership Responsibility

Just because we identify key leaders across all levels of the organization, that doesn't mean staff feel immediately prepared to take on leadership roles in improvement. We need to build their readiness for shared leadership. Rohanna (2022) found that teachers initially lacked the capacity to lead collaborative inquiry teams. They felt unprepared to lead others when they were still learning the process themselves. Even after a full year of professional development and practice, only two teachers in the study felt confident in facilitating their teams in using improvement science tools. This underscores that transitioning leadership to staff takes time, support, and ongoing coaching.

To bridge this gap, superintendents, principals, and other leaders must intentionally distribute leadership responsibilities and build the capacity of educators to join them in leading the improvement efforts. Just like the *gradual release of responsibility* that teachers use with students (Archer, 2011), leaders can use (what I'm calling) a *gradual release of shared leadership responsibility* to progress from leader-led to staff-driven inquiry. We cannot simply declare that improvement science is now staff-led. Ownership must be developed and released gradually through foundational learning (I do), followed by structured practice with regular feedback and coaching (we do), then ultimately independent real-world application (you do). This allows leaders to provide initial support, but then gradually step back, allowing staff to take more ownership (Fullan & Quinn, 2015).

Kyle described how, at first, he had to push staff to engage with improvement science.

> As a superintendent, there are times you are going to have to drive the work...But in the beginning, it's like, "Nope, we're going to try improvement processes on this, we're going to apply improvement tools to this."

Shawn echoed this, explaining that he was heavily involved in the beginning but later shifted to supporting others as they took on leadership roles.

> At first, I was really heavily involved in it. Now I've stepped out of the more hands-on role to be more supportive of others, trying to lead them to do the work.

The key takeaway is leaders must be hands-on at first but should gradually step back, allowing other leaders and staff to take increasing ownership.

I'll share an example of capacity-building through distributed leadership. In my district, we were implementing collaborative inquiry teams. We realized that leadership couldn't rest solely with principals. While there was a collective commitment that principals would be actively present and provide support to collaborative teams, the reality was they couldn't be everywhere at once. We needed to expand leadership beyond the administrative team.

To address this, we identified teacher-leaders for each team. These teacher-leaders formed a school-level leadership team, meeting monthly to build capacity, share learning, and ensure coherence across teams. This structure created a two-way flow of information—from individual teams to the school leadership team and back down. It also provided a platform for cross-team collaboration, as well as allowing the principal to get a pulse of each team and the school as a collective.

However, as the teacher-leaders stepped into their facilitator roles, they surfaced key challenges. Leading a team required time and effort beyond their typical responsibilities, and many felt they lacked the authority to facilitate their teams. While additional professional development on the inquiry process was helpful, they also needed leadership development and a space to problem-solve team dynamics with their teacher-leader peers.

In response, we formalized the role. We created a job description and an official title, reinforcing the authority that teacher-leaders needed to lead with confidence. Recognizing the additional time and responsibility, we provided a stipend to honor their contributions. To further support them, we established a district-level leadership team where teacher-leaders from all schools came together quarterly. These gatherings became critical spaces for professional learning, peer collaboration, and cross-school sharing. We modeled and practiced the next chunk of work they were facilitating with their teams. In addition to teacher-leaders deepening their own leadership capacity, they also strengthened alignment and coherence across the system.

What started as a practical solution to a logistical challenge became a shift in leadership culture. By intentionally developing grassroots leaders, we built a leadership pipeline and distributed leadership in a way that built both individual and system-wide capacity.

Build a Leadership Bench

As a result of building and distributing leadership at all levels, we are building a leadership bench that can withstand leadership and organizational transitions. A third way to build capacity in our systems is to build a strong pipeline of leaders. Anderson et al. (2024) emphasize the need for a *deep bench* of educators trained in improvement science, particularly in specialized leadership roles. "Organizations that have weaker infrastructures often fall prey to leadership changes and are not able to sustain the cultural shift" (Welsh et al., 2021, p. 375). To avoid this pitfall, leaders must build capacity across the system at all levels to develop sustainable, staff-led improvement that lasts beyond leadership transitions. This includes:

- District leaders—Must be trained to coach and support school leaders.
- School and department leaders—Must be equipped to facilitate team-led improvement cycles.
- Teacher- and staff-leaders—Should serve as liaisons between teams, schools, departments, and district leadership.
- Classroom educators and staff—Need to be trained in team-based inquiry methods so they can lead change in their own practice.

The purpose of distributing leadership is not to lighten the load for leaders. In fact, it's often more cumbersome to *lead* the work than to *do* the work yourself. But it's worth the effort. The payoff is when staff, along with school and district leaders, own improvement so that the work is embedded in the culture, making it sustainable beyond leadership turnover or organizational changes (Fullan, 2016). Leaders need to identify and support *improvement champions* within our staff who are passionate about leading change and empowered to model and scale improvement (Bryk et al., 2015). This makes distributing leadership a strategy we can use to prevent improvement work from stalling during leadership changes while, at the same time, building a long-term culture of continuous learning and shared ownership.

In sum, our three leaders provide examples of this:

- *Kyle's* ESD trained and empowered staff facilitators, ensuring that leadership was shared.
- *Melanie's* district built a coaching model, ensuring that each school had a trained staff member supporting improvement work at the team level.
- *Shawn's* district created teacher leader positions dedicated to facilitating inquiry cycles.

▶ STRATEGY 3: LEADERS PROVIDE STRUCTURES AND SUPPORTS

To increase staff ownership of improvement, leaders need to create the right conditions for inquiry and learning to happen. Even with capacity-building efforts and distributed leadership, improvement work will stall without time, tools, and structures that support continuous improvement.

Deming (1982) emphasized that, in addition to providing training, leaders need to develop systems that allow employees to engage in continuous improvement as part of their daily work. We will discuss three aspects of structures and supports to integrate new practices within existing structures: (1) collaboration time, (2) tools and protocols, and (3) learning networks.

Systematize Collaboration Time

Even when staff see the value in improvement science, they often struggle to find the time to engage in meaningful inquiry. Without dedicated time, continuous improvement competes with other pressing responsibilities and often falls to the side.

Kyle identified time as a barrier, emphasizing that if improvement feels disconnected from daily tasks, staff will struggle to sustain engagement:

> I think some of the barriers are—it is not easy work. It takes time. But are there ways that you can implement some of the small tools in the work that they're already doing? And then, from there, begin to build on them. It's hard work. And if it's not job-embedded, then it's extra work, and that alone is a problem.

Shawn recognizes that when teams see student data, they want to be able to respond to it.

> I still think it's difficult for people when they see the numbers in front of them and want to do something about it right now. They don't feel like they have the time to dig into it well.

We need to integrate collaboration time into the core functions of teaching and leadership. If collaboration is not part of the normal workflow, it feels like extra work, making it difficult to sustain. We need to bake it into the cake. For example, school leaders can integrate cycles of inquiry into professional learning communities (PLCs), professional development, building leadership teams, staff meetings, department meetings, grade-level meetings, common planning time, early release/late start collaboration times, and evaluation/coaching cycles. District leaders can integrate cycles of inquiry into the superintendent's cabinet, department meetings, principal meetings, board meetings, and leader evaluation/coaching cycles. Instead of making collaborative improvement something separate, we need to weave it into existing structures.

Provide Tools and Protocols (Including Meaningful Measures)

Bryk et al. (2015) highlight that for improvement science to be effective, data collection, reflection, and problem-solving must be embedded in the normal routines of educators, not treated as an add-on. Leaders must ensure that improvement science is not just something staff *do* when time is available or on designated professional development (PD) days. It should be a natural part of how teams function.

To increase ownership, leaders should make sure that staff understand and can independently use a step-by-step inquiry process, along with the tools for each phase of the process. We also need to make sure staff have access to practical resources in real time. For example, we can set up a shared drive or folder labeled by each step of the inquiry cycle, filled with the menu of tools specific to that phase and encourage teams to build and add their own tools as well *(Note: You can use the process and tools from Chapter 6 and Appendix 2 for this.)* This setup allows staff to access what they need when they need it. It also equips them to naturally integrate tools into their practice instead of having to wait for scheduled PD or collaboration time.

As part of the building ownership through structures and supports conversation, it is worth calling out meaningful measures and data use. This connects to Challenge 2 (Using Meaningful Measurements). True, we discussed meaningful measures as part of the strategy for capacity-building related to building data literacy and helping staff learn how to use meaningful measures. But in this *Tools and Protocols* section, let's consider how leaders attend to data collection, access, and use. Leaders should embed data collection and reflection in the authentic rhythm of leader and team routines. As Bryk et al. (2010) remind us, "data collection must be embedded into, rather than added on top of, the day-to-day work of program participants" (p. 31).

To support this, leaders can provide user-friendly data dashboards and help teams develop their own data collection tools. These tools allow teams to track micro-measures, which are small-scale, actionable, leading indicators, so they can be used to make timely adjustments in their current practice. Additionally, we need to teach and practice (not just provide) protocols for data reflection (such as the Data Analysis Protocol in Appendix 2.3). These protocols should also be easily accessible in the same online toolbox (or other organizational system) and used regularly to help teams interpret and respond to the data. Having everything in one place is key.

Finally, leaders can build alignment by setting up structures for teams to integrate their improvement measures into existing systems. For example, teams can analyze student data to set team-level goals focused on meeting student needs. Those team goals can be used to select individual growth and evaluation goals. Trends across team goals can inform the school-wide focus and guide professional learning priorities. This way, when teams are responding to the needs of their students, they are not layering on additional tasks. They are simultaneously engaging in continuous improvement in service of their own students while also accomplishing their PLC work, evaluation goals, and school improvement priorities.

Establish Learning Networks

Another way leaders can provide structures and supports is by establishing school-wide and district-wide learning networks.

These networks should be given time during existing PD, staff meetings, and collaboration time so teams can share findings and improvement strategies across the school and district. If we don't provide the time, we can't expect this sharing to happen. School leaders should establish cross-team improvement networks, while district leaders should establish cross-school and department improvement networks to create system-wide ownership from the bottom up.

Let me share an example. In my school system, when we launched collaborative inquiry teams in our district, we knew that dedicated time for teams to meet was essential. We embedded collaboration into common planning time, professional development sessions, and staff meetings. While this structure worked well in our elementary schools, it proved much more challenging at the secondary level, where schedules were more complex. If we were serious about making collaboration a priority, we needed a system-wide structure that ensured every team (even secondary) had time to collaborate.

After gathering input from stakeholders, we made the decision to implement a two-hour late start once a month. Why a late start? It minimized disruption. From a logistical standpoint, late starts were already used for inclement weather adjustments, so we already had the systems in place—bell schedules, bus routes, breakfast service, supervision, and all the operational details. It also maximized participation. Unlike the early-release model, late starts allowed our teacher-coaches and athletic staff to attend.

While many teams continued to meet during common planning and other times, the district-wide late start became a protected space for collaboration. We held this time sacred. One of the biggest risks to improvement efforts is time creep—where collaboration time slowly gets absorbed by operational tasks, administrative meetings, or urgent issues. We were intentional about guarding this time, ensuring it remained dedicated to collaboration.

By embedding collaborative time into the district's structure, we moved beyond just hoping teams would find time to collaborate. This intentional design reinforced to staff, students, and our community that continuous improvement was what we valued and invested in.

Leaders must ensure that structures enable sustained engagement (Langley et al., 2009). Leaders can ask themselves key questions:

- Are staff given structured and protected time to engage in improvement work? (Or is this just "extra" work or an add-on?)
- Are processes, tools, and protocols in place to support each step of the inquiry cycle? (Or do staff feel lost in the process or have difficulty finding scattered tools?)
- Are we creating opportunities for teams to learn from each other? (Or is learning siloed within individual teams?)

To summarize, we learn valuable lessons from our leaders about building structures and supports:

- *Kyle*'s ESD developed improvement networks across districts to scale ownership region-wide.
- *Melanie*'s district created a data equity time where teams met without administrators to discuss meaningful data.
- *Shawn*'s district reframed existing PLC time to integrate improvement science principles and tools.

▶ CONCLUSION: MAKING OWNERSHIP SUSTAINABLE

Empowering staff ownership requires more than enthusiasm and inspiration. It demands leadership moves that embed improvement into the daily fabric of schools and districts. Sure, there are challenges—namely, (a) staff initiating and leading inquiry, and (b) using meaningful measures. However, these are not insurmountable. Leaders can intentionally (a) build capacity, (b) distribute leadership, and (c) provide strong support systems for teams to be invested improvers. By embracing these user-centered strategies, leaders close the vision–implementation gap, ensuring continuous improvement is staff-owned, not leader-imposed.

> **❓ REFLECTION QUESTIONS**
>
> 1. Challenges in Shifting Ownership to Staff: What experiences have you had or seen related to the persistent challenge of staff ownership in school improvement efforts?
> 2. Leadership Strategies for Improving Staff Ownership: How might you employ one or more of the following leadership strategies to close the vision–implementation gap on staff ownership?
>   - Build capacity—How can you ensure staff feel equipped to lead improvement efforts?
>   - Distribute leadership—How might you identify, develop, and support others who can take on leadership roles in improvement efforts?
>   - Provide structures and supports—What structures and supports should be considered to integrate improvement into the culture and work?

CHAPTER 8 TRY THIS: EMPOWER STAFF AS IMPROVERS

Consider moves you might make to increase staff ownership in their improvement work.

1. Describe your vision for staff ownership in improvement efforts in your school or district.

_____
_____
_____

2. Identify a challenge related to staff ownership (vision–implementation gap).

- Challenge 1: Staff participate in the continuous improvement process when the leader provides time for it or directs them to do so, but they don't take the initiative to use it on their own or lead the process.

- Challenge 2: Staff use measurements that are required by the school, district, or state, rather than smaller, more frequent, and formative assessments that are directly tied to their students or daily work, and that help inform their improvement.
- Other _____

3. Choose a strategy and make a plan to implement it.

- Strategy 1: Build Capacity
  - Do staff know the phases of inquiry and have access and understanding to use tools associated with each phase?
  - Are staff empowered to select, monitor, and make decisions using measures that are meaningful for their students and work?
  - Do all staff engage in job-embedded improvement, no exceptions?
- Strategy 2: Distribute Leadership
  - Who are the key staff members who can take the lead?
  - What clear roles and support will you provide to scaffold success and gradually release leadership responsibly?
- Strategy 3: Provide Systems and Supports
  - How might you leverage existing meeting times or opportunities to systematize collaboration?
  - Do staff have processes and tools clearly marked, accessible, and in one place so they can easily find and use what they need when they need it?
  - How might you structure regularly scheduled learning networks across teams, across schools, and across departments?

4. Action Plan

Write your plan, including the who, what, when, where, and how. Be specific!

_____
_____
_____

 **Follow-Up & Reflection**

After one month, reflect on the impact of your chosen strategy. Did the change bring improvement? How do you know? What's next?

▶ LEADERSHIP EXAMPLE: FROM INITIATIVE TO MOVEMENT—HOW A COMMUNITY TOOK OWNERSHIP OF CHARACTER EDUCATION

One of the core elements of our district's vision was ensuring students were life-ready. That meant going beyond academics and focusing on character development—helping students cultivate traits like patience, humility, and forgiveness while recognizing those qualities in others. Each month, we focused on a different trait, learning about it, sharing resources, and putting it into action through a *Character Dare* (Norlin & Kraft, n.d.). But what started as a district initiative quickly became something much bigger. The community took ownership, and the work evolved into a movement.

Each month, a local organization stepped up to *sponsor* that month's trait. In October, for example, the senior center led the focus on patience. One of the Character Dares that month encouraged people to spend time with someone outside their usual circles. High school students took on the challenge by visiting the senior center, where they engaged in meaningful conversations with older community members. What started as a simple activity turned into something powerful—new relationships formed, and students left talking about how much they had enjoyed the experience and wanted to return as volunteers. That same month, the senior center created a video to share about patience, and they selected a student as the "Patience Character Hero" of the month—an honor that came with a yard sign from the school board.

In November, the fire department took the lead with humility. Firefighters visited elementary schools, shared stories, performed skits, and helped students see humility in action. They even awarded their own "Humility Character Hero" of the month.

Then, something unexpected happened. Driving down the main highway, we noticed the city had updated the welcome sign. It announced the character trait of the month. No one had asked them to do it. That was the moment we knew the initiative had shifted from district-led to community-led.

From there, momentum kept building. The teen center sponsored respect. The police department took on honesty. The Lion's Club led forgiveness. The character traits started appearing in the community newsletter, on coffee shop windows, and in local businesses. Videos and photos popped up on social media, and people used the hashtag to share stories and nominate character heroes.

At first, our leadership team played a key role—helping build capacity (strategy 1), intentionally reaching out to strategic community leaders (strategy 2), and establishing routines each month to keep the work moving forward (strategy 3). But by empowering the community to take ownership, the impact grew far beyond what we could have achieved alone. Students were better served, and we built community along the way (Figure 8.1).

Figure 8.1 City Sign Showing Character Trait of the Month.

References

Anderson, E., Cunningham, K. M. W., & Richardson, J. W. (2024). Framework for implementing improvement science in a school district to support institutionalized improvement. *Education Sciences*, *14*(7), 770.

Archer, A. (2011). *Explicit instruction: Effective and efficient teaching*. New York: Guilford Press.

Bryk, A. S. (2015). 2014 AERA distinguished lecture: Accelerating how we learn to improve. *Educational Researcher*, *44*(9), 467–477.

Bryk, A. S. (2017). *Redressing inequities: An aspiration in search of a method*. Paper presented at the Fourth Annual Carnegie Foundation Summit on Improvement in Education, San Francisco, CA.

Bryk, A. S. (2018). *Advancing quality in continuous improvement*. Paper presented at the Carnegie Summit, San Francisco, CA.

Bryk, A. S., Gomez, L. M., & Gunrow, A. (2010). *Getting ideas into action: Building networked improvement communities in education*. Stanford, CA: Carnegie Foundation for the Advancement of Teaching.

Bryk, A. S., Gomez, L. M., Gunrow, A., & LeMahieu, P. G. (2015). *Learning to improve: How America's schools can get better and getting better*. Cambridge, MA: Harvard Education Publishing.

Deming, W. E. (1982). *Out of the crisis* (2nd ed.). Cambridge, MA: Massachusetts Institute of Technology, Center for Advanced Engineering Study.

Elmore, R. F. (2004). *School reform from the inside out: Policy, practice, and performance*. Cambridge, MA: Harvard Education Press.

Fullan, M. (2016). *The new meaning of educational change*. New York: Teachers College Press.

Fullan, M., & Quinn, J. (2015). *Coherence: The right drivers in action for schools, districts, and systems*. Ontario, Canada: Corwin Press and the Ontario Principals' Council.

Langley, G. J., Moen, R. D., Nolan, K. M., Nolan, T. W., Norman, C. L., & Provost, L. P. (2009). *The improvement guide* (2nd ed.). San Francisco, CA: Jossey-Bass.

Lewis, C. (2015). What is improvement science? Do we need it in education? *Educational Researcher*, *44*(1), 54–61.

Rohanna, K. L. (2022). *Leading change through evaluation improvement science in action.* Los Angeles: Sage.

Spillane, J. P., Halverson, R., & Diamond, J. B. (2004). Towards a theory of leadership practice: A distributed perspective. *Journal of Curriculum Studies, 36*(1), 3–34. https://doi.org/10.1080/0022027032000106726

Welsh, R., Williams, S., Bryant, K., & Berry, J. (2021). Conceptualization and challenges: Examining district and school leadership and schools as learning organizations. *The Learning Organization, 28*(4), 367–382. https://doi.org/10.1108/TLO-05-2020-0093

Chapter 9

Addressing the Vision–Implementation Gap of Staff Vulnerability (Problem-Specific)

>  **LEARNING TARGET**
>
> I can analyze the challenges leaders face in fostering staff vulnerability and apply strategies to close the vision–implementation gap.
>
> **Success Criteria**
>
> - Justify the role of vulnerability in building a positive workplace culture.
> - Analyze how the three featured leaders prioritize and cultivate staff vulnerability in their organizations.
> - Evaluate the common challenges leaders face when encouraging vulnerability and creating a culture where staff feel safe to take risks.
> - Apply targeted strategies to bridge the gap between a leader's vision for vulnerability and the actual experiences of staff.

RELEVANT NELP STANDARDS

- NELP Standard 1: Mission, Vision, and Improvement (Disciplined Inquiry)
- NELP Standard 2: Ethics and Professional Norms (Risk-Taking, Sharing)
- NELP Standard 3: Equity, Inclusiveness, and Culturally Responsive Practices (Root Causes of Inequity, Equity-Focused Inquiry, Culturally Responsive Change Ideas, Impact on Diverse Groups, Scale Equitable Practices)
- NELP Standard 4: Learning and Instruction (Student-Centered Problems, Disciplined Inquiry)
- NELP Standard 5: Community and External Leadership (Culture of Sharing)
- NELP Standard 6: Operations and Management (Solving Operational Problems)
- NELP Standard 7 (Building-Level): Building Professional Capacity (Cross-Team Sharing, Disciplined Inquiry)
- NELP Standard 7 (District-Level): Policy, Governance, and Advocacy (Cross-Department and Cross-School Sharing for System Governance and Learning)

ICEBREAKER: RISK IT TO FIX IT

Think of a time in your professional experience when you felt safe (or unsafe) taking a risk or being vulnerable at work.

- What was the situation?
- Did you feel encouraged and supported, or hesitant and fearful?
- What role did leadership or workplace culture play in that experience?
- How did that experience impact your growth, collaboration, or willingness to take a risk in the future?

(See Appendix 1 for the Icebreaker Group Activity Facilitation Guide)

CASE VIGNETTE: SOMETIMES LEADERS GO FIRST

Background

In the central office of Steam Engine Unified, leadership meetings ran like clockwork. Agendas were tight. Updates were efficient. But something was missing. No one talked about what wasn't working. Even when a new program flopped or a school struggled with implementation, problems were glossed over or conversations stayed surface-level.

When Executive Director of Teaching and Learning, Dr. Johnson, joined the team, she sensed a culture of performance over reflection. "There's a lot of pressure to look like we've got it all figured out," a central office colleague admitted to her. Principals were mirroring the same approach in their buildings, sticking to safe strategies, hesitating to name real challenges, and avoiding conversations that might expose mistakes.

Turning Point

Dr. Johnson decided to take a risk. At the next leadership team meeting, she opened with a story about a time she'd rolled out a district-wide intervention too quickly. "I was so eager to show results that I skipped the listening phase," she said. "We lost trust, and I had to rebuild it from scratch." She didn't tie it up with a neat conclusion. She let it sit.

There was a long pause. Then, slowly, others began to share. A special services supervisor admitted to rushing a new identification process. A principal talked about abandoning a strategy too soon. The tone shifted. In time, the room became more honest, more human.

In the weeks that followed, Dr. Johnson introduced reflective protocols and learning-focused routines into the meetings. Leaders started asking deeper questions and sharing incomplete ideas. Some even modeled those same strategies with their school staff. Bit by bit, vulnerability felt less like weakness and started feeling more like learning and leadership.

Bottom Line

For continuous improvement to be genuine, educators must feel psychologically safe. If we want others to be brave, we have to go first. Modeling vulnerability opens a culture where people feel safe to take risks, make mistakes, and share their learning without fear of repercussions. You win some, you learn some!

In Chapter 4, we explored the Six Principles of Improvement. The first principle is that improvement work must be *user-centered* and *problem-specific*. In Chapter 8, we focused on the first half of this principle: making the work *user-centered* by increasing staff ownership of improvement efforts. Now, in Chapter 9, we focus on the second half of the principle: making the work *problem-specific* by helping teams work on the problems that truly matter, which requires vulnerability. This chapter explores how to create safe environments that foster staff risk-taking, problem-solving, and open learning, which are essential elements for deeper continuous improvement.

In schools and districts where psychological safety is high, educators openly analyze what's working and what's not, refining their practice together. Bryk et al. (2015) highlight that sustained improvement requires structured problem-solving, vulnerability, and iterative learning cycles, all of which depend on a trusting environment. Safety is particularly crucial when focusing on equity. Staff must be able to critically examine disparities, challenge systemic barriers, and experiment with new approaches without fear of blame. Leaders must actively disrupt the culture of fear to create spaces for authentic, equity-focused improvement (Biag, 2019).

On the other hand, in educational systems where psychological safety is low, improvement efforts, even the intentional use of improvement science, become performative rather than transformative. Staff may have surface-level compliance, but real learning, where risks, challenges, and adaptations are openly discussed, does not take place (Edmondson, 1999). Yet, many school cultures have been shaped by traditions of perfectionism and shame in failure. These norms cause staff to hesitate to share challenges and be transparent because they fear making mistakes in high-stakes environments (LeMahieu et al., 2017). As a result, improvement work can remain shallow, inhibiting teams from addressing their genuine, most persistent (even ugliest) problems.

This focus on vulnerability connects directly to two key paradigm shifts discussed in Chapter 5:

- Paradigm Shift Three: Failure is a learning opportunity
- Paradigm Shift Four: Knowledge must be shared to accelerate system learning

Drawing insights from our three seasoned leaders—Kyle, Melanie, and Shawn—we'll uncover three common challenges that make it difficult to lead a system that embraces vulnerability. To close the gap between a leader's vision for vulnerable inquiry and the deeply ingrained norms of traditional collegial interactions, we will then explore three strategies that leaders can use to overcome these challenges and help foster a culture where educators feel safe confronting hard problems in service of students on the wrong side of equity gaps.

▶ VISION–IMPLEMENTATION GAP: VULNERABILITY

Kyle, Melanie, and Shawn are like many dedicated leaders who deeply value vulnerability in education. They envision school systems where reflective practice is the norm, where staff feel safe trying new strategies, and where they are willing to make their data and practice public for the sake of organizational learning. As leaders, we know that, in the end, a culture of improvement isn't just about having the right processes and tools; it's about making sure people feel safe enough to use them.

But turning that vision into reality is difficult. Despite research affirming that psychological safety is essential for continuous improvement, even the best leaders struggle to build cultures that fully embrace vulnerability. This vision–implementation gap impedes improvement.

This is the vision–implementation gap for fostering vulnerability:

- *Vision*: Leaders want a culture where staff feel safe to take risks, tackle tough problems, and share findings.
- *Implementation Gap*: Staff often play it safe, avoid the deep equity-focused work, and teams tend to operate in silos.

To bridge this gap, leaders must address three challenges:

1. Creating conditions where staff feel safe to take risks.
2. Pushing past operational or surface-level issues to tackle persisting student-centered problems.
3. Encouraging staff to share learning, data, and work outside their immediate team.

Each challenge section includes:

- Background and research
- Leadership perspectives (vision)
- Challenges faced by leaders (implementation gap)

Following the challenges, we will look at three strategies to address these barriers to leading a culture that leans into vulnerability.

▶ CHALLENGE 1: HESITANCE TO TAKE RISKS

Risk-taking is essential for a learning and improving culture, yet it remains a persistent challenge for leaders. Many staff are tentative about trying on new instructional strategies or making their practice public due to fear of judgment, negative evaluations, or a culture of perfectionism. If educators feel that making mistakes equates to professional incompetence, they will avoid the kind of curiosity-inspired inquiry that examines deeper issues.

Edmondson (1999) found that psychological safety shows that organizations where staff feel safe taking risks outperform those where staff fear failure. Schools that encourage structured, low-stakes experimentation allow educators to iterate, refine, and improve rather than avoid risk altogether.

Seppala and Cameron (2015) explain that leaders create safety by fostering social connections, supporting collaboration, showing empathy, and making it safe for staff to share mistakes and feedback.

Risk-taking is not about reckless experimentation. Rather, it takes thoughtful, deliberate inquiry. When leaders elevate vulnerability and create routines that make failure safe, staff can take the kind of risks required to collectively improve disparate student outcomes.

Vision

Leaders often have a bold vision that values vulnerability in their systems. They want staff to feel safe trying new strategies, analyzing challenges openly, and engaging in shared inquiry.

Shawn shares the importance of leaders setting the tone:

> You don't have to have all the answers. You just need to create a culture where it's safe to ask questions.

Kyle, Melanie, and Shawn all recognize that safety is the foundation of authentic inquiry and improvement.

Kyle leads with vulnerability. He emphasizes that leaders must be willing to model vulnerability first if they expect their teams to take risks.

> Superintendents need to show others when they do not know something—that you will learn alongside them and take risks.

Too often, leaders feel pressured to project certainty. However, this is to the detriment of our learning culture. When we, as leaders, openly share uncertainties and learning moments, it sends a powerful message. Risk-taking is expected. Failure is nothing to be ashamed of as long as we use it for learning. You are not esteemed for already knowing all the answers because improvement is about active learning.

Kyle points out that improvement is about active learning.

> Teachers feel vulnerable all the time when you're looking at practice, but if they see you taking a risk—saying, "Ah, I really don't know. I have never done this. I'm going to try it"—then they feel safe to do the same.

Melanie highlights the connection between safety and risk-taking in collaboration.

> There has to be a culture of safety to have a level of vulnerability and collaboration if you're going to make real change or move the needle in data. People aren't going to be vulnerable if they don't feel safe.

Melanie also points out that vulnerability in improvement work goes beyond personal risk-taking. It also involves owning student data and taking responsibility for change.

> I have to show up with my kids' data, whatever it is, and be willing to talk about it.

This means that leaders need to build trust before they can push for vulnerability. Educators need to feel safe acknowledging instructional challenges, discussing data transparently, and exploring new strategies without fear of criticism. If improvement work is perceived as evaluative rather than a learning opportunity, staff will hesitate to share their struggles or try something new. Staff need to feel assured that their contributions will be valued, they will not be shamed for their challenges, and they will not be scrutinized as they engage in learning.

Shawn reiterates the importance of risk-taking at every level of leadership.

> Whether dealing with successes or mistakes, be vulnerable. Superintendents need to be vulnerable enough so that people can see that you are human, you can make mistakes and learn from them.

Our leaders exemplify the mindset needed to foster a culture of risk-taking and vulnerability. They model openness, create safety, and build trust, laying the groundwork for authentic inquiry. Yet, even with this vision and intentional leadership, building a culture where risk-taking feels truly safe remains a persistent challenge. That's where the gap emerges between what leaders hope to create and what staff actually experience.

Implementation Gap

Despite their efforts to normalize risk-taking, our three leaders still see patterns of caution among staff. Staff remain afraid of evaluation that equates problems or failures with incompetence. Staff can be reluctant when their efforts are connected to high-stakes rather than safe, small-scale testing. Also, making practice public feels like risky business.

As Shawn notes that even when staff engage in improvement work, it feels high-stakes. Teams sometimes revert to waiting for leadership direction rather than taking initiative:

> I want it to not just be me and those leading to feel like it is okay to innovate and take risks in a structured and low-stakes way. I think it is also very much if people are engaging in the process in their own teams, then that is a sign of success. It is not just a district thing or a building thing. It is a team-based approach to how we improve.

Part of the challenge in risk-taking is shifting from fear to learning. For risk-taking to become embedded in school culture, leaders must move beyond simply encouraging experimentation and innovation. They must create systems that honor productive struggle.

As *Melanie* points out:

> I have to show up with my data and be vulnerable about the places where it's my responsibility to move that needle. That is not going to happen in a place where there's not high trust.

Leaders need to create a culture where risk-taking is the norm and not relegated to a few courageous individuals.

PAUSE TO REFLECT ON CHALLENGE 1

- Do staff in your school or district feel safe taking risks? How do you know?
- How do you currently respond to mistakes or failures in improvement efforts? Do staff see these as opportunities for learning, or do they fear judgment?
- Think of a protocol you use for looking at data or inquiry. How can you tweak it to scaffold a reflection that fosters vulnerability?

▶ CHALLENGE 2: FOCUSING ON OPERATIONAL OR SURFACE-LEVEL ISSUES INSTEAD OF STUDENT-CENTERED PROBLEMS

If permitted, many teams default to focusing improvement efforts on (a) safe, surface-level issues or (b) operational challenges rather than the deeper, more complex student-centered challenges that get to the heart of equity gaps. One of the biggest challenges for leaders is guiding teams to use structured inquiry to confront persistent disparities.

Research emphasizes the importance of focusing on the most pressing problems. Equity-focused problems require vulnerability. Bryk et al. (2015) found that teams often gravitate toward *safe* problems because tackling deeper inequities requires vulnerability. Similarly, Deming (1994) emphasized that the most impactful improvement work is deeply human-centered, but it's also the most challenging.

One of the paradigm shifts in improvement science is learning from failure. Deming (1994) reminds improvers to *fail early and fast*, and Bryk et al. (2015) remind us to use variation as a tool rather than a problem to be eliminated.

However, embracing a learn-from-failure mindset requires us to help staff understand that identifying and addressing inequities is not a sign of incompetence. This is the responsibility of a learning organization. That notion is a radical shift from traditional school cultures that prioritize performance over process.

Vision

Leaders have a compelling vision for focusing on student-centered problems.

Kyle describes his leadership as ensuring that "each and every student is seen and supported where they are until we have reached every last one."

Melanie is passionate about serving vulnerable student populations.

Shawn emphasizes that creating opportunities for student success drives his leadership.

In Chapter 5, we read an example about Shawn's eighth-grade English Language Arts (ELA) team. Let's revisit that story through the lens of *problem-specific* practice.

Recall that Shawn's eighth-grade team originally misdiagnosed the issue until they used data dives and empathy interviews to find the root cause and design a focused intervention.

> They initially thought kids were just not engaged. Okay, that is very broad, right? When they got down to it, the actual problem was around comprehension of informational text.

Through using PDSA cycles, the team tested a three-step annotation strategy, refined it together, and then scaled it building-wide.

They used their expertise and ownership to try change ideas. Then during collaborative PDSA, we put the change ideas and data up on the screen, and we were tweaking each week based on what we learned and what we were going to try next.

The result:

We got to a product that we felt was working well for kids. Then that team shared it with their eighth-grade department and then the entire school.

This team embraced vulnerability as they pushed past their initial broad problem identification of *engagement* to uncover what was underneath it so that they could address that gap in their instruction.

Implementation Gap

However, despite their strong convictions for equity-driven improvement, leaders encounter a common challenge: Staff were not consistently focusing their improvement work on solving the most pressing equity issues.

One way leaders encounter this gap is through teams gravitating to operational problems, such as refining hiring processes, procurement workflows, or budgeting systems. These process-driven problems can feel more concrete, manageable, and less emotionally charged than tackling systemic inequities.

Don't get me wrong. These logistical improvements serve a purpose and have an important place. In addition to improving the system, they tend to be safer problems to solve. They also help leaders and teams learn structured inquiry and result in quick wins, so the team can see the immediate benefits of improvement science. While these logistical improvements are necessary and can be a great starting point, they are not the end goal.

Kyle, for example, started by using improvement science to streamline the hiring process.

> Our hiring process took 90 days to even get somebody close to being hired. So, we used that process to learn improvement science, and as a way to implement the improvement process at first.

Similarly, he applied these strategies to procurement and budgeting systems:

> We've also applied improvement science it with our purchasing and procurement systems, and we've done it with our budgeting system—like how do we budget and what's our budgeting process?

While using deliberate improvement processes improved those management issues, Kyle ultimately wanted to shift toward more student-centered problems.

Shawn took a district-wide approach when first introducing improvement science, focusing on large-scale system challenges.

> The way we approached improvement science when I first started with it was from a 30,000-foot level—us trying to solve big system issues.

Staying at the surface with problems is a common leadership encounter. While that may help build capacity in the early stages, it won't lead to the kind of transformations that equity-focused leadership aspires to—addressing student learning disparities.

Kyle acknowledged this challenge:

> One of the things I struggled with early on was when people were trying to solve what I called surface-level issues. But I let people play around with the process on these lower-stakes problems first. If they saw success, then maybe they could apply it to a more complex problem that actually needs fixing.

While these early applications help teams develop inquiry skills and build initial engagement, leaders must push past the tendency to gravitate toward general or vague improvement topics that don't produce measurable impact to identify and address the most urgent student equity gaps. For example, Kyle realized his district was not addressing the most urgent student-centered challenges. Over time, he encouraged teams to apply structured inquiry to student learning gaps, shifting the focus to equity-driven problems.

> At first, teams wanted to focus on fixing broken systems—things like hiring processes and scheduling. But those aren't the problems keeping me up at night. The challenge was helping them connect improvement science to student outcomes.

A second way leaders encounter this vision–implementation gap is that even when teams do begin to center students in their inquiry, they often start with safe, generic, or surface-level concerns rather than deeply analyzing root causes. This requires courageous leadership that is willing to challenge assumptions, engage in difficult conversations, and ensure that work remains student-centered.

Melanie recognizes that psychological safety is essential for teams to engage in equity-driven problem-solving focused on students. In her district, staff were initially hesitant to examine student equity gaps. She wanted it to be safe for staff to dig deeper.

> Staff needed to know that naming an equity gap didn't reflect negatively on them—it was an opportunity to improve. The key was creating a culture where inquiry wasn't about blame, but about learning and solving real problems together.

To close this challenge, leaders must consistently steer teams toward problem-specific, student-centered inquiry. Improvement science only reaches its full potential when the work directly impacts system disparities. By moving beyond operational or surface-level concerns, leaders create a culture where staff vulnerability pays off for students.

> **PAUSE TO REFLECT ON CHALLENGE 2**
>
> - When your team engages in improvement work, do they naturally gravitate toward surface-level issues, or do they lean in to the most difficult student-centered problems? What patterns have you noticed?
> - How comfortable are staff in identifying and discussing equity gaps and the system practices that create them? What structures or supports might help them shift from surface-level issues to deep, student-centered inquiry?

▶ CHALLENGE 3: LACK OF STAFF SHARING BEYOND THEIR IMMEDIATE TEAM

A persistent challenge in education is the culture of operating in silos. Staff often hesitate to share challenges openly, fearing judgment, reputational damage, or unintended consequences. Staff may participate in collaborative improvement, but without a foundation of trust, real learning is inhibited. Even when teams do engage in disciplined inquiry within their own groups, they are less likely to share their learning across teams, schools, departments, or districts. This limits the collective impact of improvement efforts and slows the spread of promising practices.

Bryk et al. (2015) emphasize that Networked Improvement Communities (NICs) are most effective when they intentionally break down silos to facilitate shared learning. NICs harness the wisdom of crowds, recognizing that more can be accomplished collectively than any individual or independent team can achieve alone. Yet despite these clear benefits, cross-team sharing remains elusive. Staff often work in isolation, tackling similar challenges independently instead of leveraging the collective knowledge of others.

One reason for this reluctance in sharing learning across teams is staff discomfort with making practice public. Some staff may worry that exposing challenges to others will be seen as a sign of weakness. Others worry about competition or judgment. The fact is that sharing and vulnerability are not innate in the educational culture. Actually, being open, vulnerable, and collaborative in inquiry-driven work is not an innate skill for humans. Leaders often assume that meaningful sharing will naturally happen if teams are given time and space to collaborate. But research suggests otherwise.

Rohanna (2022) found that when teachers were required to share results and reflections during collaborative inquiry, they often went through the motions rather than engaging in deep, meaningful conversations. The facilitator-leaders in the study realized a common mistake: they had expected high-quality collaboration simply because time was allocated for it. However, just as students need to be taught how to collaborate effectively, educators also need structured guidance, clear protocols, and leadership modeling to engage in deep, inquiry-based sharing. The lesson was clear. Leaders need to explicitly teach, model, and scaffold collaboration to help staff develop the skills and mindsets to be able to engage in authentic inquiry across teams.

Another barrier to sharing learning across teams is a lack of structures, such as time and protocols that facilitate cross-team sharing. Bryk (2017) emphasized that schools and districts must move away from a culture of isolated problem-solving and instead embrace shared learning. He emphasizes that when the contributions of individuals and teams are harnessed, there is an incredible collective capacity to accelerate learning and improve. For leaders, the challenge is to go beyond encouraging risk-taking to making it happen by creating structures and routines that scaffold collaboration and team-sharing.

Vision

Effective leaders value the power of shared learning and believe that improvement should not remain isolated within individual teams. They see collaboration across teams, grade levels, schools, departments, and districts as essential for accelerating improvement and ensuring that successful strategies reach as many students as possible.

Kyle sees regional collaboration as a way to break isolation between districts, leveraging NICS to tackle similar challenges:

> As an ESD Superintendent, I saw the power of a NIC and that ESDs are truly the hub. We should be pulling districts in around problems they are having and running improvement science processes.

Melanie believes that when teams share their learning, improvement becomes embedded in the district's culture:

> It is okay to show up where you are, but it is not okay to stay there.

Shawn envisions a district where learning is not isolated but is actively shared to build a stronger, more connected system:

> We had pockets of excellence, but collaboration amongst leaders and having any sort of systemic vision or way we did things was not who we were. One of my first big leadership shifts was breaking down those silos and creating K-12 systems of collaboration that still remain today.

For these leaders, vulnerable knowledge-sharing is a necessary practice for system-wide improvement. Their vision is clear. They seek to leverage what works beyond individual teams to strengthen the whole system.

Implementation Gap

While leaders strongly believe in the power of cross-team, cross-school, and cross-district learning, turning this vision into reality has proven difficult. Even when school and districts face similar challenges, such as student attendance, engagement, and achievement gaps, many continue to work in isolation.

When structures for cross-team and cross-district learning do exist, participation is still often inconsistent, and engagement remains limited. Leaders who have attempted to build systems for shared learning frequently encounter resistance, logistical hurdles, or a lack of urgency from teams that are accustomed to working independently.

For example, Shawn works to increase sharing across teams and schools within his district. However, he found that improvement efforts often stayed within teams rather than spreading across schools. To address this, he embedded structured inquiry cycles into PLCs so that collaborative learning would become the norm. This shift allowed successful strategies to be shared across different students and schools.

> We had great work happening in pockets, but unless we built structures for spreading that learning, improvement efforts stayed isolated. When we embedded disciplined inquiry into existing PLCs, scaling effective change became part of how we operated.

Across districts, both Kyle and Shawn championed opportunities for regional and cross-district collaboration but have faced persistent barriers to participation. Their experiences highlight the gap between believing in shared learning and embedding it into practice.

Kyle describes this gap firsthand in his role leading regional improvement collaboration:

> As an ESD Superintendent, our role is to bring in districts to work on shared problems. But how do we get people? Many districts choose to tackle the same problems on their own rather than collaborate regionally. They default to familiar ways of working within their own systems.

Shawn also experienced similar struggles while leading a multi-district equity initiative. Even though leaders were committed to a common goal of addressing systemic disparities, districts struggled to engage in sustained collaboration.

> We're kind of struggling right now with our work as a region with different districts in different places. We are trying to solve a problem of our own leadership and our own understanding of equity as leaders.

These stories reflect a broader educational culture issue. Even when there is a strong belief in the value of shared learning, barriers of competing priorities, logistical constraints, and ingrained habits of working in isolation prevent collaboration from becoming the norm.

To bridge this implementation gap, leaders must actively create the conditions that make cross-team and cross-district collaboration feasible, expected, and embedded into practice. Without intentional structures and leadership support, sharing will remain a vision rather than a lived reality. By fostering a knowledge-sharing culture, leaders can accelerate improvement and help successful practices benefit the entire system.

> **PAUSE TO REFLECT ON CHALLENGE 3**
>
> - When teams engage in improvement work, does the knowledge stay within their group, or is there a system for spreading insights across teams or schools?
> - What barriers might be preventing staff from sharing their learning more broadly? Are these barriers cultural (hesitancy, lack of trust) or structural (lack of time, unclear expectations and processes)?

▶ STRATEGIES TO CLOSE THE VISION–IMPLEMENTATION GAP ON STAFF VULNERABILITY

While leaders deeply value risk-taking, student-focused improvements, and open collaboration, many school and district cultures still inhibit these behaviors. To close the vision–implementation gap, leaders must create safe environments that promote vulnerability in improvement. As we shift from challenges to solutions, we will explore three actionable, research- and evidence-based strategies leaders can use to build a culture where vulnerability is embraced.

1. Choose a real problem focused on student equity gaps – Difference-making improvement begins by selecting the most pressing, equity-focused problems that center student learning rather than remaining on surface-level, logistical, or operational concerns (Bryk et al., 2015).

2. Engage in disciplined inquiry around equity gaps – Leaders safeguard and focus inquiry on those genuine student-focused problems without blame or fear. Structured problem-solving cycles help teams test change ideas designed to specifically target disparities (Bryk et al., 2015; Deming, 1994).
3. Spread and scale solutions that address equity gaps – Effective improvement work does not stay confined to one classroom, team, school, or department. Leaders must develop systems that support cross-team learning and intentionally spread and scale culturally responsive strategies tailored to the diverse needs of students in each setting to scale impact (LeMahieu et al., 2017).

Each strategy section includes research (theory) and leadership moves (practice) with examples and lessons learned from our three educational leaders—Kyle, Melanie, and Shawn. Let's examine how leaders can turn vision into reality by fostering a positive culture through vulnerability.

▶ STRATEGY 1: CHOOSING A REAL PROBLEM— EXAMINING STUDENT EQUITY GAPS

While many leaders express a deep commitment to equity, without a structured approach to identifying and solving inequities, improvement efforts can drift toward those operational or surface-level concerns. This strategy connects to Challenge 2 (Pushing Past Operational or Surface-Level Issues).

Define the Problem

One of the most powerful actions an educational leader can take is ensuring that improvement efforts directly address student equity gaps. Deming (1994) argued that failure to clearly define the problem results in wasted effort, so teams must identify the root causes of inequities before attempting solutions. Bryk et al. (2015) similarly emphasize that effective improvement work requires teams to focus on *problem-specific and user-centered* challenges, especially for closing student equity gaps. This means we need to coach teams beyond their comfort zones, supporting them in tackling difficult conversations and naming inequities directly. By doing so, we reinforce that equity is the heart of our work (LeMahieu et al., 2017).

Center Equity

To do this, leaders need to take an active role in pressing teams to identify and clearly define the most pressing student-centered inequities. For example, we need to guide teams in examining disparities in academics, attendance, discipline, and other indicators that make or break student success. We can do this by helping teams examine data with an equity lens. We need to make sure our teams have access to and use disaggregated student data to uncover patterns of inequity. We can also support teams in incorporating student and family voice through empathy interviews (Biag, 2019).

Shawn, as a hub leader, recognizes his role in "integrating equity into the network, including attending to equity both in developing the formal and social infrastructure of the network and in designing and pursuing improvement activities" (Peurach et al., 2025, p. 125). Yet, he notes that even when districts prioritize equity, many struggle to pinpoint *what specifically* they are trying to improve:

> Leaders throughout the region don't really know what they are grappling with in terms of equity, why they are stuck, and what it is they're actually trying to accomplish.

To move from broad commitments to actionable equity work, leaders must guide teams in examining who is most affected by the problem, what systemic conditions contribute to inequitable outcomes, and how we will measure if our changes are improvements.

As Shawn says:

> What is an equity gap that is keeping you up at night?

This guiding question encourages teams to identify the most pressing disparities affecting students. However, even when teams start discussing equity, they may initially land on vague or generic concerns. Leaders must coach teams into specificity, ensuring they name and measure problems with clarity (Anderson et al., 2024).

I'll share an example from my district. We had been setting achievement goals, but we realized that, despite meeting the stated goals, the same students were not consistently achieving them year after year. Our approach was well-intentioned, but it wasn't explicitly targeting the gaps that persisted in our system. We needed a shift.

Instead of setting goals that focused on *all students* (e.g., we will improve from 60% to 80% of students meeting proficiency), we reframed our approach to prioritize closing gaps (e.g., we will close the gap of students not meeting proficiency from 40% to 20%). We called these our *gap-closing goals*—an intentional, equity-driven strategy to help improvement efforts reach the students who needed them most.

This shift was more than a change in wording. Mindsets and system-wide practices changed. Gap-closing goals became the foundation of our district strategic plan, school improvement plans, and collaborative team goals. By centering our goals on the students who were underserved, we operationalized our commitment to equity. While accelerating achievement for *all*, we also shone a light on *each* student's success. (Our theme was *from all to each*.)

Make it Relevant

Too often, improvement efforts lose momentum because staff are not deeply invested in the problem being addressed. To foster meaningful engagement, teams must work on problems that are relevant to their daily practice and deeply connected to student outcomes. As Leger et al. (2023) emphasize, staff engagement in collaborative inquiry increases when the problem resonates with their professional experiences and values. However, focusing on just any problem is not enough. Teams must focus on the tough problems they are facing, particularly those related to equity. By helping teams focus on student-centered problems and equity-focused inquiry, leaders help improvement science become a vehicle for educational justice.

In sum, our leaders show us ways to help teams choose a real and relevant problem that examines student equity gaps.

- *Kyle* allowed teams to start with operational issues to build confidence in the improvement process, but pushed them toward deeper, student-centered problems.
- *Melanie* fostered a culture of psychological safety, ensuring staff felt secure discussing student data and identifying areas for growth.
- *Shawn* focused on precision in defining problems and pushing teams to go beyond vague concerns to articulate specific, measurable equity gaps.

▶ STRATEGY 2: ENGAGE IN DISCIPLINED INQUIRY AROUND STUDENT EQUITY GAPS

Identifying student equity gaps is just the beginning. Another challenge is for leaders to engage teams in the subsequent steps of disciplined inquiry to close those identified gaps. This work is high-risk, high-reward, and is not for the faint of heart. This strategy connects to Challenges 1 (Risk-Taking) and 2 (Pushing Past Operational or Surface-Level Challenges).

Both Deming (1994) and Bryk et al. (2015) emphasize that testing small-scale changes through disciplined inquiry allows teams to refine strategies before full implementation. This deliberate approach allows organizations to build system capacity, increase stakeholder ownership, and mitigate risk—all critical in equity-focused work. LeMahieu et al. (2017) reiterate that leaders must push staff to apply structured inquiry to the challenges that impact students most.

The distinction for vulnerability is the emphasis on *equity-driven* inquiry, which is a structured, scientific process for driving measurable improvements for all students and underserved students (Anderson et al., 2024). Without clear, structured inquiry into disparities, improvement work risks becoming disconnected from student outcomes (Bryk et al., 2015). This requires brave leadership.

5-Phase Equity-Focused Disciplined Inquiry

It's easy to rattle off the two words *disciplined inquiry* without thinking of the importance of each of the words.

- Disciplined—We force ourselves to slow down, follow a structured process, and resist jumping to quick-fix solutions.
- Inquiry—We get curious about problems, use data, and uncover the underlying system conditions that produce inequities.

Together, *disciplined + inquiry* ensure that teams go beyond treating symptoms to addressing root causes and transforming the systems that are failing students on the wrong side of the gaps.

This familiar cycle becomes a transformative tool when we emphasize equity. For example:

- Phase 1: Identify and clarify the problem through data-driven understanding, analyzing root causes of the equity gap, such as looking at disaggregated data to see who is most affected and conducting empathy interviews to find out how others experience inequity first-hand.
- Phase 2: Develop a theory of improvement, framing the equity gap in an aim statement and identifying drivers, which are system conditions contributing to the gap.
- Phase 3: Come up with change ideas, which are culturally responsive interventions to improve outcomes (Bryk et al., 2010; Bryk et al., 2015).
- Phase 4: Test and refine change ideas using small-scale PDSA cycles (Bryk et al., 2015), making adjustments so that actions positively impact the targeted equity gap across diverse learners and contexts.

- Phase 5: Share findings about what works, where, and for whom, so the systems that contributed to the inequities are improved (LeMahieu et al., 2017) and promising practices reach more students.

The cycle is ongoing, with teams refining and expanding improvements as they learn more over time.

As you or your team reviews the 5-phase inquiry process, ask: Where else can we elevate equity? When you engage in inquiry, pause at each step to reflect on your equity-focused practices and impacts.

Avoid the Training Trap

Caution! A common pitfall in implementing improvement science is focusing too much on the *process* of improvement and not enough on solving real *problems*. This can make teams feel like they are moving forward with implementing improvement science while still playing it safe. This is what Anderson et al. (2024) call the *training trap*. When training does occur, it should still be connected to student-centered work instead of abstract or theoretical training sessions.

Supporting training and authentic problem-solving is a real balancing act for leaders. Learning a new process is complex, but teams should not spend more time learning how to do improvement science than actually using it to solve real issues. A strong leader keeps the *why* at the forefront while the team is still learning the *how*. In other words, as leaders, we need to keep the focus on solving real equity issues, ensuring that teams spend more time improving than learning about improvement (or that they learn about improvement while they are actually improving). Learning about the process should not be a way to avoid doing it.

Equity-focused leadership is courageous. It takes bravery to press beyond surface-level improvements and directly confront inequities. Leaders must persistently guide their teams toward deeper, more impactful work, even when it is uncomfortable.

We learned this firsthand in my district. I'll share an example. Our leadership team made a collective commitment to not only be present in collaborative team meetings but also engaged. We wanted to be true partners in inquiry, actively participating alongside educators rather than observing from the sidelines. However, I had to learn—sometimes through missteps—how to balance my voice in these spaces.

To me, I was just joining the conversation as an equal voice. But to others, I was still *the superintendent*. My position carried weight, regardless of my intention. I had to recognize that my words could either foster vulnerability and authenticity or unintentionally stifle them. Over time (and likely longer than it should have taken), I learned when to speak first and when to step back.

- *I needed to be the first* to say "I don't know," to share an "Ah-ha" moment of new learning, to admit a mistake, or to spotlight others. These moments set a learning stance, signaling that inquiry and growth applied to everyone, including me.
- *I needed to be the last* to speak when teams were identifying gaps in their performance data, defining their instructional problem of practice, or generating change ideas. If I spoke first, my voice could shape the discussion before authentic inquiry had the chance to unfold, or worse, be perceived as criticism.

Leadership presence in inquiry spaces matters. But if we sit passively, we model passivity for others. The real challenge, the *art* of this work, for me was not just knowing *what* to say, but knowing *when* to say it so that training and learning remained student- and problem-centered.

Elevate Equity in Inquiry

Elevating equity in inquiry remains a challenge. It requires a willingness to challenge assumptions and confront difficult realities. Asking educators to share data across teams is already challenging, but asking them to engage in high-vulnerability equity work adds another layer of complexity. Some teams may hesitate to examine racial, linguistic, socioeconomic, or ability disparities in student outcomes due to fear of uncovering uncomfortable truths or being perceived as ineffective. Others may struggle to collaborate across teams on these complex topics, especially in schools with low trust or where improvement efforts have historically been siloed. But the potential is enormous.

Without disciplined inquiry, improvement efforts risk being reactive rather than transformative (Bryk et al., 2015). Engaging in disciplined inquiry around equity issues is critical, as our three leaders illustrate.

- *Kyle's* ESD challenges teams to engage in data analysis, empathy interviews, and root cause analysis before developing change ideas.
- *Melanie's* district cultivates psychological safety so teams feel comfortable examining and discussing equity-related data without fear of blame. She ensures that inquiry is embedded in daily routines rather than treated as an occasional initiative.
- *Shawn's* district ensures that teams use PDSA cycles to solve the equity problems that keep them up at night.

If we don't use improvement science for equity work, what are we really using it for? When we help teams remain focused on disciplined inquiry targeting the most urgent student equity gaps, we make systems better *and* more just. Let's make every inquiry cycle count!

▶ STRATEGY 3: SPREAD AND SCALE SOLUTIONS RELATED TO STUDENT EQUITY GAPS

Identifying and addressing equity gaps through disciplined inquiry within a team is a significant achievement, but the work doesn't stop there. Next, we focus specifically on the need for vulnerability when we expand that equity-centered improvement *across* teams. To create a more equitable system, educational leaders must ensure that successful solutions do not remain confined to one classroom, team, department, or school. Instead, these solutions must be intentionally spread and scaled so that more students, staff, and communities benefit from what works. This connects to challenge 3 (Staff Sharing Beyond Their Immediate Team).

Cultivate a Culture of Sharing

Vulnerability matters when we want to scale what works. As Biag (2019) found, psychologically safe teams are more likely to actively share learning across classrooms, schools, and districts. Leaders must foster a culture where sharing work, data, and ideas across contexts is safe, expected, and embedded into routine practice.

This is where sharing stories (from Chapter 7) comes into play. When teams share examples of their learning, both successes and failures, it sets a norm of transparency and collaboration. As Edmondson (1999) found, cultures that openly share encourage vulnerability because staff see others engaging in the same reflective work. Shared stories of practice don't just illustrate what's possible, but they shape norms and invite others in. This makes story-sharing more than feel-good inspiration, but a mechanism of spread! When staff see real examples of equity-focused inquiry in action, they are more likely to try it themselves.

Scale Through Adaptation

Remember, improvement science approaches spreading in a unique way, using an iterative and adaptive process instead of a copy-and-paste replication. As Deming (1994) teaches, scaling is not a final step but an ongoing opportunity to adapt and refine. Rather than assuming a solution will work everywhere, teams expand testing gradually to see whether improvements hold up across various settings and student populations (Langley et al., 2009). The goal of this phase is to understand the conditions under which the change works best, and for whom, confirming the adaptability of the strategy. By gradually increasing the scale of implementation, teams reduce the risk of failure based on real-world feedback, so they don't harm those they are trying to help.

Our equity-focused work doesn't stop after spreading and scaling what works. We need to continue to monitor and adjust change ideas. This is especially important with equity-focused change ideas. Even when a strategy has been successfully implemented across a school or district, leaders must continue to assess whether the strategy is working for *all* student groups. As leaders support the scaled effort, they should continue to ask whether student outcomes are still improving as the change expands, and how the team can continue to build knowledge to refine the approach. They should also monitor for any unintended consequences that need adjustments.

I'll share an example about scaling inquiry from my district. Before we started a deeper focus on collaborative teams, our leadership team was doing learning walks around our instructional framework (which was also our teacher evaluation tool). These learning walks were not evaluative; they were an opportunity for us to grow as instructional leaders and share learning across schools. However, publicly sharing our practice was an act of vulnerability.

Our leadership team, including my superintendent's cabinet and all school administrators, regularly visited classrooms *in each other's schools*. We refined our ability to observe instruction, sharpened our *noticings and wonderings*, and strengthened the quality of feedback we provided. Over the years, this process deepened our shared understanding and coherence as leaders.

When we established district-wide designated time for collaboration, we adapted this same approach to elevate our leadership for collaborative inquiry. During these sessions, central office and school leaders met *at each school*, where principals shared their problems of practice and where teams were at in the inquiry process. Before entering classrooms, we were briefed on each team's focus and insights. Afterward, we debriefed—sharing noticings, wonderings, what feedback or coaching the principal might offer the team, and implications for our own leadership practice.

This structure for our leadership team to share learning across schools became a built-in rhythm of the school year. Seeing collaborative inquiry *in action* was one of the most powerful tools for deepening our leadership practice. We borrowed ideas from one another, helped solve leadership challenges, and strengthened our shared understanding of improvement work across schools.

Once leaders engaged in the vulnerable work of sharing and examining practices through our equity focus, other staff members felt safe joining us. We invited teams to share at our district-wide teacher-leader collaboration facilitator meetings and board meetings. Sharing was no longer something that happened *after* improvement; it became a driver *of* improvement.

Maintain Ownership While Scaling

One of the most common mistakes in scaling strategies is assuming that staff will automatically adopt a new strategy once it has been deemed successful. In reality, however, educators are more likely to sustain solutions when they've played a role in developing and testing them, and when they are empowered to refine them for their unique contexts.

Maintaining staff ownership through the scaling process is especially critical while expanding equity-focused change ideas. When we lead in this way, we leverage staff-led knowledge-building (profound knowledge). Staff who are involved become champions of the work and support their peers in its implementation.

Of course, scaling action requires culture. By the time a school or district is ready to scale a solution that addresses an equity gap, leaders should have fostered a positive workplace culture that allows the change to take hold. We want inquiry and learning to be the norms. We want empowered staff to take ownership of improvement efforts. We want staff to vulnerably solve problems that matter. When this happens, scaling becomes an expansion of collective learning through the expansion of a strategy.

Let's see how our three leaders spread equity-focused solutions.

- *Kyle's* ESD leveraged networked improvement communities (NICs) at the regional level to support shared learning across districts. He focused on building cross-district collaboration to scale improvements beyond individual schools so all students in the region benefited from the collective wisdom of the leaders.
- *Melanie's* district prioritized alignment between school-level inquiry and district-wide goals to ensure that scaling efforts remained coherent and purpose-driven. She empowered educators to lead the spread of effective strategies so more students had access to what works while maintaining local flexibility and responsiveness to unique student and community needs, creating coherence without uniformity.
- *Shawn's* district found and shared success stories across teams to both expand promising practices and to show other teams how gap-closing and culturally responsive practices are possible through shared inquiry, making equity work feel actionable and achievable.

To truly transform student outcomes, leaders must ensure that successful improvement efforts do not remain isolated but are intentionally spread and scaled across teams, schools, and districts (Bryk et al., 2015). This work requires structured knowledge-building, continuous inquiry, and ownership to ensure customized implementation (Langley et al., 2009). As leaders, we need to help our staff get comfortable with being vulnerable or being uncomfortable and still sharing. That's how equity-focused strategies grow from promising ideas into transformative system-wide change.

▶ CONCLUSION

When staff feel safe to take risks, improvement has the potential to become more authentic, student-centered, and impactful. Schools and districts move beyond surface-level adjustments and begin addressing the root causes of inequity. This takes leadership that values trust, courage, and a commitment to equity. This isn't easy. Leaders must navigate challenges such as (a) supporting risk-taking, (b) pushing beyond operational or surface issues, and (c) fostering cross-team sharing. However, these barriers are not impossible to overcome. Leaders can (a) help teams choose equity-focused problems, (b) engage in disciplined inquiry, and (c) spread what works to deepen the system's capacity to lead and learn with equity-focused vulnerability.

Chapter 10 offers final reflections on how leaders can embed equity-focused inquiry into the daily rhythm of leadership, advancing excellence and equity across the entire system.

REFLECTION QUESTIONS

1. Challenges in Encouraging Staff Vulnerability: What experiences have you had or seen related to the challenge of fostering staff vulnerability? How have staff been encouraged (or discouraged) from taking risks, tackling the toughest student challenges, and sharing their learning openly?
2. Leadership Strategies for Improving Staff Vulnerability: How might you employ one or more of the following leadership strategies to foster a culture of vulnerability?
   - Examine student equity gaps—How can leaders ensure that problems address the most pressing student-centered problems?
   - Engage in disciplined inquiry around student equity gaps—What protocols can support deeper, equity-focused inquiry?
   - Spread and scale solutions related to student equity gaps—How can leaders ensure that the most successful strategies are shared, scaled, and customized across the district?

CHAPTER 9 TRY THIS: CREATE SPACE FOR STAFF VULNERABILITY

Consider leadership moves that foster a culture where staff feel safe to take risks, engage in disciplined inquiry, and share learning to address student equity gaps.

1. Describe your vision for vulnerability in improvement efforts in your school or district.

_____
_____
_____

2. Identify a challenge related to vulnerability (vision-implementation gap).

- Challenge 1: Staff feel safe to take risks.
- Challenge 2: Staff push past operational or surface-level issues to tackle student-centered problems.
- Challenge 3: Staff share learning, data, and work outside their immediate team.
- Other: _____

3. Choose a strategy and make a plan to implement it.

- Strategy 1: Examining Student Equity Gaps
  - How will you help teams move beyond surface-level or operational issues to examine real student equity gaps?
  - What data sources will you use to identify the most pressing student equity gaps?
  - How will you ensure teams are invested in the problem they are trying to solve?
- Strategy 2: Engaging in Disciplined Inquiry Around Student Equity Gaps
  - How will you elevate equity through each phase of improvement?

- How will you focus on solving relevant problems even while teams are learning the process?
  - Strategy 3: Spreading and Scaling Solutions Related to Student Equity Gaps
    - How will you ensure that successful improvement efforts are shared across teams, schools, and the district? What structures can facilitate shared learning?
    - How will you support staff in refining and adapting equity-focused solutions for broader implementation?

4. Create an Action Plan

Write your plan, including the who, what, when, where, and how. Be specific!

_____
_____
_____

Follow-Up and Reflection

After one month, reflect on the impact of your chosen strategy.

Did the change create a greater sense of psychological safety? Did staff engage in more risk-taking and open learning about equity gaps? What evidence do you have that staff are applying disciplined inquiry to real student-centered problems? What's next to continue building a culture of staff vulnerability and collaborative improvement?

_____
_____
_____

▶ LEADERSHIP EXAMPLE: LEADING WITH VULNERABILITY—STRUGGLING IN PUBLIC

As a leadership team, we believed in modeling what we asked others to do. If we expected teachers to embrace new instructional practices, we had to do the same. One of our district's instructional strategies was embedding learning targets and success criteria in lessons. In theory, it sounded simple—provide professional development, give teachers resources, and expect implementation. In practice, however, it was a real challenge. And if we struggled with it, we needed to be honest about that.

I started by posting learning targets and success criteria in my own professional development sessions and meetings, whether they were instructional or managerial. I caught myself defaulting to lower-level verbs on Bloom's taxonomy, so I began using a verb wheel aligned to depth of knowledge to push my thinking and elevate the rigor of the lesson or meeting.

Although I felt vulnerable, I decided to resist the temptation to present the final, polished versions of my learning targets and success criteria. I began bringing the rough drafts of my learning targets—the messy charts with crossed-out and changed words. I did a *think-aloud* about my struggle with writing the targets, sharing the different tools I was trying out. At first, my success criteria were too broad to actually be of help to learners. Then they were not rigorous enough. I wanted staff to see that this was difficult behind the scenes. I didn't want to stand in front of them, acting as if I had it all figured out. Instead, I wanted to model that it was okay to wrestle with an idea—to revise, rethink, and refine.

Next, I put myself out there and took the risk of using learning targets in lessons with students, like teachers were expected to do. Each year, I committed to substitute teaching in every school at least once. That year, I decided to practice using learning targets and success criteria in my lessons with students in addition to adult learners. Although I used this strategy when

I was a teacher, I was quickly reminded that what sounded great in theory didn't always translate into the classroom. Some learning targets I wrote confused students. Sometimes I wasn't as clear as I thought. Some targets were not responsive to the language and ability needs of different learners. I realized that sometimes I needed to teach students what a learning target was and how to use it. Other times, I didn't build in enough time for reflection and to check for understanding using the target and success criteria.

Because I experienced those struggles firsthand, I was able to have real conversations with leaders and teachers. I wasn't just saying, "This is important." I was saying, "I tried this." I could authentically join conversations about what worked and what didn't. We were problem-solving together.

I discovered that it was important for me to share the often-messy process. As leaders, we often feel pressure to show best practices only after we've perfected them. But teams really need to see the struggle, the missteps, and the learning along the way.

When we wrestle to do something well, we shouldn't act like it came easily to us. We need to share the struggle. Because when we do, we create a culture where risk-taking feels safe, where learning is valued over perfection, and where every educator, from the classroom to the boardroom, feels empowered to grow.

Figure 9.1 is an example of a learning target and success criteria that SALT and I used in our one-on-one principal budget and priority-setting meetings. Figure 9.2 is an example of a learning target and success criteria that I used with leaders to prepare for their teacher evaluation goal-setting meetings. These are just two examples to illustrate ways our team used targets for both managerial and instructional meetings, vulnerably practicing what we expected from other leaders and teachers (Figures 9.1 and 9.2).

Addressing the Vision–Implementation Gap of Staff Vulnerability 253

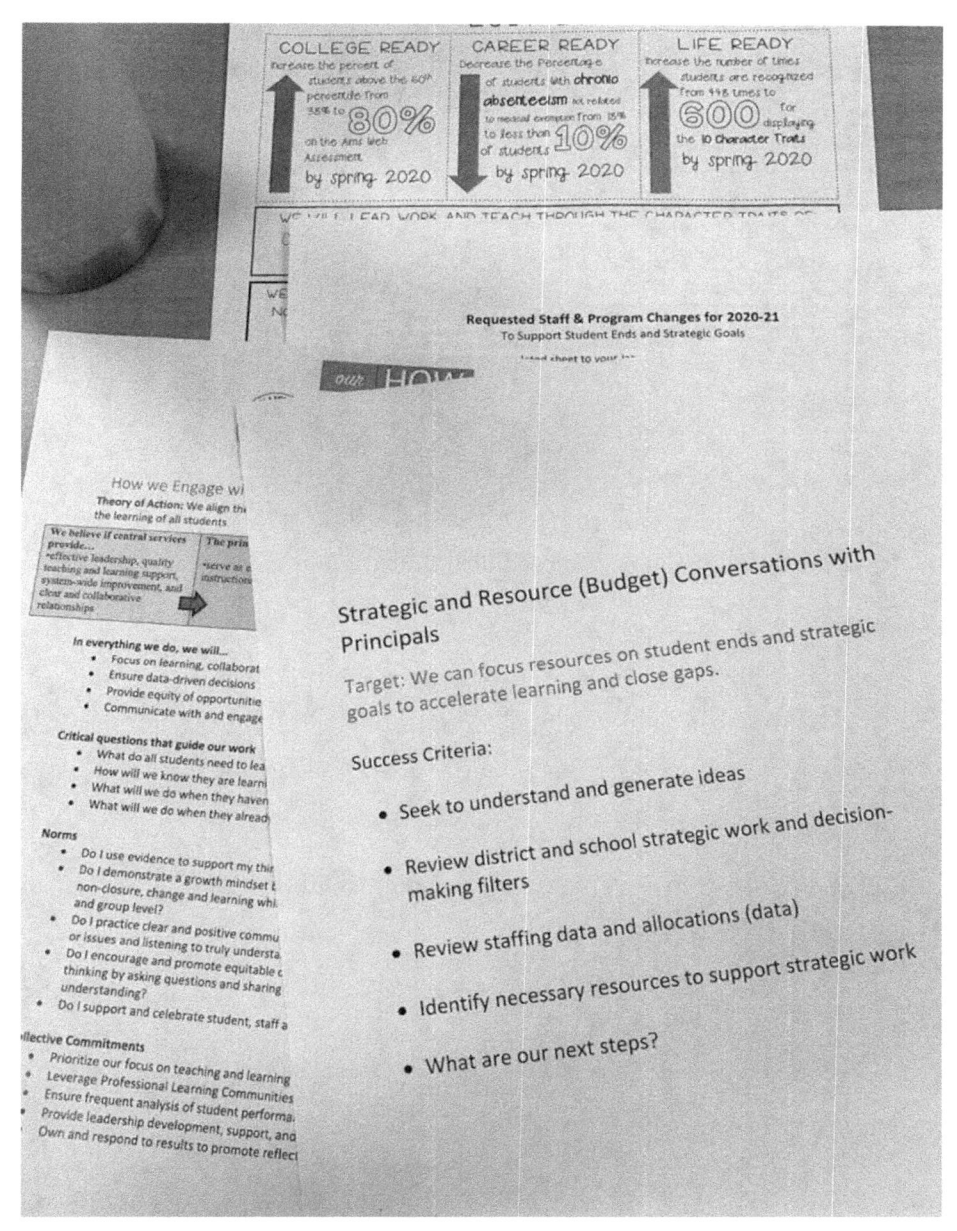

Figure 9.1 Learning Targets and Success Criteria for Principal 1–1 Budget Meetings.

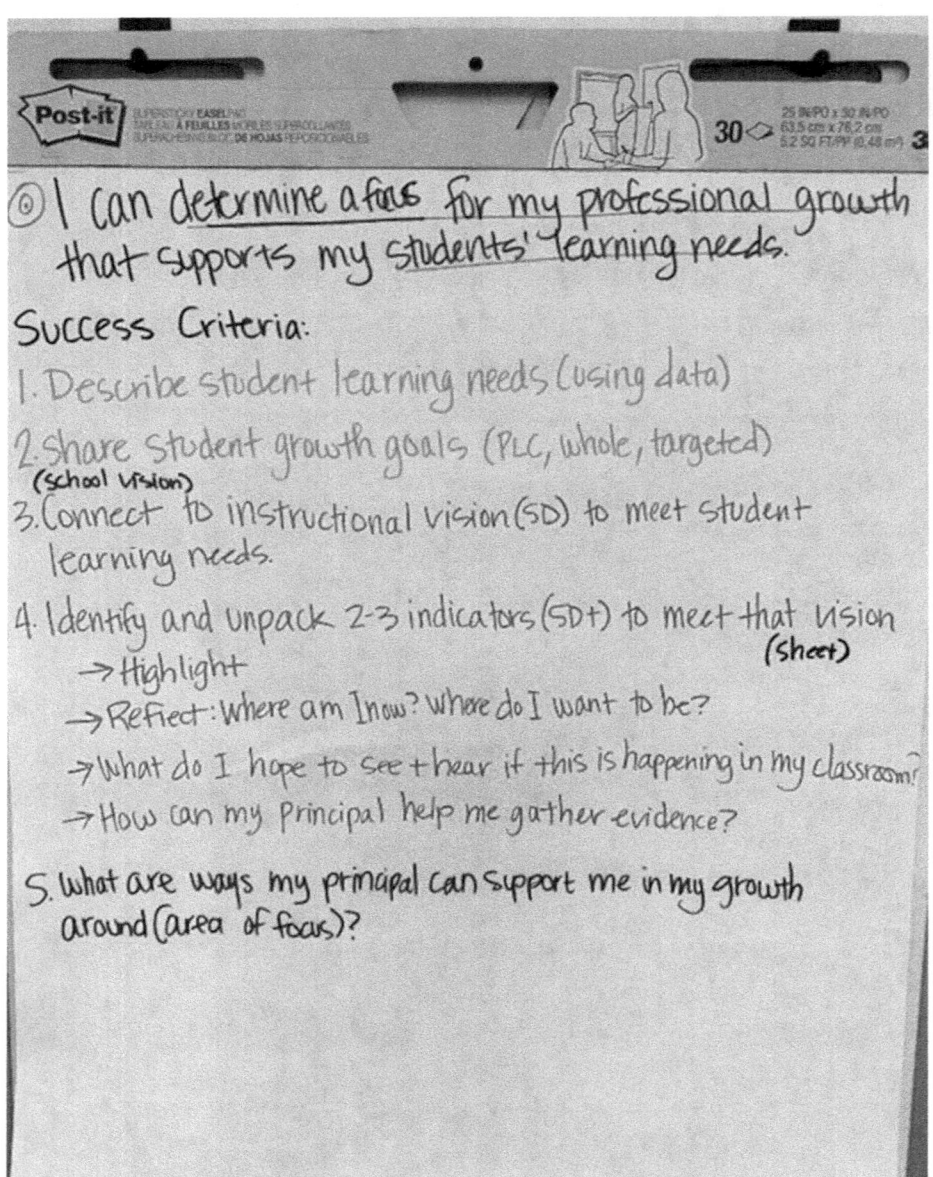

Figure 9.2 Learning Targets and Success Criteria for Teacher Goal Setting.

References

Anderson, E., Cunningham, K. M. W., & Richardson, J. W. (2024). Framework for implementing improvement science in a school district to support institutionalized improvement. *Education Sciences, 14*(7), 770.

Biag, M. (2019). Navigating the improvement journey with an equity compass. In R. Crow, B. N. Hinnant-Crawford, & D. T. Hinnant-Spaulding (Eds.) *The educational leader's guide to improvement science: Data, design, and cases for reflection* (pp. 91–125). Myers Education Press. Gorham, ME.

Bryk, A. S. (2017). *Redressing inequities: An aspiration in search of a method*. Paper presented at the Fourth Annual Carnegie Foundation Summit on Improvement in Education, San Francisco, CA.

Bryk, A. S., Gomez, L. M., & Gunrow, A. (2010). *Getting ideas into action: Building networked improvement communities in education*. Stanford, CA: Carnegie Foundation for the Advancement of Teaching.

Bryk, A. S., Gomez, L. M., Gunrow, A., & LeMahieu, P. G. (2015). *Learning to improve: How America's schools can get better and getting better*. Cambridge, MA: Harvard Education Publishing.

Deming, W. E. (1994). *The new economics for industry, government, education* (2nd ed.). Cambridge, MA: Massachusetts Institute of Technology, Center for Advanced Engineering Study.

Edmondson, A. (1999). Psychological safety and learning behavior in work teams. *Administrative Science Quarterly, 44*(2), 350–383.

Langley, G. J., Moen, R. D., Nolan, K. M., Nolan, T. W., Norman, C. L., & Provost, L. P. (2009). *The improvement guide* (2nd ed.). San Francisco, CA: Jossey-Bass.

Leger, M.-L., Gomez, L. M., & Obeso, O. E. (2023). Learning improvement science to lead: Conditions that bridge professional development to professional action. *Teachers College Record: The Voice of Scholarship in Education, 125*(9), 51–83.

LeMahieu, P. G., Grunow, A., Baker, L., Nordstrum, L. E., & Gomez, L. M. (2017). Networked improvement communities: The discipline of improvement science meets the power of networks. *Quality Assurance in Education: An International Perspective, 25*(1), 5–25.

Peurach, D. J., Jones, E. S., Duff, M., Sherer, J. Z., & Matthis, C. (2025). The practice and contexts of hub and district leadership: New directions in research on educational improvement networks. *Peabody Journal of Education, 100*(1), 117–132. https://doi.org/10.1080/0161956X.2025.2444846.

Rohanna, K. (2022). Extending evaluation capacity building theory to improvement science networks. *American Journal of Evaluation, 43*(1), 46–65.

Seppala, E., & Cameron, A. (December 1, 2015) Proof that positive work cultures are more productive. *Harvard Business Review.* https://hbr.org/2015/12/proofthat-positive-work-cultures-are-more-productive

Chapter 10

Zooming Out: Leading with a Systems Lens

LEARNING TARGET

I can lead for coherent, system-wide improvement by applying leadership strategies that move from vision to implementation.

Success Criteria

- Use systems-level thinking in improvement leadership.
- Apply targeted strategies to bridge the gap between a leader's vision for system-wide coherence and the actual experiences of staff.
- Reflect on learning and next steps for sustained personal and system improvement.

RELEVANT NELP STANDARDS

- NELP Standard 1: Mission, Vision, and Improvement (Aligned, Coherent System Improvement)
- NELP Standard 2: Ethics and Professional Norms (Reflection)
- NELP Standard 3: Equity, Inclusiveness, and Culturally Responsive Practices (Center Equity in Improvement Efforts)

- NELP Standard 4: Learning and Instruction (Share Learning Across Teams)
- NELP Standard 6: Operations and Management (System-Wide Structures)
- NELP Standard 7 (Building-Level): Building Professional Capacity (School-Wide Structures for Shared Learning)
- NELP Standard 7 (District-Level): Policy, Governance, and Advocacy (Integrating Continuous Improvement into Daily Leadership Practices, System-Wide Structures for Shared Learning)

ICEBREAKER: LOOKING BACK, LEADING FORWARD

Looking back on your leadership journey through this book, what is one key mindset shift, strategy, or insight that will change the way you lead moving forward?

- What new leadership approach or strategy do you plan to implement?
- What is one challenge you anticipate as you work toward system-wide improvement?
- How will you hold yourself accountable for sustaining improvement over time?

(See Appendix 1 for the Icebreaker Group Activity Facilitation Guide)

CASE VIGNETTE: DOING FEWER THINGS, BETTER

Background

At Pattonville City Schools, the leadership team was known for being innovative and energetic. They had vision. They had plans. They had launched 11 improvement initiatives in three years—curriculum alignment, restorative practices, equity audits, technology-integrated learning, and more. Despite all the movement, however, very little had changed in classrooms.

Staff were overwhelmed. "We just keep layering on more and more things. They're all good. But I don't feel like I have time to master any." One principal said. "It's hard to know what really matters." Teachers described a sense of whiplash. They wanted to do good work, but the priorities kept shifting.

Turning Point

When the new Superintendent, Dr. Robinson, arrived, she did something unexpected. She pressed pause. She asked the leadership team to write down every major project in motion. The list was long and sobering. Then she asked, "Which of these are we willing to do well enough that they'll still be our focus five years from now?" The room went quiet.

Dr. Robinson led the team in choosing three priorities. Everything else took a back burner or was embedded into those three buckets. Professional learning, strategic plans, evaluation systems—even budget allocations—were aligned to the district's focus areas. Leaders used the phrase "protect the focus" often, and they meant it.

When new ideas came up (and they always did), the default answer became, "That's a great idea. But does it serve our core priorities?" Many strong ideas were set aside, not because they weren't worthy, but because the system couldn't sustain more.

Over the next couple of years, people noticed the difference. Meetings were more focused. Resources were used more strategically. Schools started seeing traction on goals that had previously stalled. In fact, they found that their increased focus on a few key things was positively influencing many other things.

Bottom Line

Improvement doesn't come from trying to do everything. It comes from doing a few things well-Things worthy of intentionally teaching, that matter enough to intervene on, that warrant our investment, and that we continuously monitor for improvement. Focus means committing to the work that truly matters, doing it deeply, together, and over time. Protect the focus.

Educational leadership is filled with good intentions, but too often, well-meaning reforms fall into a vision–implementation gap where ambitious ideas fail to translate into the meaningful, system-wide, and sustained impact we hoped to see. Unlike the previous chapters that explored workplace culture (Chapter 7), ownership (Chapter 8), and vulnerability (Chapter 9) in depth, this final chapter intentionally takes a different form.

Short by design, this chapter offers a focused leadership roadmap for deepening and sustaining system-wide equity-focused improvement. Rather than introducing new content, it synthesizes systemic leadership moves that embed inquiry, center equity, and build coherence. Its brevity reflects the clarity needed to move from vision to action.

For decades, educational leaders have sought reforms that improve student outcomes. However, many initiatives have failed to scale, struggled with sustainability, or overlooked equity in their implementation (Fullan & Quinn, 2015). This book rejects sweeping, compliance-driven reform and instead embraces improvement science as a framework for user-centered, problem-specific, and equity-focused school improvement.

Improvement science is a way of leading. It provides principles, mindsets, and a structure for disciplined inquiry that supports both depth and scale. The benefits are clear: It builds system-wide knowledge, develops shared ownership, motivates innovation, fosters adaptive strategies based on real-world practice, and maintains an equity-focused commitment to continuous improvement (Deming, 1982, 1994; Langley et al., 2009; Lewis, 2015). However, these benefits require intentional leadership that sets improvement efforts in motion *and* creates the conditions for them to become the cultural mores of the organization.

- Culture must support improvement. If risk-taking, learning, and adaptation are not embedded in daily practice, improvement efforts won't take hold.
- Leadership must model inquiry. If district and school leaders are not actively modeling, engaged, and following through with supporting disciplined inquiry, staff will see improvement science as just another passing trend.
- Equity must remain central. If systems are not improved to accelerate learning for everyone—especially those on the wrong side of equity gaps and furthest from educational justice—change will fall short of meaningful improvement.

Superintendents, principals, and other educational leaders must foster an improvement culture where inquiry is the norm, risk-taking is encouraged, and betterment is woven into *the way we do things around here* (Seppala & Cameron, 2015). This requires leaders to ask themselves hard questions:

- Does our staff see improvement as integral to their role or as compliance tasks?
- Have we created a system where it is safe to try, fail, and learn?
- Do our structures, routines, and decision-making reinforce the equity outcomes we are seeking to advance?

▶ VISION-IMPLEMENTATION GAP: EQUITY-FOCUSED COHERENCE

This culminating chapter tackles a different version of the vision–implementation gap. It's not about launching improvement but ensuring it lives on coherently.

This is the vision–implementation gap for leading system-wide coherence:

- *Vision*: Leaders want the daily work of schools and districts to reflect shared equity-centered improvement that is coherent across the system yet customized to the unique context of each school and department.
- *Implementation Gap*: In practice, many schools and districts default to fragmented, episodic, and surface-level improvement that lacks alignment, sustainability, and depth needed for systemic growth.

It's a challenge to build a culture and systems where that vision is integrated into everyday leadership, internalized, enacted by staff, and sustained across leadership and staffing transitions. Improvement science offers principles, processes, and tools, but those have the greatest impact in a positive, empowering, supportive, and improvement-oriented culture.

▶ STRATEGIES FOR CLOSING THE VISION-IMPLEMENTATION GAP

To close the vision–implementation gap, leaders should consider three key areas:

1. Embed continuous improvement into leadership culture and routines
2. Position equity as the purpose of system improvement
3. Build system-wide structures for collaboration and coherence

Strategy 1: Embed Continuous Improvement into Leadership Culture and Routines

This first strategy is about the leader learning and living what they expect from others. When I was a student in the principal program at the University of Washington, we had a mantra: *You can't lead what you don't know.* In other words, we must do, teach, and lead the work, not just assign it. We also need to align the work to a shared vision, make improvement part of everyday leadership practice, and model inquiry through our own cycles of learning.

Many improvement efforts remain separate from daily leadership routines, reserved for in-services, retreats, or strategic planning meetings. This sets up improvement work to feel like an *extra task* or occasional agenda item rather than a core leadership responsibility. Also, improvement leadership is often what gets pushed aside during busier times. The urgent overpowers the important.

But Deming (1994) reminds us that improvement is not a one-off. It is a discipline that leaders must intentionally embed into their own practice and prioritize. In fact, Bryk et al. (2015) emphasize that leaders must engage in structured inquiry themselves to create the culture for staff to do the same. We help make leadership strategies part of our culture and routines by:

- Using our Theory of Action statement to connect equity-focused actions to the shared vision.

- Making improvement a standing agenda item in all leadership meetings.
- Ensuring district and school leadership teams run their own PDSA cycles to model an inquiry stance, grow their own leadership, and build capacity to support others.

Strategy 2: Position Equity as The Purpose of Improvement

We lead with our why. For me, equity—ensuring everyone has what they need to succeed—is the heart of my work. It is a stance of service and responsibility. As leaders, it is important to be able to articulate our own moral imperative and make it overt, while also co-creating a collective purpose. When equity is positioned as our purpose, it guides how we define problems, design solutions, and measure progress.

Yet, in many systems equity work is treated as a separate initiative rather than the foundation of improvement. Bryk (2015) emphasizes that improvement efforts must be explicitly designed to close equity gaps in addition to improving overall performance. Similarly, Fullan & Quinn (2015) found that districts that center equity in their improvement culture are more likely to sustain change more effectively over time.

These findings reinforce the need for leadership moves that operationalize equity by centering equity in how systems improve:

- Frame problems of practice through equity-focused data and empathy work to identify and address systemic disparities.
- Ensure all improvement cycles include equity measures there are qualitative (such as empathy interviews, observations, and process efficacy) and quantitative (such as outcome and survey data).
- Establish consistent, structured time for teams at all levels to reflect on the real impact of their strategies on all students, including those in the gaps.

Strategy 3: Build System-Wide Structures for Collaboration and Coherence

Establishing structures is the way we don't leave this work to chance. This is where the rubber meets the road, where we walk our talk. One of my former superintendents used to say, "What gets calendared gets done." Structures make the difference between improvement work that lives and breathes across a system versus work that quietly fades when we get busy, distracted, or hijacked by the tyranny of the urgent.

Systems naturally default to silos and fragmentation, so achieving collaboration and coherence requires persistence. Without intentional and scheduled structures for knowledge-sharing and joint problem-solving, even effective practices remain contained in small pockets. Deming (1994) argued that systems do not improve unless learning is systematically shared. Structures like networked improvement communities (NICs), cross-leadership, sharing and cross-team routines accelerate improvement by leveraging collective expertise and reinforcing a collective approach (Bryk et al., 2015).

When structures are intentionally designed, calendared, taught, and supported, they promote collaborative learning, system alignment, and long-term capacity.

- Establish regular district-wide improvement networks where teams come together to share learning, provide feedback loops, and align efforts across schools and departments, ensuring leaders are actively engaged in them.
- Facilitate cross-school and cross-department leadership networks that focus on shared problems of practice using consistent routines, such as data-sharing, learning walks, and artifact review (including student work, outcome data, and improvement process artifacts), to normalize transparent learning across teams, build leadership capacity, and calibrate leadership expectations.
- Help leaders build capacity at all levels within their schools and departments through structures like mentorship, co-facilitation, coaching, and training in processes and tools to ensure improvement efforts are not dependent on

individuals and can sustain momentum through leadership transitions.

I'll share an example of using structures to reinforce collaboration and coherence. In the two districts where I served as superintendent, we wanted to schedule and see connections across improvement teams in our district, so we created a single calendar to help us align the work of individual collaborative teams, school leadership teams, the district leadership team, the administrative team, and the board. Each level had a distinct cadence:

- Individual teams met weekly
- School leadership teams met monthly
- District leadership team met quarterly
- Admin team met ahead of those cycles to preview and plan
- Board reports were scheduled to follow district-level cycles so the board could hear what teams were learning and support what they were working on

Mapping this on a single page helped us coordinate timelines, surface connections, get in front of the work instead of reacting to it, follow through with our commitment to collaboration, and ensure there were no surprises. Even though we mapped out a plan, we were flexible, honoring site-based variation while building system-wide coherence.

To support improvement-focused district governance, we created an Annual Board Calendar as a tool to embed the district's improvement focus into the board's work throughout the year. It looked a bit different in each district, but we built it in three phases:

1. Understand the Tradition
   My secretary and I reviewed three years of board agendas to identify patterns, such as what topics appeared when. In this phase, I also asked the board about traditions they wanted to keep and I gathered their preferences.

2. Align to Board Policy
   My secretary and I reviewed every policy, keeping track of required reports and actions. Some were clearly defined ("report biannually"), while others were vague ("report periodically"), so we defined what made sense. Then we talked to district leaders to learn when each report naturally fit into their workflow. For example, our special services director already compiled restraint data each June for the state. So we scheduled that board report for June to align with her process, not add to it. We plugged the policy requirements into the calendar tool. This helped ensure compliance and revealed gaps where reports had previously fallen off the radar.
3. Make Space for What Matters
   This gets to the point of the example. Once traditional and required items were scheduled, we stepped back and asked: How do we make room for board improvement-focused learning, not just policy-related updates? To focus on each aspect of our vision, we built quarterly presentations aligned to the district's ABC data (Attendance, Behavior, and Course Performance) to show progress on our academic goals. We added monthly recognition and student voice features aligned to our character goals. We embedded the strategic plan and superintendent evaluation throughout the year to mirror the model and timelines used in other staff evaluations.

   Now that we had calendared our vision and improvement focus areas, we had a new problem. By simply adding these items, we were not shifting focus, and we were in for some very long meetings! To free space, we shifted certain compliance reports from live presentations to written memos. Board members and the public still had access and could ask questions, but this protected *airtime* for more improvement-focused, vision-aligned learning that required our collaboration. We also coded the agenda items to our vision and improvement focus areas. This helped us spot imbalances, like a tendency to focus on academics over character.

To expand improvement-focused district governance, I organized my weekly board updates around our vision and improvement priorities. Each weekly update used the vision and priorities as headings, and I bulleted my actions under the appropriate heading, showing how my work directly supported our vision and improvement focus. (It was also a great self-check to make sure I was balancing my time across our vision and focus areas.) I used consistent formatting, color coding, and arrows pointing back to our vision/priorities graphic. This helped board members track progress and tangibly see alignment between our stated vision, priorities, and actions.

The same structure showed up in district leadership agendas, admin meetings, and communications. We used the vision heading, priorities graphic, color coding, and shared language everywhere. Schools began using the same structure for their newsletters, organizing staff shoutouts around priority areas and even color-coding agendas. The visual became a practical tool for coherence across the system. Staff knew the vision, priorities, and how the work they were doing explicitly connected to it.

▶ CONCLUSION

Let's hear from our three leaders about their experiences with sustaining coherent, systemic improvement.

Kyle: "We realized improvement science wasn't working because it was always treated as an event rather than a habit. Now, every leadership meeting starts with an inquiry-based check-in—what are we learning? What needs refinement?"

Melanie: "We stopped treating improvement science as something staff 'do' and instead made it how we lead every day."

Shawn: "Our leadership team uses improvement cycles at every level—if we want staff to see this as a normal way of working, we have to model it ourselves."

Take a moment to reflect on the journey from this book, moving from foundations to action as we walked through the *why*, *what*, and *how* of leading equity-focused improvement. Each Part has built toward one goal: supporting equity-focused leaders in closing the vision–implementation gaps that limit the impact of an improvement culture.

- Part 1—The Why: Framed equity, leadership values, and workplace culture as the foundation for improvement.
- Part 2—The What: Introduced improvement theory, principles, and paradigm shifts necessary for leading change.
- Part 3—The How: Offered structured processes and strategies to close gaps in culture, ownership, vulnerability, and coherence.

As Bryk (2018) reminds us, the role of superintendent and principal is not to enforce. We are called to lead an ever-evolving profession that learns together, grows together, and continuously improves in pursuit of equity. "Advancing better, more equitable educational outcomes—that is our shared aim. The improvement principles, they are our guidance system. And learning together, this is the work of a profession getting better at what it does" (p. 19).

The heart of improvement work is about equity and improving the experiences of our students and staff. The most pressing student equity gaps cannot be addressed through compliance or charisma. They'll be solved through the science of disciplined inquiry and collective learning that happens in a culture of trust, owned by the people closest to the work, and led with courage.

▶ PERSONAL VISION AND THEORY OF ACTION

My vision is to *close equity gaps by helping educational leaders improve systems.*

My theory of action (described more fully in Chapter 6 and Appendix 2.13) outlines how I believe that can happen in an *if–then–which will* format.

If educational leaders cultivate positive workplace cultures grounded in shared ownership and vulnerability, **then** schools and districts will sustain coherent, continuous improvement **which will** lead to solving the most pressing student equity gaps at scale.

—Marci Shepard

I hope this book is in service of that vision and theory of action. I invite you to join me in this work, or to craft your own vision and theory of action as a reminder to lead with both heart and science.

> **REFLECTION QUESTIONS**
>
> *Final Reflection: 3-2-1*
> 1. Key Takeaways from the Book: What are 3 ideas from this book that resonate most with you and will influence your equity-focused leadership moving forward?
> 2. Action Planning: What are 2 specific actions you will take to foster a culture of collaborative, continuous improvement in your school or district?
> 3. Commitment to Growth: What is 1 way you will continue to grow your leadership practice using principles of improvement?

CHAPTER 10 TRY THIS: BE THE LEADER WHO CHANGES THE SYSTEM

Throughout this book, we've explored how improvement science can transform leadership, culture, and outcomes for students. We've examined the barriers that impede well-intentioned reforms and how ownership, vulnerability, and a culture of inquiry are key ingredients for authentic, continuous improvement.

This is your moment to reflect on what kind of leader you will be. Will you lead from compliance or curiosity? Will you create mandates or momentum? Will you chase quick wins or build lasting change?

 It starts with YOU! Use this activity to close your own vision-implementation gap and be the leader who changes the system.

1. Vision: Define Your Leadership Legacy

Imagine it's five years from now. You are about to receive an award for transformational leadership in education. The room is filled with your staff, students, families, and community members. As they introduce you, they reflect on the impact you've had.

What do you want them to say?
- How did your leadership change the way continuous improvement is embedded in your school or district?
- What did staff say about the culture you built?
- How did students' experiences improve because of the work you led?
- How did your leadership advance equity?

Write your leadership legacy statement:

We are honored to give this award for leading in a way that ...

_____
_____
_____

2. Shift Your Mindset

Identify the mindset shift you need to make to bring that vision to reality.
- What do I need to unlearn, rethink, or let go of to lead in this way?
- What leadership habit must I strengthen?

My leadership mindset shift:

_____
_____
_____

3. Take Action

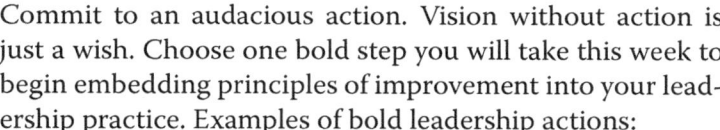

Commit to an audacious action. Vision without action is just a wish. Choose one bold step you will take this week to begin embedding principles of improvement into your leadership practice. Examples of bold leadership actions:
- Empower your team—Identify a key decision or improvement effort and shift ownership to staff. (Remember to build capacity and support the shift!)
- Make vulnerability safe—Publicly share a challenge you've faced, and what you learned from it.
- Center equity—Analyze a problem of practice. Press in until you get to the root of the equity gap and improve the system that contributes to it.
- Change a structure—Revise an ongoing leadership meeting format, data process, or collaboration routine to better reflect an improvement culture.

My bold leadership action:
_____
_____
_____

Use your legacy, mindset shift, and bold action to close the gap between your vision and implementation. Equity-focused leadership comes to life through integrity—alignment between what we believe, say, and do.

▶ LEADERSHIP EXAMPLE: BUILDING AN ALIGNED SYSTEM FROM THE BOTTOM UP

When people think about a school district's strategic plan and evaluation system, they often picture a top-down model—something created at the central office with schools aligning to the district plan and teams aligning to the school plan. In my district, however, we flipped that model. We designed a system of reciprocal accountability, where leaders were responsible for serving those closest to students, not the other way around.

We had a theory of action that flowed from the central office to principals, to teachers, and to students, showing how leadership responsibility for providing support moved through the system. However, the way we built our annual focus started from the bottom up, driven by the needs of students (Center for Educational Leadership, 2014).

Students. Everything began with students. If we wanted meaningful change, we had to go beyond focusing on overall progress to focusing on students who were being left behind. In Chapter 9, I shared an example about our gap-closing goals. Traditionally, student goals focused on raising averages (e.g., 80% of students will reach proficiency). But that approach allowed the same students to be missed year after year. We shifted the question to, "Who are the students in the gap, and how do we close it?" (e.g., If 60% of a student group was meeting the standard while 40% were not, our goal became, "We will close the gap from 40% to 20%.") This reframing meant teams had to identify the root causes, understand the students being underserved, and center those students in our inquiry.

Teachers. Once student learning goals were set, teachers aligned their professional goals with the needs of their students. The shift was from *What do I want to work on this year?* to *What do my students need me to work on?* This reflected a servant leadership mindset. Teachers then reviewed their evaluation criteria and identified which professional standards would help them improve their practice in service of what their students needed. This helped evaluations feel less like another disconnected task, as student, teacher, and team growth were part of one connected effort.

Principals. Principals engaged in the same process at the school level. They examined teacher and team goals across their buildings, looking for patterns and trends. Instead of setting leadership goals based on personal preference, they took a servant-leadership stance and asked themselves, *What do teachers need from me to better support their students?* Then they identified a leadership evaluation standard so that principals' professional learning, coaching, and support from the central office were directly tied to school support.

Central office. At the district level, we mirrored the same approach. Instead of deciding what we thought schools needed or what we wanted to work on, the Superintendent's Cabinet (SALT) reviewed principal goals and identified common needs across schools. We asked: *What do our schools need from us?* Based on those needs, we looked at our own evaluation frameworks and selected criteria that would help us grow in ways that would help us better serve school leaders and schools.

Even my own superintendent evaluation followed this pattern. Instead of choosing goals based on what *I* wanted to work on, I focused on what central office leaders and principals needed from me to better serve departments and schools.

In the end, our entire system—from students to teachers to principals to central office—was aligned from the bottom up:

- *Student* goals focused on closing equity gaps.
- *Teachers'* professional goals were directly tied to student learning needs.
- *Principals'* leadership goals addressed patterns in teacher needs.
- *District* leadership goals were tied to school and principal support needs.

Instead of evaluation, collaborative inquiry, professional learning, and strategic improvement focus areas feeling like separate efforts, they were one unified work. We built a system where everyone was focused on gap closing goals and could clearly follow the throughline from their work to student impact.

We found a way to systematize our core value of servant leadership by building a system that wasn't top-down but was driven by and focused on students. We maximized impact through aligned, coherent, equity-focused leadership for continuous improvement (Figure 10.1).

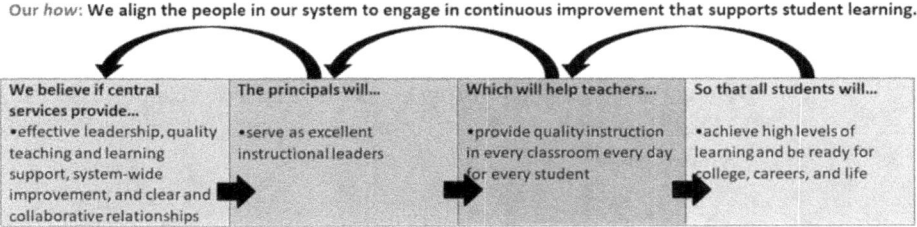

Figure 10.1 Our District's Theory of Action to Align the System for Student Impact.

▶ FINAL THOUGHTS: KEEP LEADING, KEEP LEARNING

This is not the end. Continuous improvement is about progress, not perfection. It's about turning values and vision into action that creates equitable outcomes, nurtures a positive culture, and builds capacity for system-wide improvement. It's about getting better, driven by a relentless pursuit of equity and excellence that refuses to accept the status quo.

As you, your team, and your system continuously get better on behalf of those you serve, embrace the journey. Find joy in the work. This is where the science of improvement meets the heart of leadership.

References

Bryk, A. S. (2015). 2014 AERA distinguished lecture: Accelerating how we learn to improve. *Educational Researcher, 44*(9), 467–477.

Bryk, A. S. (2018). *Advancing quality in continuous improvement.* Paper presented at *the Carnegie Summit*, Stanford, CA.

Bryk, A. S., Gomez, L. M., Gunrow, A., & LeMahieu, P. G. (2015). *Learning to improve: How America's schools can get better and getting better.* Cambridge, MA: Harvard Education Publishing.

Center for Educational Leadership. (2014). *Creating your theory of action for districtwide teaching and learning improvement* (Adapted by the University of Washington Center for Educational Leadership and Meredith I. Honig, commissioned by the Wallace Foundation). University of Washington. https://k-12leadership.org/tools/creating-a-theory-of-action/

Deming, W. E. (1982). *Out of the crisis* (2nd ed.). Cambridge, MA: Massachusetts Institute of Technology, Center for Advanced Engineering Study.

Deming, W. E. (1994). *The new economics for industry, government, education* (2nd ed.). Cambridge, MA: Massachusetts Institute of Technology, Center for Advanced Engineering Study.

Fullan, M., & Quinn, J. (2015). *Coherence: The right drivers in action for schools, districts, and systems*. Ontario: Corwin Press and the Ontario Principals' Council.

Langley, G. J., Moen, R. D., Nolan, K. M., Nolan, T. W., Norman, C. L., & Provost, L. P. (2009). *The improvement guide* (2nd ed.). San Francisco, CA: Jossey-Bass.

Lewis, C. (2015). What is improvement science? Do we need it in education? *Educational Researcher, 44*(1), 54–61.

Seppala, E., & Cameron, A. (December 1, 2015). Proof that positive work cultures are more productive. *Harvard Business Review*. https://hbr.org/2015/12/proofthat-positive-work-cultures-are-more-productive

Icebreaker Group Activity Facilitation Guide

Appendix 1

1. Post the Icebreaker Prompt.
   - Display the chapter's opening prompt.
2. Individual Reflection (2–3 min.)
   - Have participants reflect quietly, jotting down thoughts on the prompt.
3. Discussion Formats (Choose One or Mix and Match):
   - Think–Pair–Share
     - Participants pair up and discuss their reflections (3–5 min.).
     - Invite a few pairs to share key takeaways with the whole group.
   - Small-Group Discussion
     - Groups of 3–4 share experiences and identify common themes.
     - Have one person summarize small-group insights for the whole group.
   - Whole-Group Discussion
     - Ask for volunteers to share one key takeaway from their reflection.
     - Write themes on chart paper or a whiteboard to visualize patterns.

4. Debrief and Transition to Chapter (3 min.)
    - Connect to Learning Target: What common themes emerged?
    - Set the Stage for the Chapter
        - Connect to the purpose: "Now that we've reflected on the [topic of prompt], we'll explore how improvement science can help leaders [share the big idea of the chapter topic and learning target]."
        - Build inquiry and ownership: What wondering are you carrying into this chapter?

Chapter 6
Try This—Tools for Leading Disciplined Inquiry

▶ 2.1 ASSEMBLE A TEAM CHECK-IN

Use this tool to assess whether your improvement team is inclusive and positioned for success.

1. What level is your improvement effort focused on?

☐ Grade-level or content team
☐ School-level team
☐ District department-level team
☐ District-level team
☐ Other _____

What is the problem area and scope of the problem you are addressing?

_____
_____
_____

2. Who is on the team?

List all team members and their roles (e.g., teacher, coach, principal, student, family member, central office leader):

TABLE A2.1 Team Members and Their Roles

Name	Role	Perspective/Expertise

Is this team representative of those experiencing or affected by the issue and/or responsible for implementing the solution?

☐ Yes
☐ Somewhat—Considerations needed: _____

☐ No—Action needed: _____

3. Leadership Involvement

☐ A leader serves as a facilitator
☐ A leader is actively engaged in the team's inquiry work
☐ A leader is present, providing support, and championing the project
☐ Leadership presence or support is limited

What is the leader's role in this team?

_____

How can leadership engagement be strengthened?

_____

4. Structures for Success

- ☐ The team has regular meeting times and clear routines
- ☐ Improvement work is part of existing structures (e.g., PLCs, department meetings, staff meetings, collaboration time)
- ☐ The team has access to the process, relevant data, tools, and resources

What supports or adjustments are needed to strengthen team function?

_____

_____

5. Equity and Action

- ☐ Norms are established and ensure all team members are heard, valued, and influence decisions

What is one step you can take to strengthen this team's foundation for improvement?

_____

_____

_____

PHASE 1: UNDERSTAND THE PROBLEM AND THE SYSTEM THAT PRODUCES IT

▶ 2.2 IDENTIFY AN ISSUE TOOL

Use this tool to identify one problem area you would like to explore.

Ask yourself: What is one inequitable outcome that keeps you up at night?

Note: At this point, your problem may not be narrow and focused. That will take shape after you use strategies to deeply understand the problem. For now, identify a problem area to explore.

Copyright material from Marci Shepard (2026), *Where the Science of Improvement Meets the Heart of Leadership*, Routledge

Problem Area:
_____
_____

Check your issue to ensure your problem is:

- Phrased as a negative—Clearly defines the issue as a problem
- Not disguising solutions as problems—Does not say what should be done
- Not placing blame—Focuses on patterns and systems, not individuals
- Actionable—Eventually leads to actions that are within the team's control

▶ 2.3 DATA ANALYSIS PROTOCOL

This protocol helps teams explore data, identify patterns, and inform hypotheses about the root causes of issues.

Step 1: Data Overview and Understanding

- What dataset are we analyzing?
- What is the timeframe of the data?
- Who is represented in the data?
- What is being measured?

Step 2: Notice—Identify Patterns and Trends

- What do we see? (Record observations without interpretation or judgment)
  - Examples: Trends, differences between groups, variations

Step 3: Wonder—Generate Questions

- What questions emerge from the patterns?
- Why are certain student groups outperforming or underperforming?

- What additional data and information do we need to deepen our understanding?

Step 4: Interpret—Hypothesize Root Causes

- What might be contributing to these trends?

What additional data or information is needed to confirm or challenge these hypotheses?

▶ 2.4 FIVE WHYS PROTOCOL

Use this tool to get to the root cause of a problem.

Note: Dig deeper into each why instead of going wider by listing different reasons.

Problem:
_____
_____

1. Why is this a problem?
   _____
   _____
   _____

2. Why is that?
   _____
   _____
   _____

3. Why is that?
   _____
   _____
   _____

4. Why is that?

_____

_____

_____

5. Why is that?

_____

_____

_____

Root cause:

_____

_____

_____

Check:
- ☐ Do we want to do the protocol again to follow another line of *whys*?
- ☐ Is the root cause in the team's control?
- ☐ Can it be solved through the actions of adults in our system?
- ☐ Does it make sense—is it a logical connection to the problem?
- ☐ If we address the root cause, will it solve or improve the problem?

▶ 2.5 FISHBONE DIAGRAM

Use this tool to identify multiple lines of reasoning that point to the root causes of a problem.

1. Write the problem statement at the "head" of the fishbone.
2. Create major "bones" (categories) of contributing factors (e.g., processes, policies, resources, training, student factors).

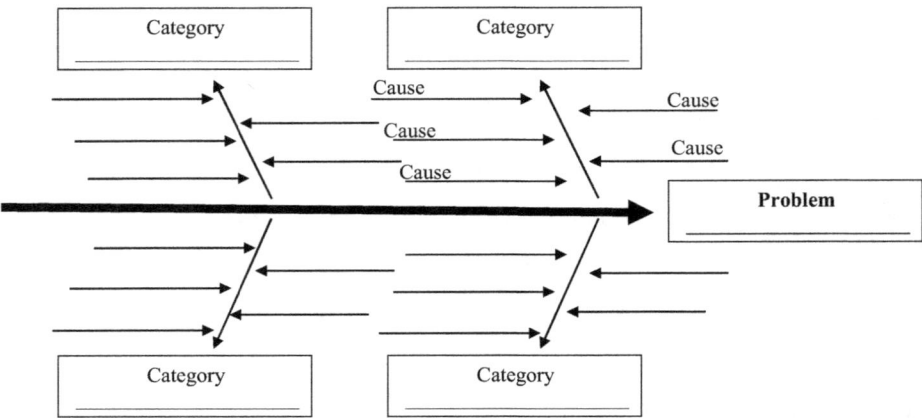

Figure A2.1 Fishbone Diagram.

3. Brainstorm sub-causes under each category by asking "Why?" multiple times.
4. Ask:
   • What trends or patterns do we see across multiple sources?
   • Which root causes are within our control?
   • Which root cause(s) would make the biggest impact?
5. Select the most impactful cause(s) to focus on.

▶ 2.6 PROCESS MAPPING

Use this tool to understand the system producing the problem.

1. Identify the system related to the problem—What process produces or influences this outcome?
2. Have each team member sketch their understanding of the process individually. (No peeking!)
3. Compare team members' maps through a gallery walk. Notice:
   • Where do interpretations differ?
   • What are the similarities and differences in how we see the process?
   • Do we all experience the system the same way?
   • Where are the breakdowns, bottlenecks, or inconsistencies happening?

4. Create a shared process map with:
   - Compiled understanding of the process (sticky notes can help so you can move the boxes around)
   - Steps and decision points
   - Time duration of each step
   - Roles, who is involved, or who is responsible for each step
5. Analyze the map for improvement opportunities:
   - Where are the breakdowns, bottlenecks, lack of clarity, or inconsistencies happening?

▶ 2.7 EMPATHY INTERVIEWS

The purpose of an empathy interview is to listen to those experiencing the problem to better understand their needs, feelings, and perspectives.

Before: Steps for Planning Empathy Interviews

1. Identify whose perspectives need to be heard e.g., (students, staff, families). Consider diverse voices and experiences.
2. Brainstorm questions that will help the team understand the problem and surface root causes contributing to it. Narrow the list to approximately five questions. Craft open-ended questions that invite storytelling (e.g., "Tell me about a time…").
3. Determine who will conduct the interviews. *Note: High trust is needed for honest responses.*
4. Plan for note-taking and sharing insights (use actual quotes).

During: Conducting Empathy Interviews

Person interviewed (include role and other pertinent information):

Interview questions:
1.
2.
3.
4.
5.

Note: Include exact words and phrases as much as possible.

After: Reflecting on Empathy Interviews

- What did we hear?
- How do users experience the system?
- Where do users identify system breakdowns or rough patches?
- What emotions, frustrations, or needs are emerging?
- What are we learning about the root causes that contribute to the problem?
- Is there someone else we need to talk to?

▶ 2.8 RESEARCH AND EVIDENCE TO UNDERSTAND THE PROBLEM

Use this tool to explore research-based practices (proven strategies) and evidence-based practices (what has worked for others) to deepen your understanding of root causes and connect your local challenge to broader knowledge in the field.

1. Define Your Focus

What is the specific problem area or issue you are trying to understand more deeply?

_____
_____
_____

2. Search for Relevant Research and Evidence

Check multiple sources:
- Research articles
- Improvement science case studies or process stories
- Reports or white papers from trusted education organizations
- Practitioner resources
- Other schools or districts engaging in similar efforts

3. What Did You Find?

Summarize 2–3 key ideas, findings, or strategies related to your problem of practice.

TABLE A2.2 Summarize Information from Research and Evidence Sources

Source	Insight or Strategy	Evidence Type (research- or evidence-based)

4. Make Meaning as a Team

Discuss:
- What insights feel relevant or transferable to our context?
- What surprised or challenged our assumptions?
- How might we apply or adapt these ideas?

_____

_____

_____

5. Connect to Root Cause Analysis

How does this research- or practice-based evidence inform your understanding of the root causes of your problem?

_____

_____

_____

▶ 2.9 AFFINITY PROTOCOL

This protocol helps teams analyze insights from multiple data sources so they can identify key themes and zero in on a specific, defined problem.

1. Capture insights from different data sources on sticky notes.

2. Cluster sticky notes into themes based on commonalities.

3. Label categories and identify major patterns.

4. Discuss and document key takeaways across themes.

5. Use findings to hone in on the team's specific problem.

Based on the affinity chart, determine which problem area you should prioritize first. Ask:

- Which part of the problem can we most effectively address right now?
- Where can we have the greatest impact?
- What improvement efforts are within our control?

Finalize the narrowed, specific problem:

_____
_____
_____

PHASE 2: FOCUS COLLECTIVE EFFORTS

▶ 2.10 SET AN AIM

This template helps teams create a clear, measurable, and time-bound aim statement to guide shared understanding of targeted outcomes.

TABLE A2.3 Set an Aim

Component	Guiding Question	Your Response
What	What specific root cause do we want to improve?	
Who	Who will benefit, or who is the target of this aim?	

TABLE A2.3 (Continued)

Component	Guiding Question	Your Response
How Much and How Measured	How will we know the change is an improvement (*from* baseline outcome *to* goal outcome), and how will we measure progress?	
By When	By when do you plan to meet the aim?	

Final Aim Statement (Put It All Together)

"By [when], we will improve [what/root cause] for [who/target group] from [baseline data] to [goal data] as measured by [how we will track improvement]."

By _____, we will improve _____ for _____ _____ from _____ to _____ as measured by _____.

▶ **2.11 DRIVER DIAGRAM**

Use this tool to identify and make connections between an improvement aim, key drivers, and change ideas aligned to achieve the goal.

1. Copy your aim statement (using the template from Appendix 2.10) into the box on the far left.
2. Fill in the primary drivers—These are the aspects of the system that need to change to impact the aim. (There are two in this example. Each problem will have a different number of primary drivers.)

3. Fill in the secondary drivers—These are more specific opportunities for change in the system. (There may be one or more secondary drivers for each primary driver.)

(Leave Change Ideas blank for now. We will add them later in Phase 3.)

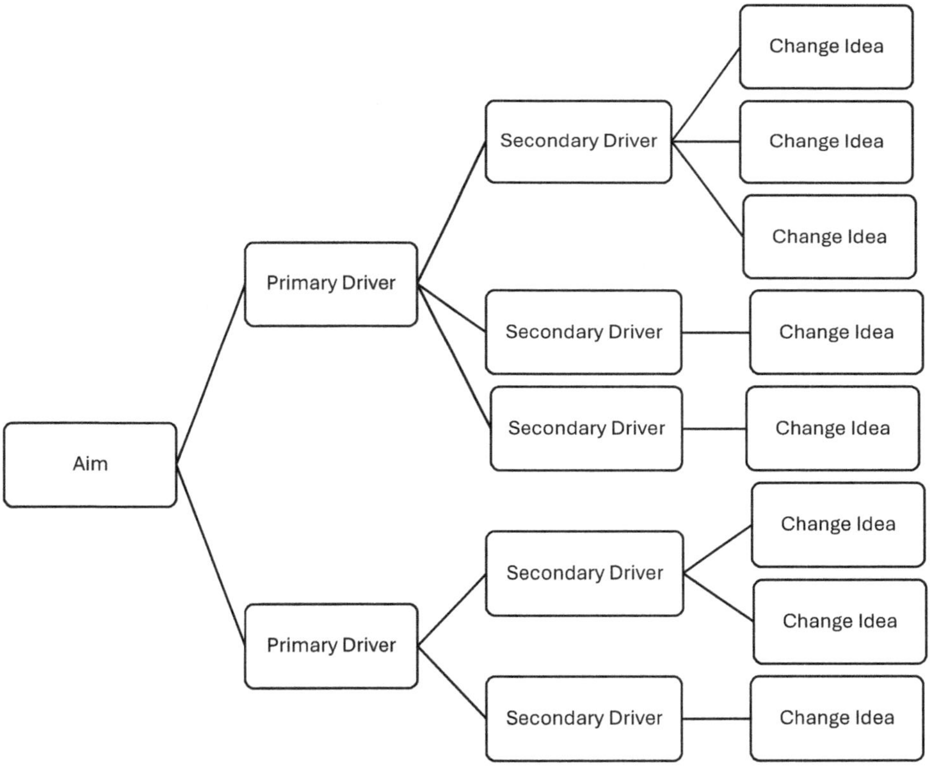

Figure A2.2 Driver Diagram

PHASE 3: GENERATE IDEAS FOR CHANGE

▶ 2.12 CHANGE IDEAS

Use this tool to guide your team in generating, organizing, and prioritizing actionable change ideas on the Driver Diagram (Appendix 2.11) that connect to your drivers and support your improvement aim.

1. Brainstorm Change Ideas

Use the prompts below to generate a range of change ideas. These should be specific actions that could disrupt the status quo and influence one or more secondary drivers. Brainstorm change ideas based on:
- Research—What strategies or interventions does the evidence suggest?
- Practice—What have others tried that worked in similar contexts?
- Design—What creative or locally personalized ideas might work here

2. Add Change Ideas to Your Driver Diagram

- Return to your existing Driver Diagram (Appendix 2.11).
- Write each change idea under the corresponding driver.
- Draw arrows to show logical connections:
- One change idea may influence multiple drivers.
- One driver may support multiple change ideas.
- Group or bundle related change ideas, if appropriate.

3. Select a Change Idea to Test First

Not all change ideas can be tested at once.
a. Evaluate your options and select one high-impact change idea (or bundle) to start testing:
- Is it aligned with a key driver?
- Is it specific, actionable, and measurable?

Copyright material from Marci Shepard (2026), Where the Science of Improvement Meets the Heart of Leadership, Routledge

- What is the potential impact (high, medium, or low)?
- How feasible is it (resources, time, support)?
- Can we learn from it quickly?
  b. Choose the change idea (or bundle) you will test.

▶ 2.13 THEORY OF ACTION

Use this tool to connect and communicate how your strategy supports the vision.

Write a Theory of Action statement that summarizes how a change idea is expected to drive improvement.

"*If we (change idea),* **then** *that will lead to (driver),* **which will** *impact (aim).*"

If we (change idea)

___

Then that will lead to (driver)

___

Which will impact (aim)

___

Review your Theory of Action to ensure the cause-and-effect is clear.

Leadership Communication

Where will you use this Theory of Action to connect actions to the vision (e.g., meetings, professional development, board presentations, community events, newsletters, social media)?

___

___

___

___

PHASE 4: TEST AND BUILD EVIDENCE

▶ 2.14 PDSA-PLAN

Plan the change idea.

TABLE A2.4 PDSA–Plan

What is your change idea?			
What do you predict will happen?			
Plan to conduct the test.			
Tasks	Who—Person(s) responsible	When	Where
1.			
2.			
3.			
4.			

▶ 2.15 PDSA-DO

Test the change idea.

TABLE A2.5 PDSA–Do

Process Measures (Change Idea)	Outcome Measures (Aim)
What did you do to implement the change?	What results(s) did you collect or observe?
Process data:	Outcome data:

▶ 2.16 PDSA–STUDY

Learn about the change idea.
Was the cycle carried out as planned? What happened during the testing phase?

_____

_____

_____

Data summary or evidence (as needed): Charts, student work, quotes, etc.

TABLE A2.6 PDSA–Study

Process Measures (Change Idea)	Outcome Measures (Aim)
Did the implementation of the change go as planned?	What results(s) did you collect or observe?
Did the process measures match your prediction(s)?	Did the outcome measures match your prediction(s)?
What did you learn or experience that was surprising or different than expected?	What did you collect or observe that was surprising or different than expected?

▶ 2.17 PDSA-ACT

Make a decision about what to do with the change idea test results.

- ☐ **Adopt** – This idea worked well. We plan to spread or scale it.
- ☐ **Adapt** – This idea has potential. We will revise and test it again.
- ☐ **Abandon** – This idea didn't work or isn't the right fit. We'll test a different idea.

Why did you make this decision? What evidence or learning from the test informed your choice?

_____

_____

_____

_____

_____

_____

PHASE 5: SPREAD AND SCALE

▶ 2.18 USE THE SPREAD AND SCALE DECISION-MAKING TOOL

This tool will help you decide when to spread and scale a change idea.

1. Assess Your Confidence in the Change Idea

Do you strongly believe this change will lead to improvement?
- ☐ High degree of belief that the change idea will lead to improvement
- ☐ Low degree of belief that the change idea will lead to improvement

2. Consider the Cost of Failure

If this change does not work, will it have a large or small negative impact?
☐ Large cost of failure (e.g., major disruption, financial loss, negative student outcomes)
☐ Small cost of failure (e.g., minimal disruption, easy to reverse)

3. Identify Your Organization's Level of Commitment

How committed is your school or district to this change?

☐ No commitment – We are just exploring the idea.
☐ Some commitment – There is interest, but not widespread buy-in or ownership yet.
☐ Strong commitment – Leadership and staff are invested in making this change work.

4. Determine the Appropriate Spread or Scale

Use your responses in questions 1–3 to complete the table below and determine the right spread for testing or scale for implementation.

TABLE A2.7 Determine the Appropriate Spread or Scale (Langley et al., 2009)

	Belief in Effectiveness	*Failure Cost*	*No Commitment*	*Some Commitment*	*Strong Commitment*
Option A	Low belief	Large cost	Very small-scale test	Very small-scale test	Very small-scale test
Option B	Low belief	Small cost	Very small-scale test	Very small-scale test	Small-scale test
Option C	High belief	Large cost	Very small-scale test	Small-scale test	Large-scale test
Option D	High belief	Small cost	Small-scale test	Large-scale test	Implement

5. Plan Your Next Steps

Based on the table, what level of testing or implementation is next?

☐ Option A: Very small-scale test (try with a small group of students, one class, or a short timeframe)
☐ Option B: Small-scale test (pilot in one grade level, department, or school
☐ Option C: Large-scale test (expand to multiple schools or grade levels)
☐ Option D: Full implementation (system-wide adoption)

To test, run additional PDSA cycles.

To implement, adapt and monitor the strategy in different contexts.

▶ 2.19 NETWORKED IMPROVEMENT COMMUNITY (NIC) SHARED LEARNING TOOL TO SUPPORT SPREADING AND SCALING

This tool supports NIC members in learning across teams, schools, or districts by sharing tested change ideas, comparing contexts, identifying adaptations, and planning for scale. Use this after completing small-scale testing to determine what can be learned and spread more broadly.

1. Summary of Tested Change Idea

TABLE A2.8 Summary of Tested Change Idea

Team/Site (e.g., Grade Level, Content, School, Department	Change Idea Description	Driver Addressed	Targeted Aim

---

Copyright material from Marci Shepard (2026), *Where the Science of Improvement Meets the Heart of Leadership*, Routledge

2. What worked, where, and for whom?

TABLE A2.9 What Worked, Where, and For Whom (Bryk et al., 2015)

What worked?	Where did it work? (e.g., grade level, content, school, department)	For whom did it work? (e.g., specific student groups or demographics)
How do you know? (e.g., process, outcomes, artifacts)	How do you know? (e.g., process, outcomes, artifacts)	How do you know? (e.g., process, outcomes, artifacts)

3. How did local conditions influence implementation and outcomes?

_____
_____
_____

4. Emerging patterns, promising practices, and pitfalls

Common patterns:

_____

Promising practices:

_____

Copyright material from Marci Shepard (2026), *Where the Science of Improvement Meets the Heart of Leadership*, Routledge

Pitfalls to avoid:

5. What adaptations might be needed for other contexts?

TABLE A2.10 Adaptations for Spread and Scale

Site/Team	Adaptation Needed	Support/Resources Needed	Opportunities for Co-Design or Shared Learning

Appendix 3: Connecting NELP Standards to Improvement Science in Schools and Districts

The National Educational Leadership Preparation (NELP) standards define the knowledge and skills that school- and district-level leaders need to lead effectively across a broad range of leadership domains (NPBEA, 2018). The leadership mindsets, principles, and strategies in this book help aspiring and current leaders bring standards to life.

▶ OVERVIEW OF NELP STANDARDS

The NELP standards are divided into two sets:

- School-Level Standards (for Principals and Building Leaders)
- District-Level Standards (for Superintendents and Central Office Leaders)

Each set of standards consists of eight domains that provide a comprehensive framework for leadership.

For each NELP standard, this appendix:

- Connects improvement science principles to leadership actions
- Links to chapters and leadership strategies from the book

- Provides sample internship activities and discussion prompts to support in-the-field learning and reflection

▶ NELP STANDARD 1: MISSION, VISION, AND IMPROVEMENT

Improvement Science Connection: Vision-Driven Leadership and Systems of Continuous Improvement

Book Connections

- Part 1 (Preface, Chapters 1–2) introduces the improvement science framework (Chapter 1) and key leadership dispositions like systems thinking, reflection, and collaboration that ground vision and improvement work (Chapter 2).
- Part 2 (Chapters 3–5) deepens understanding of *constancy of purpose* and improvement theory (Chapter 3), the principles of disciplined inquiry (Chapter 4), and the mindset shift toward staff as knowledge creators (Chapter 5).
- Part 3 (Chapters 6–10) applies vision and improvement science through a five-phase inquiry process (Chapter 6), casting a clear vision and engaging teams (Chapter 7–8), focusing improvement on equity gaps (Chapter 9), and building coherent, aligned systems that maximize and sustain improvement (Chapter 10).

Examples of Internship Activities

- Facilitate a Vision-Focused Meeting or Learning Session
  - Connects to: Chapter 7, NELP 1.1
  - Intern co-designs and facilitates a meeting introduction that links the district or school vision to team goals and improvement efforts.
- Engage in Strategic Improvement Planning
  - Connects to: Chapters 3, 6, 10, NELP 1.2

- Intern participates in developing or refining a district or school improvement plan using in data, stakeholder input, and iterative cycles of inquiry.
- Analyze and Reflect On Improvement Data
  - Connects to: Chapters 4, 6, 9, NELP 1.2
  - Intern helps lead a team in reviewing outcome or process data to assess whether current strategies are advancing the vision and closing equity gaps.
- Conduct a "Vision-in-Practice" Audit
  - Connects to: Chapters 1, 10, NELP 1.1 & 1.2
  - Intern creates and uses a simple tool to observe how the vision is showing up across schools, departments, meetings, and communications.
- Interview Stakeholders About the Vision and Improvement Work
  - Connects to: Chapters 7, 8, NELP 1.1
  - Intern gathers input from students, staff, or families to understand how they perceive and engage with the system's vision and improvement priorities.
- Contribute to Public Communication of the Vision
  - Connects to: Chapter 7, NELP 1.1
  - Intern drafts communications (e.g., newsletters, board updates, social media) that reinforce the vision and improvement focus.

"Try This" Tools from the Book

- Chapter 1: Build a Workplace Culture for Continuous Improvement
- Chapter 5: Apply the Six Leadership Paradigm Shifts
- Chapter 6: 2.10 Setting an Aim
- Chapter 6: 2.13 Theory of Action
- Chapter 10: Be the Leader Who Changes the System

Intern-Mentor Discussion Prompts

- What is our mission and vision? How do we ensure that our school or district's mission and vision are clear, shared, and connected to improvement efforts?
- What improvement process do we use?
- How do we integrate improvement principles, processes, and tools into the existing work of schools and teams?
- How do we engage teams in identifying problems and using data to determine priority areas for improvement?
- What structures and routines ensure that teams engage in collaborative improvement?

▶ NELP STANDARD 2: ETHICS AND PROFESSIONAL NORMS

Improvement Science Connection: Positive Workplace Culture, Ownership, Vulnerability, and Collaboration

Book Connections

- Part 1 (Preface, Chapters 1–2) explores how to build a positive workplace culture (Chapter 1) and how leadership that models and fosters vulnerability, reflection, and collaboration encourages ethical systems (Chapter 2).
- Part 2 (Chapters 3–5) highlights how leaders learn from failure (Chapter 3), support user-centered and transparent inquiry through NICs (Chapter 4), and shift culture through collaboration, trust, and learning (Chapter 5).
- Part 3 (Chapters 6–10) presents strategies to model professional norms and support reflective practice (Chapters 6–7), create psychological safety for risk-taking (Chapter 9), and sustain ethical, equity-centered systems (Chapter 10).

Examples of Internship Activities

- Identify and Communicate Your Core Values in the Context of Improvement Work
  - Connects to: Chapter 2, NELP 2.1 & 2.3
  - Intern identifies their leadership values and uses them to ground a decision, presentation, or facilitation connected to an ongoing improvement effort (e.g., leading a PLC, presenting a PDSA cycle, or responding to resistance).
- Co-Establish Norms that Promote a Culture of Continuous Improvement
  - Connects to: Chapters 1, 5, 7, NELP 2.1
  - Intern helps a collaborative team co-create or revisit working norms during an improvement training or team launch meeting, explicitly linking them to equity, collaboration, and psychological safety.
- Model Ethical and Reflective Leadership During an Improvement Cycle
  - Connects to: Chapters 2, 3, 9, NELP 2.1 & 2.3
  - Intern leads or co-leads a segment of an inquiry team meeting, modeling vulnerability by sharing a personal learning moment or misstep related to the improvement cycle (e.g., flawed data use, missed voices) and inviting group reflection.
- Build Reflection into Collaborative Inquiry or Improvement Meeting
  - Connects to: Chapters 6, 10, NELP 2.1
  - Intern designs and facilitates a short reflection protocol or closing activity in an inquiry team, PLC, or leadership meeting to surface learning, reinforce norms, or improve future cycles.
- Facilitate an Equity-Centered Ethical Dilemma Protocol for a Stalled Team
  - Connects to: Chapters 5, 9, NELP 2.2
  - Intern identifies a real tension in an improvement group (e.g., lack of engagement from staff, shallow equity practices, or conflict avoidance) and leads a structured discussion using ethical and improvement frameworks.

- Apply a Decision-Making Filter to an Improvement Leadership Choice
  - Connects to: Chapters 5, 6, 9, NELP 2.2
  - Intern uses a values-based or equity-centered decision-making tool to guide an action related to the design, implementation, or communication of an improvement strategy.
- Observe and Reflect on How Leaders Shape Norms During Improvement Work
  - Connects to: Chapters 1, 7, NELP 2.1
  - Intern observes a principal, coach, or central office leader during a meeting related to improvement (e.g., data review, coaching session, PD) and reflects on the leadership moves that reinforced or missed opportunities to model professional norms.

"Try This" Tools from the Book

- Chapter 1: Building a Positive Workplace Culture for Continuous Improvement
- Chapter 2: Identify Your Leadership Values
- Chapter 7: Deepen a Positive Improvement Culture
- Chapter 8: Empower Staff in Continuous Improvement
- Chapter 9: Create Space for Staff Vulnerability

Intern-Mentor Discussion Prompts

- How do we model vulnerability and reflection by sharing mistakes and lessons learned?
- How do we empower staff to take ownership of improvement efforts?
- How do our leadership moves and team norms reflect values that support improvement, such as trust, equity, and collaboration?
- What actions do we take during improvement efforts to foster a culture where staff feel safe taking risks, reflecting openly, and learning from mistakes?

- How are we building structures and routines that help teams develop and uphold shared professional norms?
- How do we navigate ethical dilemmas in improvement work, such as teams focusing on surface-level problems rather than deeper equity issues?

▶ NELP STANDARD 3: EQUITY, INCLUSIVENESS, AND CULTURAL RESPONSIVENESS

Improvement Science Connection: Addressing Student Equity Gaps Through Inquiry and Implementing Culturally Responsive Change Ideas

Book Connections

- Part 1 (Preface, Chapter 2) centers equity as the purpose of system change (Preface) and emphasizes equity-focused leadership (Chapter 2).
- Part 2 (Chapters 3–5) highlights failed reforms and the need for collaborative, user-centered learning structures.
- Part 3 (Chapters 6–10) presents strategies for uncovering systemic inequities through inclusive inquiry and root cause analysis (Chapter 6), building inclusive team cultures that elevate diverse voices (Chapter 7), leading equity-focused inquiry cycles and testing culturally responsive change ideas (Chapter 9), and scaling equity-centered practices using empathy interviews, disaggregated data, and equity-focused outcome measures (Chapter 10).

Examples of Internship Activities

- Analyze Disaggregated Student Data to Identify Equity Gaps
  - Connects to: Chapters 6, 9, NELP 3.2
  - Intern works with school or district teams to examine outcome or process data (e.g., achievement, attendance, discipline) to pinpoint disparities across student groups.

- Conduct Empathy Interviews to Elevate Marginalized Voices
  - Connects to: Chapters 9, 10, NELP 3.1 & 3.3
  - Intern gathers qualitative insight by interviewing students, families, or staff experiencing inequity, ensuring that voices often excluded from system design are heard and valued.
- Lead Root Cause Analysis to Investigate Systemic Inequity
  - Connects to: Chapter 6, NELP 3.1 & 3.2
  - Intern facilitates or participates in using tools like the 5 Whys, fishbone diagrams, or affinity protocols to explore student-centered equity problems and their causes.
- Map the System to Understand Structural Barriers
  - Connects to: Chapters 6, 10, NELP 3.2
  - Intern uses process mapping or driver diagrams to uncover how practices, policies, or routines contribute to inequitable access to resources or opportunities.
- Ensure Inquiry Cycles Address Equity Gaps
  - Connects to: Chapters 4, 6, 9, NELP 3.2
  - Intern helps a collaborative team focus their improvement cycles on disparities, aligning change efforts with real student needs.
- Design and Test Culturally Responsive Change Ideas
  - Connects to: Chapter 9, NELP 3.3
  - Intern supports the testing of change ideas that reflect students' culturally responsive practices.

"Try This" Tools from the Book

- Chapter 6: 2.2 Identify an Issue
- Chapter 6: 2.3 Data Analysis Protocol
- Chapter 6: 2.4 5 Whys Protocol
- Chapter 6: 2.5 Fishbone Diagram
- Chapter 9: Create Space for Staff Vulnerability

Intern-Mentor Discussion Prompts

- How do we identify and address disparities in student experience and outcomes? How do we define problems and test solutions?
- How do we engage those most affected by inequities to help us understand problems and inform solutions?
- How do we ensure that culturally responsive mindsets and practices are reflected in change ideas and the testing of change ideas?
- How do we foster an inclusive, caring culture where diverse perspectives are heard, valued, and used to shape improvement work?
- How do we use system-level tools (like driver diagrams or process tools) to evaluate how our policies, routines, or resources impact and reinforce inequities?

▶ NELP STANDARD 4: LEARNING AND INSTRUCTION

Improvement Science Connection: Using Meaningful Measurements, Data for Learning, and Inquiry for Instructional Improvement

Book Connections

- Part 1 (Preface, Chapters 1–2) introduces the importance of instructional leadership in shaping system-wide improvement (Chapter 2), with a focus on values, reflection, and culture that support student success.
- Part 2 (Chapters 3–5) explores variation in performance and the use of practical, real-time data for improvement (Chapter 4) and the role of educators in sharing knowledge and using meaningful data to drive instructional and professional learning (Chapter 5).
- Part 3 (Chapters 6–10) provides a process and tools for generating and testing instructional change ideas (Chapter 6), user-centered, purposeful measurements (Chapter 8),

disciplined inquiry into student-centered problems (Chapter 9), and creating coherent systems (Chapter 10).

Examples of Internship Activities

- Support Teams in Using PDSA Cycles to Improve Instructional Practice
  - Connects to: Chapters 6, 9, NELP 4.2 & 4
  - Intern co-facilitates an instructional team using Plan-Do-Study-Act cycles to test and refine teaching strategies aligned to student needs.
- Analyze Variation in Instruction Across Classrooms or Schools
  - Connects to: Chapter 4, NELP 4.1 & 4.4
  - Intern helps collect and interpret instructional data to inform instructional improvement (building) or identify patterns and opportunities for system-level improvement across teams, grade levels, or buildings (district).
- Design or Facilitate Data Meetings that Prioritize Learning and Adjustment
  - Connects to: Chapters 4, 5, 8, NELP 4.2 & 4.3
  - Intern leads or supports data discussions focused on diagnosing learning patterns, fostering shared reflection, and driving responsive instructional changes.
- Pilot and Reflect on Small-Scale Formative Assessments to Inform Instruction
  - Connects to: Chapters 4, 8, 9, NELP 4.3
  - Intern collaborates with teachers (building) or leaders (district) to implement short-cycle, team-based assessments that inform instruction and promote student learning without adding assessment overload.
- Use Disciplined Inquiry to Refine Strategies Before Scaling
  - Connects to: Chapters 6, 9, NELP 4.1, 4.2, 4.3
  - Intern supports teams in applying inquiry tools to test instructional ideas in a small setting before district- or school-wide implementation.

- Integrate Improvement Science into Collaborative Team Structures
  - Connects to: Chapters 5, 8, 10 | NELP 4.2 & 4.4
  - Intern supports a collaborative team (building) or NIC (district) to embed routines for reflection, data use, and iterative instructional improvement as part of ongoing professional development.

"Try This" Tools from the Book

- Chapter 6: 2.14 PDSA–Plan
- Chapter 6: 2.15 PDSA–Do
- Chapter 6: 2.16 PDSA–Study
- Chapter 6: 2.17 PDSA–Act
- Chapter 6: 2.12 Change Ideas

Intern-Mentor Discussion Prompts

- How do we support educators in using data-driven, iterative approaches, like PDSA cycles, to improve instruction and student supports?
- How do we/might we integrate cycles of inquiry into instructional improvement practices?
- How do we/can we shift from using assessment data for accountability to leveraging real-time, formative data that informs teaching and learning?
- How are we systemically improving academic and non-academic supports, and what data helps us do that well?

▶ NELP STANDARD 5: COMMUNITY AND EXTERNAL LEADERSHIP

Improvement Science Connection: Engaging Stakeholders in Problem Understanding and Solving

Book Connections

- Part 1 (Preface, Chapters 1–2) introduces collaboration as a core leadership disposition (Chapter 2).
- Part 2 (Chapters 3–5) emphasizes the importance of collective learning through networked improvement communities (Chapters 3–4) and reframes improvement as a collaborative, team-based effort rather than individual responsibility (Chapter 5).
- Part 3 (Chapters 6–10) reiterates importance of engaging diverse voices through empathy interviews and collaborative inquiry (Chapter 6), building a culture of storytelling and visibility (Chapter 7), systematizing time and structures for professional collaboration (Chapter 8), and creating a culture of sharing ideas and learning across teams (Chapter 9).

Examples of Internship Activities

- Conduct Empathy Interviews with Students, Families, Staff, and Partners
  - Connects to: Chapter 6, NELP 5.1 & 5.2
  - Intern conducts empathy interviews with diverse stakeholders to inform improvement efforts, with attention to elevating voices often left out of decision-making.
- Co-Lead or Participate in Networked Improvement Communities (NIC)
  - Connects to: Chapters 3, 4, 8, NELP 5.2
  - Intern co-leads, participates in, or observes diverse NIC meetings across departments or schools, sharing learning, promising practices, and cross-team collaboration.
- Facilitate Two-Way Communication with Internal and External Stakeholders
  - Connects to: Chapters 6, 7, NELP 5.1, 5.2, 5.3
  - Intern evaluates and recommends improvements to communication structures that invite feedback, share stories of learning, and joint work on shared goals with

families and community partners, attending to those most affected by the decision.
- Visibly Integrate Stakeholder Voice into Vision and Strategic Graphics
  - Connects to: Chapters 7, 10, NELP 5.1, 5.2, 5.3
  - Intern incorporates internal and external constituents to anchor charts that communicate your values, vision, culture, and continuous improvement work. Frequently make connections to it.
- Map Community and External Partnerships to Improvement Goals
  - Connects to: Chapter 10, NELP 5.2
  - Intern collaborates with leaders to connect existing partnerships to improvement goals. Then, identify gaps and suggest opportunities to expand the involvement of stakeholders in academic or well-being priorities.

"Try This" Tools from the Book

- Chapter 6: 2.1 Assemble a Team Check-In
- Chapter 6: 2.7 Empathy Interviews
- Chapter 6: 2.19 NICs Shared Learning Tool to Support Spread and Scale

Intern-Mentor Discussion Prompts

- What structures do we have in place to authentically engage teachers, students, families, and community partners in identifying and solving problems together?
- How do we collect and use qualitative data (such as student, staff, and family interviews and stories) to understand problems and inform improvement efforts?
- How are community voices represented in our leadership decision-making processes (e.g., how they experience the system, helping us understand the problem, engaging inquiry, making sure our change is an improvement)?

- How do we use what we are learning through our improvement work to represent and advocate for school and district needs?

▶ NELP STANDARD 6: OPERATIONS AND MANAGEMENT

Improvement Science Connection: Improving Operations and Transforming Systems

Book Connection

- Part 1 (Preface, Chapters 1–2) introduces the importance of systems thinking as an improvement leadership disposition (Chapter 2).
- Part 2 (Chapters 3–5) deepens viewing schools and departments as interconnected systems (Chapter 3) and introduces the principle of "seeing the system" to diagnose system-level barriers (Chapter 4).
- Part 3 (Chapters 6–10) includes solving operational problems (Chapter 6); structures and supports (Chapter 8), operational examples (Chapter 9); and coherent, system-wide structures that align leadership, resources, and learning systems (Chapter 10).

Examples of Internship Activities

- Use Process Maps to Identify Inefficiencies in Management Systems
  - Connects to: Chapters 4, 6, 10, NELP 6.1
  - Intern facilitates or supports teams in mapping processes to reveal operational breakdowns or inefficiencies.
- Track Improvement Using Data
  - Connects to: Chapters 6, 8, NELP 6.1 & 6.2
  - Intern gathers and visualizes data from PDSA cycles to inform decisions and monitor progress.

- Solve an Operational or Managerial Issue Using an Inquiry Process
  - Connects to: Chapters 6, 9, NELP 6.3
  - Intern co-leads or engages in solving operational issues such as purchasing, hiring, safety, technology integration, transportation, facilities, or food service using an inquiry cycle.
- Ensure Operational Decisions are Guided by Data
  - Connects to: Chapters 4, 9, 10, NELP 6.1 & 6.2
  - Intern evaluates the implementation of a recent operational or managerial change (e.g., schedule revision, staffing model, transportation route), analyzes relevant data (e.g., time use, equity of access, efficiency), and identifies what supports or adjustments are needed to sustain and improve the effort.

"Try This" Tools from the Book

- Chapter 3: Apply Deming's PDSA Cycle to Your Own Leadership Practice
- Chapter 6: 2.6 Process Mapping
- Chapter 6: 2.11 Driver Diagram
- Chapter 6: 2.18 Spread and Scale Decision-Making Tool

Intern-Mentor Discussion Prompts

- Think of a recent problem you helped solve in your school or district. How did you zoom out to examine the broader system contributing to the issue, and how did your response improve operational and resource supports for those experiencing the system?
- How do we apply improvement principles and tools to refine operational processes such as budgeting, hiring, safety, technology, and communication systems so they are more equitable and efficient?

- How do we create feedback loops so that our improvement work informs our resource allocation decisions e.g., (budget, staffing, time)?
- How do we build systems that promote better coordination across departments, teams, or initiatives? What structures, routines, and tools help make this happen?

▶ NELP STANDARD 7: BUILDING PROFESSIONAL CAPACITY (BUILDING-LEVEL)

Improvement Science Connection: Developing People, Building Culture, and Strengthening Professional Capacity for Improvement

Book Connections

- Part 1 (Preface, Chapters 1–2) places a collaborative professional culture (Chapter 1) and leadership dispositions like reflection and shared leadership as foundational for growth (Chapter 2).
- Part 2 (Chapters 3–5) includes job-embedded professional learning and evaluation (Chapter 3), a shift toward staff as knowledge creators and learners (Chapter 5), and the value of collaboration and learning from failure.
- Part 3 (Chapters 6–10) leverages inquiry as a form of professional learning (Chapter 6), leadership strategies to build trusting, collaborative cultures (Chapter 7), and staff-led inquiry and distributed leadership (Chapter 8).

Examples of Internship Activities

- Integrate Improvement Cycles into School Leadership Meetings
  - Connects to: Chapters 6, 8, NELP 7.2 & 7.3
  - Intern designs or facilitates a segment of a school leadership team meeting focused on a real-time PDSA cycle.

- Position Staff as Knowledge Creators and Learning Leaders
  - Connects to: Chapters 5, 8, NELP 7.2 & 7.3
  - Intern supports staff in sharing tested practices and presenting lessons learned.
- Redesign Professional Learning to Be Ongoing, Job-Embedded, Collaborative, and Staff-Driven
  - Connects to: Chapters 6, 7, NELP 7.3
  - Intern works with a mentor to co-plan or refine PD that aligns with improvement principles and responds to emerging classroom needs.
  - Intern evaluates the existing professional learning model and makes recommendations to better align it with improvement principles and processes.
- Support a Culture of Sharing and Collective Efficacy
  - Connects to: Chapters 5, 8, NELP 7.2 & 7.3
  - Intern facilitates a cross-classroom, cross-grade, or cross-department protocol for surfacing and spreading promising instructional practices.
- Participate in a Hiring Process Aligned to Improvement
  - Connects to: Chapter 3, NELP 7.1
  - Intern assists with applicant screening and interviews, reflecting on how the process explicitly reflects an improvement vision and culture (e.g., interview questions align with the improvement focus and collaborative culture).
- Use The Evaluation Process to Support Teacher Growth
  - Connects to: Chapter 3, NELP 7.4
  - Intern observes instruction and practices offering formative feedback connected to improvement efforts, such as implementing change ideas.
- Create or Support a Teacher Leadership Opportunity
  - Connects to: Chapter 8, NELP 7.3
  - Intern helps co-design and support the implementation of a leadership role or professional learning segment facilitated by teachers.

"Try This" Tools from the Book

- Chapter 4: Apply the Six Principles of Improvement
- Chapter 5: Apply the Six Paradigm Shifts
- Chapter 6: Tools that Support Disciplined Inquiry
- Chapter 8: Empower Staff as Improvers

Intern-Mentor Discussion Prompts

- How does our leadership team intentionally support and empower staff across teams to lead and share improvement work?
- How do we create a school-wide culture where staff actively engage in continuous improvement cycles to improve instruction and student learning?
- How do we/might we align team goals, teacher evaluations, and professional growth to our school's student learning goals?
- How does our feedback and supervision system live out our culture of improvement, learning, and trust?
- How do our hiring practices and onboarding ensure we're building a diverse, equity-minded, and improvement-focused staff?

▶ NELP STANDARD 7: POLICY, GOVERNANCE, AND ADVOCACY (DISTRICT-LEVEL)

Improvement Science Connection: Leading System-Wide Coherence and Governance for Equitable Improvement

Book Connections

- Part 1 (Preface, Chapters 1–2) introduces equity as a system-wide lens for leadership and decision-making (Preface) and systems thinking as a foundational mindset for district coherence and governance (Chapter 2).

- Part 2 (Chapters 3–5) includes the theory of profound knowledge and quality management as drivers of effective governance (Chapter 3), then applies improvement principles (Chapter 4) and paradigm shifts (Chapter 5) to frame leadership and governance.
- Part 3 (Chapters 6–10) shares how district leaders embed disciplined inquiry into cabinet- and central office-level routines (Chapter 6), dismantle top-down structures and cast a shared vision (Chapter 7), build the supports and structures for coherence (Chapter 8), scale promising practices across schools and departments (Chapter 9), and institutionalize shared learning through system-wide leadership practices (Chapter 10).

Examples of Internship Activities

- Pilot a Small-Scale Test of Change to Inform Policy
  - Connects to: Chapters 6, 9, NELP 7.1 & 7.3
  - Intern co-designs and supports a small-scale pilot of a new district policy or practice and evaluates its impact before broader implementation.
- Engage Stakeholders in Policy or Governance Design
  - Connects to: Chapters 4, 5, 8, NELP 7.2 & 7.4
  - Intern facilitates a listening session, empathy interview, or workshop with stakeholders e.g., (staff, families, board members, community partners) to inform a district policy or governance decision or to follow up to see if an implemented change was an improvement.
- Evaluate a Policy's Impact on School-Level Autonomy and System Coherence
  - Connects to: Chapters 3, 7, 10, NELP 7.2 & 7.4
  - Intern assesses whether a district policy or practice supports local school- or department-level problem-solving while maintaining system-wide coherence.
- Model Improvement Science in Board or Cabinet Work
  - Connects to: Chapters 4, 6, 7, NELP 7.1 & 7.3
  - Intern co-leads, supports, or observes a segment of a board or cabinet meeting where improvement science

principles are applied, such as using a PDSA cycle, to learn and model what is expected from others.

"Try This" Tools from the Book

- Preface: Self-Assessment: Where Are You in Your Leadership Journey
- Chapter 3: Apply Deming's PDSA Cycle to Your Own Leadership Practice
- Chapter 4: Apply the Six Principles of Improvement
- Chapter 5: Apply the Six Leadership Mind Shifts
- Chapter 6: 2.19 NIC Shared Learning Tool for Spreading and Scaling
- Chapter 10: Be the Leader Who Changes the System

Intern-Mentor Discussion Prompts

- How do our district's policies and governance structures support continuous improvement by modeling inquiry, responding to local needs, building coherence, and supporting innovation at scale?
- How do we use improvement principles to evaluate and refine district policies to ensure they promote equity, inclusivity, and student success across the system?
- How do we structure cabinet, board, and leadership routines to embed disciplined inquiry and accountability into governance and decision-making?
- How do district leaders build schedules and routines that embed a focus on continuous improvement in accountability and governance throughout the system, ensuring information flows both bottom-up and top-down across the system?

For Product Safety Concerns and Information please contact our EU representative GPSR@taylorandfrancis.com
Taylor & Francis Verlag GmbH, Kaufingerstraße 24, 80331 München, Germany

www.ingramcontent.com/pod-product-compliance
Lightning Source LLC
Chambersburg PA
CBHW061425300426
44114CB00014B/1549